class

and its

others

J. K. Gibson-Graham

Stephen A. Resnick

Richard D. Wolff

Editors

class

and its

others

Foreword by

Amitava Kumar

University of Minnesota Press

Minneapolis / London

MINNESOTA

The University of Minnesota Press gratefully acknowledges permission to reprint an earlier version of chapter 8, which originally appeared as "Remapping Los Angeles; or, Taking the Risk of Class in Postmodern Urban Theory," in *Economic Geography* 75, no. 2 (April 1999). Reprinted with permission from *Economic Geography,* Clark University.

Published by the University of Minnesota Press
111 Third Avenue South, Suite 290
Minneapolis, MN 55401-2520
http://www.upress.umn.edu

Printed in the United States of America on acid-free paper

Library of Congress Cataloging-in-Publication Data

Class and its others / J. K. Gibson-Graham, Stephen A. Resnick, and
     Richard D. Wolff, editors ; foreword by Amitava Kumar.
        p.   cm.
     Includes bibliographical references and index.
     ISBN 0-8166-3617-6 (hc : acid-free) — ISBN 0-8166-3618-4
     (pb : acid-free)
        1. Working class—Economic conditions. 2. Working class—
     Social conditions. 3. Social classes. 4. Communism and society.
     I. Gibson-Graham, J. K. II. Resnick, Stephen A. III. Wolff, Richard D.
     IV. Title.
     HD4901.C576 2000
     305.5—dc21
                                                        00-008821

11 10 09 08 07 06 05 04 03 02 01 00   10 9 8 7 6 5 4 3 2 1

Contents

In Class

Amitava Kumar

I have just finished teaching the first month of an undergraduate course on Marx. The course is one in the "critical thinkers" series that we offer in my department for those students who have opted for the cultural studies track. This is the first time I—or anyone else—has taught this course here. It is impossible for me to introduce *Class and Its Others* without my thoughts reflecting, in some measure, what we have been involved in reading and discussing in our classroom.

In my case, the owl of Minerva is swooping into flight even later than usually expected. It is nearly two years now since a copy of the *New Yorker,* marketed as "The Next Issue," predicted that the next university would be "Drive-Thru U," the next president, Elizabeth Dole (someone "who is better at tea and sympathy than Bill Clinton"), and the next thinker—Karl Marx! The magazine presented him to us as a now-little-read nineteenth-century German writer whose basic insights were reintroduced in recent times by James Carville with the phrase "It's the economy, stupid."

And the "next" fashion outrage? Ozone chic. To quote the *New Yorker's* cosmopolitan astrologers: "A pink polyester minidress with a singing-cricket sound module, a bloodstain-print animal-rights T-shirt, a raincoat with a bondage mask, and a lacy spiderweb dress with gloves attached to the sleeves." With such a buildup, it was only right that we begin the course by taking up Howard Zinn's fine little play *Marx in Soho.* A bureaucratic mix-up has landed the venerable but feisty philosopher in New York's fashionable Soho rather than London. He has come back to clear his name. "I have had it up to here," he says. The newspapers have been proclaiming that his ideas are dead. He asks, "Don't you wonder: why it is necessary to declare me dead again and again?"

In Zinn's play, Marx reads the day's newspapers. We decided to do the same. On the first day of class, *New York Times* carried an obituary entitled "Wilbert J. Oliver at 89; Fought Funeral Color Line." Mr. Oliver had died at a hospital in Marksville, La. The newspaper said that he had sued the Escude Funeral Home in Mansura, La., for discrimination after it refused to provide visitation for his deceased mother because she was black. Mr. Oliver's lawsuit in 1973 "had the practical effect of forcing funeral homes throughout the nation to provide equal services to blacks and whites." The case had been fought by the lawyers of the Southern Poverty Law Center.

There was a photograph of the dead man printed beside the headline. The *Times* story said that Rev. August Thompson, who was Mr. Oliver's priest when his mother had passed away, remembered Mr. Oliver as being distraught when he was told that the funeral home would not permit visitation. "He lived in what used to be called a shotgun house because it was so flimsy that if you fired a shotgun at the house it would go right through it. He wanted a better place for visitation for his mother."

While we read and discussed the story, I looked at the photograph several times. What do such photographs convey anyway? "He was just an ordinary man, one of the common people and not a crusader," the priest was quoted as saying. So I saw in the picture the man I was discovering through this report: a salesman for John Deere who, after his mother was denied visitation, had arranged to hold the wake in "a run-down storage building on the grounds of Our Lady of Prompt Succor Church." At first none of the lawyers helped him. To quote Father Thompson's words again: "Life was a little harder for him because he had lost his left arm in an accident, but none of the local lawyers would touch the case."

Several of my students had picked up on other stories that day. There was one about "the young and the determined" on Wall Street. Someone else wanted to discuss the phenomenon of Bill Gates's wealth: "If you laid his money out in $1 bills end to end it would make a trail that would go back and forth to the moon 15.8 times." But I could not shake out of my mind the story of Mr. Oliver, a man who was ashamed to deny his mother the dignity of a decent visitation. When I returned to class the next day I asked my students: Is it not the shame of a poor man, his plain indignation, that we—precisely as readers of Marx—should see as a weapon in a class struggle?

The editors of *Class and Its Others,* as well as the contributors, would be interested, I believe, in addressing and refining the above question that I had posed to my students. They would do so partly because they rightly understand that it's never *just* the economy, stupid! And partly also because they signal in this volume their clear commitment to sharpening traditional perceptions of class: "We are keen to enlarge the domain of class narrative and widen the affective register of class politics."

Why is this necessary?

The editors are in agreement with Raymond Williams who wrote that there were diverse concepts of class present in Marxism and that they make their appearance in "a whole range of contemporary discussion and controversy . . . usually without clear distinction." However, the editors, especially Resnick and Wolff, also share a history of negotiating these contending meanings in order to establish a concept of class that is particular to Marx himself. This concept is different both from the two-class theory of traditional Marxism as well as the alternative theories of differential class formations in the writings of Nicos Poulantzas, Erik Olin Wright, Barbara and John Ehrenreich, among others. In their founding work, *Knowledge and Class,* Resnick and Wolff have put forward the reading of "class as process" in Marx's writings. In this interpretation, Marx's work is an explanation of class processes and their relationship to the processes of interpersonal domination and property ownership as conditions of one another's existence. The opposition to essentialist and fixed notions of class was announced in Resnick and Wolff's declaration: "Class is an adjective, not a noun." More recently, this dynamic, nonessentialist notion of class was taken up and elaborated in Gibson-Graham's influential book, *The End of Capitalism (As We Knew It).* Like the latter work, *Class and Its Others* takes on the task of enriching our understanding of class. It does so by prompting us to see in a broad range of subject positions the possibility of class identifications and the promise of discerning—and protesting—exploitation in places previously repressed.

A few years ago, in their introductory remarks to the volume *Marxism in the Postmodern Age,* Antonio Callari et al. had remarked on the intellectual project of a mature Marxism that might be called "anti-economism." They added: "Insights from poststructuralist and postmodern thought have been woven into Marxian discourse in ways that have both challenged and extended traditional Marxism. The works of Michel Foucault, Jacques Derrida, and Jean-François Lyotard, among many others, have raised profound questions about the centrality of master narratives of unidirectional progress" (1995, 6). The essays in *Class and Its Others,* to my mind, repeat that gesture but also inscribe a difference. They critically foreground poststructuralist issues of language and articulation, and hence rescue class from its traditional a priori status; at the same time, going beyond the duties of opening the category to contestation, they productively focus attention on hitherto un-examined sites of class processes and their effects. That is how I understand, for instance, Harriet Fraad's essay in the volume that challenges traditional Marxism to be serious about exploitation and ask what's love got to do with it. In a similar vein, Marjolein van der Veen calls into question the deploy-ment of a monolithic notion of exploitation in the context of prostitution. Van der Veen's article throws into relief questions of moralistic and mas-culinist ideologies, the agency of sex-workers, and their collective strengths that fissure traditional understandings of class and sexuality. I could also mention here Jacquelyn Southern's well-written, almost belle-lettristic, de-construction of the blue-collar, white-collar distinction (following Kocka, she calls it the "collar line"). Southern's demonstration of the binaristic preju-dice that has governed so much of the classificatory systems emphasizes one of the volume's central concerns: a protest against the identical condition mandated by much of the accepted terminology around class. When she concludes that "the collar line supports the dangerous idea that only like people can organize and work together," Southern echoes the concern voiced in earlier essays that solidarities must be built across differences, which await rearticulation in the interest of a new political future.

When the editors of this volume write of their desire to conceptualize identity more dynamically and fragmentarily in relation to class, we find evi-dence and strong justification for this in some of the essays presented here. Jenny Cameron's essay "Domesticating Class: Femininity, Heterosexuality, and Household Politics," for instance, will compel the analysts of class to think about fluid identities where masculinity and femininity are queered and unstable; that essay will also challenge critics of a more radical, egalitari-an stripe to alter a theoretical worldview where the feminine and the familial are negated and the domestic sphere understood only as a realm of bond-age. A similar kind of labor is performed by Susan Jahoda's cross-genre piece "Spring Flowers." In what is also a meditation on cross-gendering, we find images and words that institute in the space between them a process of class: the process of *making flesh* the abstract ideas of bodies and exchange, race and sexuality, class and desire.

It will not come as news to many in cultural studies that while there has been a return in radical theory to issues of the economy, following the de-cline of the moment in high theory, there are very few sophisticated studies that mix a good understanding of the claims of recent theory with rigorous analyses of aspects of the economy. The essays in *Class and Its Others* deliver exactly that. It is true of the chapters I have mentioned above. It is also true of Cecilia Marie Rio's essay on African American female domestics who rewrite stereotypically left class-narratives, Janet Hotch's paper on the self-employed, and Enid Arvidson's postmodern mapping of the city of Los Angeles that tries to complicate the picture provided us by Mike Davis's brilliant, earlier work.

Before I conclude, I'd like to return once more to the scene of my classroom on Marx. We have just finished reading the book of communiqués of Sub-commandante Marcos, *Shadows of Tender Fury*. Currently, we are plodding through Hegel's *Reason in History*. We are also reading *The German Ideology*. Next week, we will take up sections of the *Grundrisse*.

No one who has passed the last couple of decades with their eyes open can deny that we have been faced with the need to work out in new ways the relationship between what had been familiar as the working class and now its many others—the prisoners, overwhelmingly black, the immigrants, queers, or, for that matter, the gays in the military, our institutional others who are the adjuncts, the aged, the sick, the angry janitors, the triumphant UPS part-timers, the migrant cyberworkers who are the high-tech braceros, all our youth who are organizing.

Many of the essays in this book are sharply aware of that trajectory, and this is also how I understand the emphasis the editors put on "connecting class to its historical others—sites from which class has been excluded, subjects to whom class has been denied, activities that have been devalued and subordinated to class." But, more than the other materials my students are reading in our class, it is the writings of Marcos that, in their incessant, ineradicable footnotes, reveal the struggles as well as the fecundity of the others in our contemporary moment.

When Marcos was queried by a San Francisco reporter whether he was gay, the communiqué that was sent back from Chiapas said in part: "Marcos is gay in San Francisco, black in South Africa, an Asian in Europe, a Chicano in San Ysidro, an anarchist in Spain, a Palestinian in Israel, a Mayan Indian in the streets of San Cristóbal, a gang member in Neza, a rocker in the National University, a Jew in Germany, an ombudsman in the Defense Ministry, a Communist in the post–Cold War era, an artist without a gallery or portfolio, a pacifist in Bosnia, a housewife alone on a Saturday night in any neighborhood in any city in Mexico, a reporter writing filler stories for the back pages, a single woman on the subway at 10 P.M., a peasant without land, an unemployed worker, a dissident amid free-market economics, a writer without books or readers, and, of course, a Zapatista in the mountains of south-east Mexico."

The effervescent logic articulated here—linking disparate social actors

and contexts in a logic that makes intuitive sense—finds its theoretical justification in the pages that follow. More than that, there is a resonance between the Sup's words and the openness that the essays in this book show to
questions of affect and hope. The editors of *Class and Its Others,* following
Wendy Brown, do not want *ressentiment* to overtake the place of freedom as
a collective project. Marcos knows this all too well. Hence, the indefinable
resolve: "Here we are, the forever dead, dying once again, but now in order
to live." And his declaration in a letter to a thirteen-year-old boy in Baja
California: "Our profession: hope."

Acknowledgments

Putting together an edited collection is a collective endeavor and in this case especially so. Each of the authors worked intensively with the editors, responding to two and even three rounds of comments with exemplary fortitude. At the outset, then, we would like to acknowledge our contributors not only for their good work but also for their extraordinary grace under criticism, time pressure, and the general jostling that is always an aspect of collective projects.

Certain resources were made available to this project without which it could not have been undertaken and completed. We are indebted to Monash University and the Small Grants Scheme of the Australian Research Council and to Linda Slakey, Dean of the College of Natural Sciences and Mathematics at the University of Massachusetts, Amherst, for funding the June 1996 workshop at which the first drafts of all the papers were presented and discussed.

We are also indebted to the many individuals who helped the book take its final form. Jack Amariglio, David Ruccio, and the other members of the editorial board of *Rethinking Marxism* buoyed our spirits with their unflagging enthusiasm for the project. Carole Biewener and two anonymous reviewers provided us with a full set of very useful comments on the first draft. Ken Byrne was involved in every aspect of producing the manuscript, from tracking down stray references to printing out the final copy. Without his stalwart and good-humored efforts, this work would literally not exist. Sandra Davenport did an excellent job of proofreading and producing the index. At the University of Minnesota Press, our editor Carrie Mullen encouraged and supported the project from its inception, Nancy Sauro provided elegant and unobtrusive copyediting, and Robin A. Moir has made the arduous process of completing and submitting a manuscript seem relatively stress free. We are very lucky to have been able to work with them.

Finally, we would like to express our deepest thanks to the many other members of the Association for Economic and Social Analysis who laid the theoretical groundwork for *Class and Its Others* and created a variety of forums for exploring the ideas developed here, including the initial workshop at which the project took shape. We hope that the book is an appropriate tribute to your individual and collective creativity, vision, and hard work.

Introduction

Class in a Poststructuralist Frame

J. K. Gibson-Graham, Stephen A. Resnick,

and Richard D. Wolff

Class and Its Others draws deeply on two sources of energy that commingle in this introduction and in the editors themselves (or in the spaces between them). The first and most profound is an affective commitment to the experience of the laboring body. In this we feel an affinity with the growing number of movements that are centered on or circling around economic exploitation: among these, a revitalizing labor movement, the living wage campaigns being fought in many U.S. communities, the stakeholders' rights movement in deindustrialized regions, associations of self-employed workers like the National Writers Union, employee buyouts of capitalist firms, and the widespread interest in worker cooperatives and "intentional economies" in the United States and around the world. Where we overlap with these movements, our links to modernist emancipatory traditions are activated and strong. Yet we feel a need to stretch and attenuate these links. For while we would wish to stay within the flow of passionate energy that circulates around labor, we also hope to extend that energy beyond the constricted range of projects, subjects, and emotions that has historically confined it. We want to draw from the reservoir of feeling that the theory and politics of exploitation has collected while at the same time opening the political field to an expanding array of subjects, visions, and desires.

The second is the desire for a contemporary political discourse that has a purchase on the dread and disavowed terrain of the economy. The nearly ubiquitous tendency to view economic activity as taking place in a separate and rarefied social location—the so-called economy—signals the urgency of speaking the *language of economy* in unfamiliar ways. For to the extent that the economy has been taken from us—represented as removed from

1

the forces of social and discursive construction—it becomes important and urgent to take it back, not as a homogeneous and unified level, sphere, or system, but as a discursive terrain, a set of concepts, issues, contradictions, identities, and struggles that falls outside the purview of most contemporary social theory. If we fail to inhabit this territory, treating it as already ceded, we risk setting too much aside—too many memories, violences, and miseries, too many political and emotional possibilities.

For us at this moment, repossessing the economic terrain entails producing (or fostering) a discourse of class—not in the familiar and widespread sense of *social* distinction but in the more restricted *economic* sense first systematically expounded by Marx.[1] In this essay and the ones that follow, the processes of producing, appropriating, and distributing surplus labor are identified as the "processes of class." Around these processes social practices are organized, struggles are galvanized, and identities and experiences transformed. Setting forth this single (and simple) understanding of class as the magnetic center of the book allows us to highlight, amidst the confusing welter of class meanings, a salient meaning deriving its emotional power from the knowledge and experience of exploitation. It creates a strategic point of confluence between the desire to produce a politically enabling discourse of economy and the intense feelings attached to the experience and witness of the laboring body.

Sometimes haltingly and rudimentarily, *Class and Its Others* heeds its twin impulses by speaking a language of class, one that may allow us to retrieve memories and adumbrate possibilities; one that can authorize projects, interpellate subjects, and proliferate identities; one that can connect gender, race, sexuality, and other axes of identity to economic activity in uncommon ways. Such a language has the potential to liberate a vision of economic difference, outside the theory and practice of capitalist reproduction. It may suggest openings for class politics by expanding the range of actors, emotions, and relationships associated with class.

Like other languages, the language of class is inevitably performative—it participates in transforming economic and other social relations. Not only may it provide a new discursive foothold on the terrain of the economy, giving us different ways to make sense and take action, but it offers new possibilities for connecting class to its historical "others"—sites from which class has been excluded, subjects to whom class has been denied, activities that have been seen as "noneconomic," identities that have been devalued and subordinated to class. In the process it may create a desire for new forms of class politics, perhaps even in those with no desire for that desire.

Languages of Class

Crisscrossing the historical field of class discourse are two prominent streams of meaning that often flow together, masking their different origins as they intertwine. The first, and most familiar, gives us class as a place in a social ranking, a hierarchy of upper, middle, and lower classes with gradations in between. The second refers to an economic relation (of exploitation) between producers and nonproducers, working and nonworking classes. As Raymond Williams points out, these two sets of distinctions/relations are often partially and confusingly combined.[2]

Class as social hierarchy is arguably the more popular and pervasive meaning. Deriving from the medieval language of estates, orders, and degrees (in which social places were associated with social functions), it has devolved to complex and multifaceted taxonomies in which the various classes have no clearly specified boundaries or functional roles. Contemporary metrics of class are diverse and their calibrations highly unstable, yet no dimension of social existence escapes the anxious and invidious ordering that is the hallmark of the hierarchical conception of class. Everything can be read as a class marker, and anything and anyone can be placed in a class.

This hierarchical and classificatory conception of class has recently become the focus of considerable attention.[3] But it is from the other stream of meaning—where class is associated with labor and an economic relation—that we wish to draw our own understanding of the term. Williams traces the headwaters of this stream to "the fierce argument about political, social and economic rights" (63) that took place in late eighteenth- and early nineteenth-century England, when a language of class was used to distinguish the "unproductive and useless" aristocracy (and occasional capitalists) from the "productive and useful" persons whose labor sustained them. Drawing from this language and the political energies eddying around it, Marx produced in volume 1 of *Capital* a theory of the capitalist's exploitative relation to the laborer/producer.[4]

In the work of Marx we recognize a project of creating meaning, one that involved reworking the language of political economy to produce a novel yet extraordinarily resonant (for the political reasons just suggested) understanding of capitalism. This project turned on the deployment of a set of distinctions—between necessary and surplus labor, between the production and appropriation of surplus labor and the moment of its distribution, and between different forms of exploitation, including slave, feudal, and capitalist, among others. Taken together, these distinctions constitute the rudiments of a language of class.

While the notion of a surplus above and beyond what was necessary for reproduction had long figured in classical political economy,[5] Marx was the first to produce a discourse of exploitation that hinged on the distinction between necessary and surplus labor. As he defined it, necessary labor "is the quantity of labor time necessary to produce the consumables customarily required by the producer to keep working," while surplus labor is "the extra time of labor the direct producer performs beyond the necessary labor" (Resnick and Wolff 1987, 115). In an exploitative relation this unpaid or unremunerated surplus labor (or its product in physical or value forms) is appropriated by someone other than the producer.[6]

Any attempt to differentiate categories of labor (time) must be seen as an accounting exercise in which boundaries are ultimately arbitrarily drawn. Thus the necessary/surplus labor distinction cannot be grounded in the ostensible reality of the body's "basic needs" for subsistence but must be seen as a particular way of fixing meaning, one that has certain social and political effects. It is important, not because it marks a bodily limit, but for what it makes visible, the feelings it prompts, the differences it allows us to imagine and create. The boundary is an accounting device, inscribed on the body rather than emerging from within it, and the desire to move it can be seen to have motivated political struggles historically and to this day.

Marx used the distinction between necessary and surplus labor to identify what for him was the principal violence of capitalism: the existence of an "invisible" flow of labor (taking the form of "surplus value") from the worker to the capitalist. Each worker in a capitalist enterprise produces in a day enough wealth to sustain her or himself (for which the worker is compensated in the form of a wage) and also a surplus that is appropriated by the capitalist.[7] The exploitative process in which surplus labor is produced and appropriated is for Marx a *class* process, and the positions of producer and appropriator are *class* positions.

But the class positions identified by Marx are not limited to these two. The structure of *Capital* turns on a second distinction, between what might be called the appropriative moment and the distributive moment of the · capitalist class process. (Resnick and Wolff [1987] call these the fundamental and subsumed class processes, respectively). The former is the moment of exploitation in which surplus labor is produced and appropriated in value form (explored in volume 1), while the latter and no less important moment involves the distribution of appropriated surplus value to a range of recipients (explored in volumes 2 and 3). In the distributive moment the surplus labor that has been "pumped out of [the] direct producers" and temporarily condensed in the hands of the appropriating capitalist can be seen to be dispersed in myriad directions—out into the wider society to, for example, financiers, merchants, landlords, advertising agents, governments, charitable organizations, or organized crime, who provide conditions of existence of surplus value production), as well as within the enterprise (into the accumulation of productive capital, or management salaries and benefits, or compensation for nonproducing workers in marketing and sales).

Traditional class analyses generally focus on the class positions of surplus producer and appropriator while neglecting the flow of surplus labor from the appropriator (who is also the first distributor) to the receivers of surplus labor distributions. But these distributive flows can be seen as constituting a range of distributive class positions. They can also be understood as connecting the moment of class exploitation to the ways that society is organized and enacted, highlighting the interdependencies within any economy and society. In class analyses that account for distributions of surplus labor and the class positions they entail, what emerges is a complex vision of the social ramifications of class.

So far we have focused on two discursive fixings that we take from Marx—the distinction between necessary and surplus labor and the distinction between the appropriative and distributive moments of the class process.[8] In *Capital,* each of these distinctions is elaborated with respect to capitalism. But while capitalism was Marx's principal object of investigation, he also employed the language of class to identify noncapitalist class processes that predated capitalism, have always coexisted with it, or indeed might succeed it. His theory of capitalism was formulated, for example, via a comparison with feudalism, with the differences specified in terms of the ways that surplus labor was extracted and distributed within feudal as opposed to capitalist social arrangements. In addition, Marx identified a range of other class processes, including primitive communist, slave, ancient or independent, and communal or communist. What distinguishes each from the others is the way that surplus labor is produced, appropriated, and distributed (for example, as feudal rent, as surplus value, under various types of force or agreement). In this rudimentary typology of class forms, we can discern the elements of a language of economic difference and the possibility of complex class readings of internally differentiated social and economic formations.

Like all systems of accounting, Marx's language of class highlights certain things and not others, potentiates certain identities and not others, and has the capacity to energize certain kinds of activities and actors while leaving others unmoved. As a movable boundary, the distinction between necessary and surplus labor has made exploitation a visible, tangible object of discourse and politics. The further division of appropriated wealth into various surplus distributions suggests its formative and proliferative potential and allows us to trace some of the ways that exploitation participates in constituting other social practices and institutions. It also places surplus distribution alongside exploitation as a potential object of political struggles. Finally, the open-ended list of different class processes suggests the scope for creative enactment of different (nonexploitative) economic futures.

The language of class does not merely enable us to explore the socially constitutive role of exploitation (though that is something that it does), but in its proliferation of terms it opens up the economic field—offering a range of identity positions that could potentially be inhabited, providing a rudimentary typology of forms of surplus appropriation that might prompt imaginative extension and normative valencing. As always, a world of possibility is created through the drawing of boundaries and positing of distinctions. The essays in this volume highlight and explore that world, or at least some of its regions and byways.

Re-Presenting Class

The Marxian tradition has (often though not always) conspired to situate class within a realist epistemology, a determinist approach to social explanation, and an essentialist conception of identity/being. Ordained as the central contradiction of the social totality, class is seen as the principal axis of social transformation, and actual classes appear as the political collectivities charged with *the* transformative historical task. What is dauntingly familiar in this recapitulation is the closed and univocal social ontology (the structured "capitalist totality" of classical Marxism) and the resultant fixity of the meaning and role of class.

Confronting a tradition in which class is laden with meaning but resistant to resignification, we find ourselves in need of radical epistemological redress. It is not enough to say that the meaning of class is socially and discursively constructed. The bald restatement of this view seems an insufficient challenge to the many reductions—of knowledge to reflection, of complex effects to simple determinations, of identities to categorical commonalities—that have shadowed the classical Marxian conception of class (Resnick and Wolff 1987). Dislodging the forms of thought in which class is mired requires something more concrete and deliberate—a specific practice of anti-essentialism, a self-consciousness about epistemological mechanics, an alternative procedure for thinking class. For what it can offer along these lines, we have been drawn to Althusser's concept of "overdetermination."

In Althusser's brief formulation (1977, 89–116), overdetermination stands as an ontological presumption or starting place that does not assign causal or constitutive privilege to any social instance or process. Instead, causation and identity are complex unfoldings that yield themselves differently to every analysis and every analytical moment. From this perspective, each identity or event can be understood as constituted by the entire complex of natural, social, economic, cultural, political, and other processes that comprise its conditions of existence. None of these can be eliminated or assigned prior or fundamental importance, though every analysis singles out one or several for emphasis and investigation.

Overdetermination derives its power (to contradict and undermine, to radically reframe) from its relation to economic determinism, its essentialist counterpart in the Marxian tradition. As a practice of anti-essentialism, it is uniquely positioned to destabilize the reductive forms of thought that have haunted and truncated Marxian theory and politics over the course of the twentieth century. Offered in their stead is what Althusser termed an "aleatory materialism": the refusal to reduce an event or being to a root cause or to an idea or principle (this tendency he calls "idealism"), the recognition and honoring of contingency and historicity.[9]

In a less ontologizing vein, overdetermination functions as an antidote to epistemological realism, with its tightly bound association of words to things: "the presence of some objects in others prevents any of their identities from being fixed" and conveys the "incomplete, open and politically negotiable character of every identity" (Laclau and Mouffe 1985, 104).[10] Working against the understanding of class as given and known, what is given in this instance is something *to be* known, as yet a theoretical "emptiness"—the processes of producing, appropriating, and distributing surplus labor. Creating a knowledge of class involves filling this emptiness, always partially and incompletely, constructing particular understandings of the ways that specific class processes are constituted by their "class" and "nonclass" conditions of existence.[11] Through that contextualized and contextualizing practice, a variety of class narratives will emerge. The emaciated and emotionally spare categories will take on flesh, become animated and animating, realize their performative and interpellating potential.

Continuities and Discontinuities

The process of animating a language of class is constructionist and neologistic; as a prospective endeavor, its political implications can only be guessed. But it takes place in a field that is already inhabited (by other class languages and their histories), presenting both options and obstacles to those who would enter.

Attempting to bring class and exploitation into visibility, to end their

sojourn in the theoretical shadows, we would hope to move outside the clo-
sures and constrictions that have become the historical signatures of class.
This involves not only a self-conscious practice of resignification, but also
divorcing class from the dominant narratives and forms of essentialism to
which it has historically been linked. Within Marxism in particular, narrative and categorical universalism has enlarged the ostensible purview of
class discourse while greatly restricting its political effectivity.

Some of the humanist universals that haunt class theory can be traced to
the political and intellectual context in which it emerged. In producing a
theory of capitalism, Marx drew from the late eighteenth-century discourse
of exploited producers and "parasitic" nonproducers, classes who obtained
their differential normative and affective weightings in the context of liberal
democratic revolutions. Despite Marx's strong disavowals,[12] *Capital* is indebted for much of its potency and resonance to ideas he disavowed, including most notably an Enlightenment humanist understanding of labor as the
origin of all wealth and a discourse of rights in which man's entitlement to
the fruits of his labor is naturally ordained.[13] This ambient discourse of rights
(to property in labor and its fruits) was a volatile source of the political energies circulating around Marx's project. Even today, whatever frisson of outrage we may feel in the presence of exploitation derives, to some undecidable
extent, from a politically charged discourse of natural property rights that
renders the exploitative relation fundamentally "unjust."

While the modernist discourse of rights cannot be abjured without emp-
tying class politics of much of its programmatic and emotional content, the
universalism that attends this legacy is now unsustainable. Not only is it not
required,[14] but it stands in the way of a politics in which class discourse can
coexist (nonhierchically) with discourses that have other starting places, emphases, and affective entailments.[15]

Humanism is of course not the only legacy that shadows this project. Any
attempt to develop a contemporary discourse of class must also confront the
history of political formations that have coalesced around class and exploitation. Animated by a vision of working-class transcendence, class-centered
revolutionary movements have not only amplified the affective charge of the
laboring body but have had a simultaneous constricting effect—narrowing
the class imaginary to a preeminent narrative of working-class agency. This
familiar story foregrounds an economy centered on industry, class subject
positions limited to workers and capitalists, class embodiment as quintessentially male (not to mention white and heterosexual), and class destiny as
the fate of society as a whole.

We would hope to carry forward the intensity of feeling that has been politically affixed to the experience of exploitation, while unyoking this affective energy from the essentialist commitments and confining narratives to which it has been contingently attached. In positive terms, this requires diversifying the social compass of class narration and treating the political significance of class as an effect rather than a ground of class discourse. In the discussions that follow—of identity, power, economic difference, and political affect—we draw out some of the implications of such a project.

Class and Identity

"Class is an adjective, not a noun."
—Resnick and Wolff, *Knowledge and Class*

In attempting to produce a discourse of class, we feel an affinity with other poststructuralist theorists who are concerned with destabilizing established and restrictive identities constructed along the axes of gender, sexuality, race, ethnicity, and other forms of categorization and distinction. Like them we are interested in opening up the field of class identity. But we are also (as they may or may not be) engaged in a positive process of potentiating identities where none has previously been perceived or enacted.[16] To invigorate economic innovations centered on exploitation and distribution, we are interested in generating a discourse of class that offers a range of subject positions that might prompt identification.

It is not immediately obvious how to move beyond the categorical notions of class(es) that have created such a powerful undertow in the Marxian tradition—to conceptualize identity more fluidly and fragmentarily in relation to class. But it is clear that class can no longer be understood as the organizing center of individual and collective identity.[17] Nor can it be seen as ordained by or founded on positions in a larger social structure or as constituting social groups (classes) unified by commonalities of power, property, consciousness, etc.[18] By defining class simply in terms of the processes of performing, appropriating, and distributing surplus labor, we have detached it from an a priori social structure (in which both its reproductive and emancipatory functions are given and known) and freed it from the intractable and unrewarding problems of class-ification. How class processes relate to individual and collective identities, the formation of social groups, and to other complexities such as power and property becomes an open question, something to be theorized rather than assumed.

One of the paradoxical consequences of defining class more narrowly is that the possibilities for constituting class identities proliferate. Without the vision of a social and economic structure that fixes the identity of its constituent elements, we can begin to see class processes being enacted in multiple forms and social sites—not just in the capitalist enterprise but in noncapitalist ones, and also in the household, the state, the prison, the community, and any other place or relationship in which the accounting of flows of necessary and surplus labor might be illuminating or compelling. Individuals may participate in multiple class processes at any one time and over their life spans, all of which may (or may not) contribute to a class identity.

Consider, for instance, a married manual laborer in a rural mining enterprise who spends his weekends hunting for game that is consumed by his family and also sold through a marketing cooperative. This individual may participate in a capitalist class process "at work" (where he works for a wage and produces surplus value that is appropriated by the board of directors of the enterprise); a communal class process "at home" (where he and his spouse jointly engage in housekeeping and childrearing, collectively producing, appropriating, and distributing their surplus labor); and an independent class process on the weekends in the outdoors (where he works on his own and appropriates and distributes his own surplus labor). His class identity could be fixed in any number of ways—as a worker in a capitalist firm, as a new age communard, as an independent producer—or not at all. With a conception of the multiplicity of class relations that intersect in an individual's life, we cannot assume that participation in any one class process is a basis for self-identification or establishing common cause with others. This is not to say that individual and collective class "interests" or desires cannot be constituted, but to suggest that they cannot be presumed.

The potential for an anti-essentialist language of class to participate in constituting new identities and social articulations rests, of course, on the refusal to enforce any predetermined rules of translation from class to other languages of identity. To return to our rural subject with multiple class positions, given his location and activities, he could display an active political interest or a passive disinterest in union organizing, species protection and environmental management, day care, the New Age men's movement, the Christian right and/or rural boosterism. None of these political (in)activities can be seen as more influenced by class relations than by other dimensions such as gender, sexuality, race, spirituality, or age. Yet in all aspects of his subjecthood—as a rural white male, a father, a hunter, a domestic worker, a Christian—the class processes he participates in could be seen as contributing to the constitution of his self-identifications as well as the other way around. So, for instance, his work as an independent self-appropriating hunter whose performance of surplus labor is directly related to issues of environmental/species management may overdetermine his identity as an environmental activist. And his participation in the New Age men's movement and interest in redefining masculinity may overdetermine his participation in a communal domestic class process in the household, encouraging him to perform an equal share of once gender-coded jobs. As Daly (1991) has suggested, identities constituted outside production are powerful origins of desires to resist or transform exploitation within it.

Our task is to open up new discursive spaces where a language of class can articulate with other aspects of social existence that are themselves potential sources of identity. The emphasis we place on a language of process rather than of social structure suggests the possibility of energetic and unconfined class identities, where the compelling question is not "What is my class belonging?" but "What is my class becoming?"[19] Whenever individuals or collectivities are mobilized around flows of surplus labor, a class relationship is (in our understanding, at least) enacted. What difference might it make if such an understanding were more widespread? What new social possibilities might emerge if a class language existed to call forth identities, motivate projects, and produce desires for economic and social transformation?

Class and Power

For many theorists class *is* a power relation, a relation of domination. But this collapsing together of exploitation and domination can be seen as an impoverishing move. We want instead to separate and distinguish power/domination from class/exploitation, to open up their relations to the contingencies of theory.[20]

Even when power and class are not understood as identical, the relations between them have almost always been theorized as relatively simple. The power associated with class in the traditional Marxian view emanates from a location in a structure in which the capacity to dominate is already inscribed. The ruling capitalist class "possesses" power vested in its ability to subordinate and control the working class, which "lacks" structural power. Power is conceived as a negative force from which to be liberated; it is something that is "held" and must be "seized."

Against this broad-brush picture of hierarchically structured and unequally distributed quantities of negative force, Foucault's refusal of essential forms of power (1988, 18) and attention to power as a "multiplicity of force relations" (1990, 92) suggest the possibility for exploring the workings of power in relation to class, of developing a microphysics of class and power.

When labor flows are disaggregated into necessary and surplus, appropriations and distributions, a plethora of interactions and transactions comes into view—all sites for the enactment of capacity, for the creation, harnessing, and dispersion of power.

Only some (or perhaps none) of these sites exist in a stable state of domination, that is, in an extreme or terminal form of power in which the "subordinated have relatively little room to manoeuvre" (Hindess 1997, 97–98). Yet this is the state emphasized by traditional class analyses when, for example, ownership of the means of production is positioned as ultimately (if not totally) constraining the exercise of power by workers vis-à-vis capital. What if we were to focus instead on the enactment of power by subjects who are understood to be relatively "free?" What if class relations were seen as unfixed and malleable, presenting opportunities for "strategic games between liberties"? (Foucault 1988, 19). In this "freed up" milieu, power might be seen as affecting class processes in unexpected ways.

Callon and Latour (1981) speak of power as a process of "enrolling, convincing and enlisting" associations of bodies and materials. We might think here of the strategic actions of a housewife (traditional homeworker) convincing family members to participate in the communal production and distribution of domestic surplus labor when she seeks a job outside the home, or the repeated strategic decision by members of a worker cooperative not to hire temporary employees and to minimize wage differences between categories of workers, or the traditional labor union "enrolling" and "enlisting" members who will exert power (in the form of strikes or consumer campaigns or shareholder organizing) to shift the boundary between necessary and surplus labor or to influence the conditions under which their labor is performed, or community stakeholders threatening legal action against a local firm and effecting a new distribution of appropriated surplus value toward environmental cleanup. Each of these acts marshals bodies and materials and affects flows of surplus labor, in the process constituting power, class, and subjects.

This conception of power refuses to see itself as vested in any place or thing—the market, property, corporations, a state or institution—from which it emanates as a steady, radiating force (Latour 1986). Power as a force is void until it is performed, transformed, and translated. In the absence of an overarching structure of power, a familiar script of dominance and defeat cannot be drawn on to smother the potential for different sorts of class politics and possibilities to emerge. We are left with the contingencies of power in all social sites. Our interest is to differentiate and disaggregate power in a heterogeneous economic field, and to discover novel and productive powers where power-as-domination once reigned.

Class and Economic Difference

Despite the extraordinary contemporary flowering of theories of difference, when it comes to class we are faced with the "same." The contemporary economic (and therefore also the social) field is represented as dominated by a single class process—capitalist exploitation; the class descriptors we encounter are those that "belong" to capitalism—working class or proletariat, capitalist class, or bourgeoisie.[21] Such economic monism is perhaps the most telling legacy of the structural, systemic, and hegemonic conceptions that have colonized the economic terrain.[22]

Feminist theorists have challenged the omission from conventional economic representation of the economic activities in which most people are engaged—nonmarket-oriented, noncapitalist, household-based production (of cooked food and cleaned houses and cared-for elders and children, etc.), which absorbs more hours per week in both rich and poor countries than does laboring for capitalist firms (Folbre and Abel 1989; Beneria 1996). But their attempts to produce a representation of economic difference often fall into the binary trap that is laid for those who would differentiate capitalist from noncapitalist practices. True to the binary template, the latter are usually seen as less significant, less productive, less world-shaping, less real.

Here we can detect the workings of what might be called "capitalocentrism" (Gibson-Graham 1996). Whenever noncapitalist economic processes (such as independent commodity production) are seen, for example, as obsolete remnants of a precapitalist "traditional" economy, or as seedbeds of truly capitalist endeavor, or as ultimately "capitalist" because they involve commodification or markets, we confront the operations of a discourse that places capitalism at the defining center of economic identity. All other forms of production are seen as opposite (and therefore deficient), complementary, the same as, or contained within capitalism; they are measured against a capitalist norm. Such "capitalonormativity" confines the proliferative potential of economic difference within a binary frame.

A conception of class that is not limited to structural positions and functional roles in a capitalist totality offers one way to destabilize the equivalence between Capitalism and Economy and to render economic identity open, multiple, and differentiated. The language of class makes intelligible a range of slave, feudal, independent, and communal class relations that coexist in the formal, market-oriented, and legally regulated economy, as well as in those more hidden or devalued sectors characterized as informal, domestic, and nonmarket. Naming and coming to terms with these can be seen as a political project of differentiation. To view the economic landscape not as colonized by a sameness called Capitalism, but as only discursively colonized by capitalist rhetoric, is to open up "realistic" possibilities for economic activism around class transition and transformation.

A language of economic difference presents a heterogeneously classed landscape, one that both offers and suggests hitherto unglimpsed opportunities for projects of change. In such a landscape the possibility of appropriating surplus labor in nonexploitative ways (in households, firms, and other organizations) and of distributing it to potentiate different social orders becomes present and proximate, instead of unlikely and strange.

Class and Political Affect

"[R]essentiment is the primal class passion." (Jameson 1995, 86)

Class politics is traditionally aligned with a truncated affective regime in which anger and resentment are the preeminent emotions. In the scripted scenarios that provoke and channel class feeling, humiliation and outrage attach to the "victims" of exploitation,[23] producing recognition and antagonism, solidarity and division, protection and persecution as political "behaviors" of class.

Perhaps the narrative that pulls most powerfully on class emotions today is the story of global capitalism circulating widely in a number of forms. This representation of an expansive, naturally hegemonic system of exploitation positions workers (and the left more generally) in relation to a massive revealed antagonist—calling forth the familiar emotions of moral outrage or victimized self-regard, pure animus in the face of a powerful enemy, and desire for fundamental redress accompanied by bitterness, resignation, and guilt in the face of the thwarting of that desire. These feelings may be accompanied by a moral and epistemological certitude that is akin to contempt. As Wendy Brown characterizes the later modern liberal (and here we read leftist) subject, "starkly accountable yet dramatically impotent, s/he quite literally seethes with ressentiment" (1995, 69).

Though the narrative of working class exploitation and oppression interpellates subjects with a presumptive desire for freedom, another more hidden process of subjectification is also at work. And that, of course, is the production of desire for the narrative itself, with its familiar actors and subject positions, its heroes and foes, its utopian terminus or telos. This may even translate into a desire for Capitalism, the antagonist without which self-recognition is difficult and emotional energy diffuse.

We are concerned about losing Marx's focus on the bodily intensity of performing surplus labor and on the affective intensity associated with exploitation. But we would also like to "undo" the ties that have harnessed those intensities to a limited range of emotions. If we follow the insights of Silvan Tomkins and Brian Massumi, that "undoing" will involve the production of more and different class narratives.

Tomkins argues that

> because affect is inherently brief, it requires the conjunction of other mechanisms to connect affective moments with each other and thereby increase the duration, coherence and continuity of affective experience. Cognition plays a major role in such magnification. (Sedgwick and Frank 1995, 179)

Massumi makes a related point about the contextualization of affect, distinguishing affect and emotion. "Affect is intensity" while

> emotion is qualified intensity, the conventional, consensual point of insertion of intensity into semantically and semiotically formed progressions, into narrativizable action-reaction circuits, into function and meaning. It is intensity owned and recognized. (1996, 221)

Within the Marxian political tradition the affect of exploitation—its bodily intensity—has been "owned and recognized" through a narrative of alienation and injury and the organizing emotion of ressentiment. Over the last century or more, these have been constitutive of a vigorous and morally authoritative form of class politics. But alongside their positive and successful effects are others—resignation (at least where revolutionary possibility is concerned), the tendency to focus on pain and injury rather than hope and possibility, blaming and moralizing rather than envisioning and acting. In Brown's terms, "ressentiment takes the place of freedom as a collective project" (1995). Revolutionary possibility is relegated to the future and the present becomes barren of real possibility. It is therefore also empty of the kinds of emotions (like creative excitement, pleasure, hope, surprise, pride and satisfaction, daily enjoyment) that are associated with present possibilities.

We are keen to enlarge the domain of class narrative and widen the affective register of class politics. Given the different types of class relations, the different moments of the class process, and the different relations of class to other dimensions of identity, narrative and emotional possibilities are infinite. Some corollaries of this pronouncement:

1. We cannot presume that any particular emotions, including ones like anger, resignation, or resentment that are typically associated with class, are uniquely appropriate class emotions. An individual may experience exploitation not in the context of domination (presumably allied with anger), but as a positive index of dutifulness, or as an act of love or of gender identity

or of ritual self-abnegation. A person may be exploited but not necessarily oppressed (for example, the familiar case of the individual who works in an otherwise communal enterprise but is not involved in communal surplus appropriation because of not wanting the duties and responsibilities associated with appropriating and distributing the surplus). Exploitation may be scripted into very different narratives, social arrangements, and emotional structures.

2. Class processes involve not only appropriation but also distribution; emotions associated with letting go and largesse may overshadow proprietary emotions and those associated with fairness and redress. Class politics may be animated by stories not merely of justice and freedom but also of potentiation, as politicized class subjects activate some of their visions and goals by distributing appropriated wealth to the sites and subjects they wish to enliven. (Here the example of the Mondragon cooperatives comes to mind, where much of the surplus is used to capitalize other cooperatives.) In such stories there is room for visionary speculation and channels for hope—as well as other unfamiliar left emotions.

3. If class is not embedded in a vision of a systemic totality, a singular macronarrative cannot suffice to structure class affect. The stories that mobilize class emotions may be incompatible and divergent as well as diverse. Theorizing a site like the sex industry, we may find different class stories in the industry and different emotional possibilities associated with them. If some sex workers are not exploited but are involved in communal or individual surplus appropriation, will they have the same feelings as those who are enslaved, or those who work for a capitalist appropriator, or those who labor in feudal "serfdom" for a pimp? Will those who affiliate politically with them feel the same toward all these workers? Economic difference and the narratives through which it is manifested allow for class politics in the absence of a central and unifying story line.

4. Finally, class affect is retemporalized when freedom from exploitation becomes not merely a future possibility but also a present one. The politics of class transformation loses its association with longing and self-denial and becomes less entangled with self-aggrandizement (often taken as compensation for loss of possibility). The present opens up to the full range of emotions and class possibilities.

Finding the Words, Telling the Stories

Each of the essays in *Class and Its Others* takes the language of class into arenas where class has seldom been theorized (such as household and emotional life), or connects class to the themes of identity, power, economic difference, and political affect in unusual ways. Taken together, the essays intimate the potential of an anti-essentialist class discourse to "take back the economy," to constitute new domains of identity, and to suggest possibilities of political (re)construction.

"'This Job Has No End': African American Domestic Workers and Class Becoming" tackles the elusive "mutual constitution" of race, gender and class. Cecilia Rio traces the way that African American women working as paid domestic workers in the nineteenth and early twentieth centuries actively sought a new class position, struggling to define themselves as "not slaves" or, in positive terms, as independent self-appropriating producers and sellers of domestic services. Rio's reading of the struggles of African American women shows them exercising decisive power in this class transition, which was never recognized by the union movement, or by historians, as a struggle around class. In Rio's reading, class touches identity lightly but affects subjectivity profoundly and pervasively. Never self-identified in class terms, African American domestic workers create new self-understandings, new gender and racial meanings, and new forms of empowerment through enacting a relatively invisible class transition.

Jenny Cameron's essay, "Domesticating Class: Femininity, Heterosexuality, and Household Politics," takes on the political/affective complex that links power, domination, and ressentiment. Using a close reading of interviews with women about their domestic labor practices, she undermines the familiar alignment of exploitation and oppression, suggesting that some women who are "exploited" in their households may be simultaneously engaged in the process of performatively producing their gender and sexual identities and may not necessarily be dominated or oppressed. Cameron highlights the possibility that very different emotions might accompany class exploitation (enjoyment or fulfillment, for example) and connects the affective experience of class to the distribution of surplus labor, which, like exploitation, may be associated with a wide and contradictory range of emotions.

In "Exploitation in the Labor of Love," Harriet Fraad extends the theory of emotional labor from the service industries and "caring" professions to the intimate, carceral realm of the family. Using the distinction between necessary and surplus labor to illuminate her concerns, Fraad focuses on the surplus emotional labor performed by children in service to parents. Many individuals who, as children, were subject to a high rate of emotional exploitation by family members suffer from emotional and mental illness in adult life. This essay provides a powerful example of the insights to be gained by taking class analysis into realms, like the family and emotion, where a consideration of labor and exploitation has rarely ventured.

"Spring Flowers" by Susan Jahoda is a story with accompanying images that represents the complex intertwining of race, sexuality, place, power, gender, class, and love. In "Spring Flowers" labor is produced in different forms and appropriated and distributed in complex transactions and flows. Jahoda focuses on the disjunctures (including surgical) that accompany the formation of bodies, subjects, and relations. Breaking the familiar association of female, penetrated, exploited, and colored bodies with relative powerlessness, she suggests the different political and social possibilities that become visible when power is not conflated with any aspect of identity, experience, or form of embodiment. Jahoda's piece does not highlight or emphasize class but lets it emerge surreptitiously, to shape and indeed to queer (or suggest the queerness of) subjectivity and identity.

Marjolein van der Veen's essay, "Beyond Slavery and Capitalism: Producing Class Difference in the Sex Industry," works against the vision, produced by both radical and Marxist feminists, of prostitution as uniformly exploitative and degrading. Drawing on sex radicalism and the discourse of the rights of prostitutes, van der Veen produces a representation of economic difference in the industry in which slave, capitalist, feudal, independent, and communal class relations can be seen to coexist. By acknowledging the existence of different class narratives, she makes visible the very different economic, moral, political, and emotional possibilities associated with prostitution, offering a range of social possibilities outside simple condemnation and celebration.

Janet Hotch's chapter broaches the possibility of collective projects among the self-employed—a set of workers usually associated with independence and organizational isolation. In "Classing the Self-Employed: New Possibilities of Power and Collectivity," Hotch argues that acknowledging the differences among these workers might actually help rather than hinder efforts to bring them together. Her class analysis of self-employed workers yields no invariant commonalities among them, even of class experience, highlighting the need to construct rather than presume the grounds of solidarity. Bringing together a politics of difference with a politics of solidarity, Hotch's essay suggests ways that poststructuralist theory can contribute new directions and possibilities for class politics.

"Los Angeles: A Postmodern Class Mapping" by Enid Arvidson takes on the familiar representation of Los Angeles (the paragon of "postmodern" urbanization) as characterized by class polarization and/or class decline. Using an empirical study of different class relations, she finds class to be a ubiquitous if largely unrecognized feature of the Los Angeles landscape. In case studies of Fontana and Malibu, she discovers radically different kinds of class experience but at the same time the possibility of recognizing class commonalities across space. What Arvidson's essay suggests is the potential fruitfulness of a class reading of the social landscape for "taking back the economy" discursively and politically.

The desire to make distinctions, to set up different valuing frames, to class-ify and categorize subjects has permeated class politics since its inception. In the concluding essay, "Blue Collar, White Collar: Deconstructing Classification," Jacquelyn Southern scrutinizes the most prevalent classificatory device used to disaggregate the labor force in the twentieth century. Taking on the distinction between blue-collar and white-collar workers, Southern explores the difficulties inherent in a categorical conception of class. She shows how assumptions about unity, commitment, and alignment are made when classification and politics are intermixed, alluding to the divisive effects of these assumptions on struggles to alleviate or transform exploitation. This final chapter helps to make explicit some of the problems of organizing political movements and actions around identity-based collectivities, clearing the ground for a class politics mobilized across differences.

Each of the essays in *Class and Its Others* is a contribution to a nascent class discourse. To produce a discourse of class is to make visible economic relations that exist and could exist, to catalyze desires, to attempt to re-enliven the socialist imagination. It is a project beginning with a language, an open-ended matrix that frees as well as confines.

A language provides a provisional ontology—a set of boundaries, contours, and emphases—but it cannot tell you what to say. Its terms are redefined each time they are recontextualized, in the endless and political process of making meaning. What we would hope in attempting to develop and build on a language of class is not that everyone would learn to speak it or come to understand their experience primarily in its terms, but that new connections would be made, projects forged, and identities constituted on the social and economic terrain.

Notes

1. Though tracing its roots to popular movements of the early nineteenth century and before.

2. When "working class" is used in the same breath with "middle class," the meanings come together with a familiar clash: "Middle class implies hierarchy and therefore implies lower class," Williams writes, whereas working implies nonworking,

leaving all those "who are not *working class* unproductive and useless (easy enough for an aristocracy, but hardly accepted by a productive *middle class*)" (1983, 65).

3. Dimock and Gilmore (1994), Kumar (1997), Wray and Newitz (1997) are among the fascinating recent books that explore this conception of class. Collections that embrace class as an economic relation of exploitation (as well as the other meanings of class) include Hall (1997), Joyce (1995), and Nielsen and Ware (1997).

4. The theory of exploitation in volume 1 is animated by a compelling representation of the laboring body. See, for example, the chapters on the length of the working day.

5. Economic theory has generated a variety of surplus theories, often characterized by a vision of original scarcity, a resultant general imperative of economic necessity (constituting economic activity as necessary to sustenance and reproduction), and a corresponding concept of surplus as a residual in excess of what is required for sustenance and reproduction. Marx's alternative view was that scarcity, rather than necessarily being a pregiven starting point located in the material world, was also created as an effect of certain class processes and their role in constituting society—as, in fact, a problematic by-product of a productive abundance.

6. Exploitation can be seen as one of the processes that presents the problem of economic necessity to the individual or other social unit. The process of appropriation of surplus labor itself delineates and defines the surplus (i.e., what is not going to go into the subsistence or reproduction of the producer). What is necessary and what is surplus is not predefined or given, in some humanist or cultural essentialist sense, but is established at the moment of appropriation itself.

7. Or by a collective of capitalists, such as the board of directors of a capitalist firm.

8. Marx also developed another distinction, that between productive and unproductive labor, in order to distinguish those workers who are engaged in capitalist commodity production and production of surplus value (and are therefore involved in an exploitative class process) from those who are not (for instance, workers in advertising and marketing or in the financial sector, or workers like domestic servants who sell their labor power but are not involved in commodity production). In other words, the term "unproductive" refers to any labor that in Marx's particular accounting system was deemed not to be productive of surplus value for a capitalist. The unfortunate realist interpretation of this distinction as designating who was truly "productive" in society has fueled divisive practices ranging from blue-collar privilege within the union movement in capitalist countries to the active persecution of "mental laborers" in the Chinese cultural revolution. This does not mean that one can or should attempt to function without boundaries and distinctions, but rather points to the critical vigilance that must be exercised in their use.

9. "The character of this aleatory materialism is not denoted by reference to a world of 'matter' (e.g., the economy or the physical body as opposed to a separate world of ideas) but rather by its irreducibility to *any* given order" (Callari and Ruccio 1996, 26). In the words of Laclau (1984, 43), "the only meaning of the term 'material-

ism' which seems valid to me is that which opposes the reduction of the real to the concept."

10. "The most profound *potential* meaning of Althusser's statement that everything existing in the social is overdetermined is the assertion that the social constitutes itself as a symbolic order. The symbolic—i.e., overdetermined—character of social relations therefore implies that they lack an ultimate literality . . . there is no possibility of fixing an *ultimate* literal sense for which the symbolic would be a second and derived plane of signification. Society and social agents lack any essence." (Laclau and Mouffe 1985, 97–98; emphasis in the original).

11. As perhaps the preeminent example of this constructive analytical process, *Capital* can be read as a social analysis undertaken from the "entry point" of class (Resnick and Wolff 1987, 25–29). In its three volumes Marx produced a detailed theoretical examination of the ways that capitalist class processes overdetermine and in turn are overdetermined by other social processes, generating a knowledge of capitalist exploitation that he believed (rightly it turned out) would have profound political effects.

12. See "The Critique of the Gotha Program" (1978).

13. In the Chartist imagination, for example, the disenfranchised producers of social wealth were sustaining a class of politically powerful nonproducers who could only be seen as parasitical. When the Chartists demanded that the laboring classes be included in the national polity, they did so on the basis of a doctrine of natural rights and a vision of labor as the ultimate and only source of wealth (Stedman Jones 1983).

14. As Chantal Mouffe (1995) argues, the logic of self-assertion associated with modernism is independent of, and does not require, the logic of self-grounding with which it is historically associated.

15. Judith Butler contends that "any totalizing concept of the universal will shut down rather than authorize the unanticipated and unanticipatable claims that will be made under the sign of 'the universal.'" She is not trying to do "away with the category, but trying to relieve the category of its foundationalist weight in order to render it as a site of permanent political contest" (1992, 8).

16. Other contemporary theorists of identity are concerned to destabilize given identities such as woman, homosexual, white, or Asian, and while these projects are implicitly designed to clear the space for new meanings of these identity categories to emerge (as well as for identities in general to dissolve into fluidity), they are often less concerned to positively identify or enact new meanings.

17. We are not arguing for the abandonment of terms such as "working class," but for an approach to their use that does not know in advance what they mean.

18. The conception of class as an aspect or feature of social structure is allied with a taxonomic vision of social groups or classes constituted by characteristics common to their members. Under capitalism, for example, class identity is associated not only with a distinct position in relations of exploitation, but also with particular relations with power in the labor process (belonging disproportionately to the

"ruling" or capitalist class) and property in the means of production (again a capitalist prerogative). These relations with *exploitation, power,* and *property* are seen as the principal commonalities that unify and differentiate working and capitalist classes (Resnick and Wolff 1986). Of course, allocating all societal members to class positions within this singular (capitalist) totality has been hard to do, and countless projects have tried to smooth over differences or tidy up class identity by placing recalcitrant citizens in hybrid structural positions/identities occupying the space between true workers and true capitalists (see, for example, Wright 1978, 1985).

19. In the same vein, Foucault (1981) speaks of gay identity as a zone of potential rather than a fixity: "We must be aware of . . . the tendency to reduce being gay to the question: 'Who am I?' and 'What is the secret of my desire?' Might it not be better if we asked ourselves what sort of relationships we can set up, invent, multiply or modify through our homosexuality? . . . We must therefore insist on becoming gay, rather than persisting in defining ourselves as such" (quoted in Cohen 1993).

20. This does not mean that we would position power as an "exteriority" (Foucault 1990, 94) with respect to these economic processes, but merely that we do not want to treat them as the same.

21. Complicating terms, such as middle class, petit bourgeoisie, and lumpen proletariat, are all understood in relation to capitalism. The middle class, for example, may be seen as occupying contradictory class locations, with some aspects of their identity aligned with the working class and others with the capitalist class.

22. This seems to be truly a legacy of the Marxian tradition rather than of Marx, who went out of his way to study and theorize noncapitalist class structures while focusing his major work on a critical analysis of capitalism.

23. This "class passion," to use Jameson's phrase, has a broad lineage deriving not just from Marx's representation of relations between the capitalist and laborer, but also from Hegel's master-slave dialectic, Nietzsche's base-noble distinction, and countless classical formulations.

"This Job Has No End":

African American Domestic Workers

and Class Becoming

Cecilia Marie Rio

Miss Grand-lady turns to me and says, "And what do you do?" . . . Of course
I told her! "I do housework," I said. "Oh," says she, "you are a housewife."
"Oh, no," says I, "I do housework, and I do it everyday because that is the
way I make my livin'." . . .

Miss Timid turns to me and says, "I do housework too but I don't always
feel like tellin'. People look down on you so."

Well, I can tell you that I moved in after that remark and straightened
her out! . . .

Of course, a lot of people think it's *smart* not to talk about *slavery* any-
more, but after freedom came, it was domestics that kept us from perishin'
by the wayside. (Childress 1995, 33–37; emphasis in original)

Though slavery "officially" ended with the passage of the Thirteenth Amendment, African Americans struggled to free themselves from the deeply en-
graved emotions, oppressive daily practices, and material deprivations of
slavery that continued to saturate the social landscape well into the twentieth century. As domestic workers who were legally free and paid, rather than
enslaved, many African American women fought to break the continued association of their race with slave exploitation and servitude—despite being
relegated to an occupation that smacked of it.[1] This chapter examines how
these women found ways to radically transform the economic and social conditions of paid domestic labor during the first half of the twentieth century.

After the abolition of slavery, African American women who were domestic workers were often sellers of labor power and hence at the mercy of
expectations and desires of people they worked for. They were expected to

perform a variety of chores, with diffuse obligations, frequently under dehumanizing conditions. Postbellum paid domestic work was usually based on a fusion of workplace and home. Work days and weeks had no end for many domestic workers, and remuneration was irregular and often in kind. Over time, however, African American women gradually and through small-scale, incremental changes redefined their work. Most notably, they standardized their jobs as domestic workers so that they were increasingly able to exchange predefined services for a specified amount of money, modeling themselves after other petty producers and vendors in the African American community. Individually and collectively, African American women struggled to assert their right to a dignified and meaningful existence by redefining their working conditions and the processes that shaped their labor and gave it meaning. This historic cultural and economic transformation in the way that paid domestic work was carried out can be theorized in part as a class transition. As more and more African American women began to occupy new class positions as independent producers and sellers of domestic services, the social relations of paid domestic labor changed significantly.

Intertwined with struggles over class transition in the realm of paid domestic labor were other equally important processes, notably the reinvention and reiteration of new gender and racial identities and the protection and maintenance of social life in African American communities. The desire to sustain and nurture family life within their own community was a particularly powerful catalyst of change for African American women. Protecting the relative autonomy of black family life has been a critical area of struggle and resistance for the African American community since slavery (Hogan 1984). Such autonomy was achieved with the help of African American women (many of whom were domestic workers) in the face of severe cultural, political, and economic violence, including widespread lynching, rape, criminalization, debt peonage, and Jim Crow segregation (Davis 1981). As domestic workers, African American women found ways to nourish and protect family life even under these severe conditions by striking a more generative balance between their work in public and private realms (Joseph 1981; Dill 1988). In the process new representations of black womanhood emerged to challenge the existing racial and gender stereotypes.

The resulting transformation in domestic work does not appear in any of the dominant narratives about paid domestic labor. One effect of the invisibility of this process of change has been the denial of the role of African American women as active subjects who resisted and remade social life not only for themselves but for society in general. To help make the invisible visible, this chapter offers a series of theoretical interventions. First, I explore the mutually constitutive meanings of race, gender, and paid domestic work that were socially constructed within the United States in the period after slavery was abolished. The aim here is to highlight how meanings and representations forged in the symbolic realm during slavery continued to function within social and material practices now designated "free."

Second, I examine the dominant discourses on the transformation of domestic labor for the hidden assumptions, denied possibilities, and predetermined outcomes associated with paid domestic work. The point here is to challenge the narrative of occupational change that represents it as part of a teleology or series of ordered steps in the development of capitalism (Gibson-Graham 1996; Unger 1987b), and to undermine the widespread view of African American women as victims of the undiminishing power of a set of interconnected structures of oppression. This critical destabilization then serves as the rejected ground from which a creative rethinking of domestic labor transformation can be launched. In the remainder of the chapter I employ an anti-essentialist class analysis to help map out the subtle changes that took place in the performance of paid domestic labor by African American women and the exchanges of labor, money, and meaning that constituted this practice. My aim here is to help fortify the affirmative task of composing an alternative story about African American domestic workers that foregrounds their role as makers and shapers of the American social and economic landscape.

The Social Construction of Race, Gender, and Domestic Work

In the United States, the problem is complicated by the fact that for years domestic service was performed by slaves and afterward up till today largely by black freedmen—thus adding a despised race to a despised calling. . . . Thus by long experience the United States has come to associate domestic service with some inferiority in race or training. (Du Bois 1899, 136)

In *The Philadelphia Negro*, written in 1899, Du Bois recognized that the social construction of paid domestic work in the United States as a despised and degraded occupation was intensified by its increasing association with race. The social and discursive connections between domestic service, slavery, and African Americans had important implications for the ways in which the meanings of femininity, race, and housework were reshaped in the post-slavery era. New representations of gender, race, and women's work were mutually constituted in a milieu in which ideals of freedom and equality jostled with still fresh memories of slavery and ardent beliefs in social hierarchy and differential racial competencies.

African American women had few employment options available after the abolition of slavery. Severe racism and discrimination meant that the majority of women had to work, even after marriage.[2] Since they were largely excluded from higher paying capitalist wage labor, most continued to work in agriculture or domestic service.[3] For those that left rural areas for towns and cities in the South or migrated north, domestic service became an increasingly important occupation (Greene and Woodson 1930; Jones 1985).[4]

The increased affluence and urbanization that accompanied capitalist development contributed to important changes in family lifestyles, gender differences, and racialized identities. Throughout the second half of the nineteenth century and the beginning of the twentieth, more and more household goods were manufactured in factories and sold as commodities. White married women became increasingly dependent on their husbands for their survival (Strasser 1987), and new wealth allowed a growing number of white families to copy a privileged lifestyle in which the "ideal" wife stayed home. The economic contributions of full-time housewives to the family became more elusive and devalued, and feminine attributes like companionship, personality, and attractiveness grew in importance (Wilson 1979).[5] The home became seen as a (white) man's private kingdom where his dependent wife, untouched and unsullied by public life, remained attentive to his needs.

In this fluid society the social meanings attached to race, gender, and work were changing under the influence of newly dominant discourses of humanity, freedom, and equality. With the abolition of slavery, practices and beliefs that were once familiar to many were legally outlawed and socially challenged. Many households that had depended upon slaves as domestic laborers now were forced to employ African American women to perform domestic labor. And in those increasingly affluent households in the North, the domestic laborers who were employed were Southern migrants who had once been enslaved, or whose family members had been slaves. New meanings and representations of womanhood, racial identity, and domestic work were socially constructed in response to this altered social landscape.

Importantly, new models for women and the home were promulgated—all of which had important implications for the construction of racial difference. Prior to the Civil War the ideals of "true (white) womanhood" had emphasized "piety, purity, submissiveness and domesticity" (Welter 1976, 21). In the postwar period, especially during the rapid industrialization and urbanization of American society from 1870 to 1920, the gendered and

racialized meanings associated with the "cult of true womanhood" intensified. The ideal household came to be represented as a private sanctuary for
men, an escape from the turmoil of the competitive world, and for women
a place of leisure and reflection. And the ideal domestic work came to be
seen as that of nurturing—what women did out of love for their families
and as their civic and moral responsibility, an activity that was not to be valued in economic terms or seen as labor.[6] These ideals required white women
to be free from dust, dirt, and other impurities resulting from hard, sweaty,
physical labor. Yet clothes had to be washed, children had to be bathed and
their messes cleaned up, floors had to be scrubbed and polished. Such physically demanding labor stood in direct contrast to the representation of a
white woman's delicate constitution, her purity and submissiveness.

Against the ideal images of essentially *white* homes, *white* women and
unpaid domestic labor were their devalued "others"—representations of
the black shanty or ghetto dwelling, the "black/negro" woman and paid
domestic labor.[7] With slaves no longer legally defined as chattels but designated human, a whole new set of discursive hierarchies became part of the
regulation of the strict boundary between black and white (Kayatekin forthcoming). The enforcement of racial difference centered less upon representations of blacks as animal or subhuman and shifted to other meanings still
tied up in a slave semiotic. Associations of childishness, dependence, dirti-
ness, bodily strength, and servitude remained folded into the subordinated
images, and these qualities were clearly present in the cultural representation of domestic service.

Paid domestic labor was women's work that was dirty, physically demanding, and degrading. Dirt signified blackness; its absence (purity) signified whiteness.[8] The strength of this association of dirt with impurity and
racial inferiority can be seen in the common portrayal of African American
domestic workers as pathological carriers of disease and contamination, especially tuberculosis (Hunter 1997). A female paid domestic worker was
seen as dependent on her physical strength and fortitude for economic survival. Black women were represented as strong and able to do heavy physical
work. In contrast the idealized (white) female body could not bear visible
evidence of dirt or sweat or other signs of manual labor. The rhetoric of race
was continually drawn on to differentiate unpaid domestic labor (white,
feminine, nurturing, and pure) from paid domestic labor (dirty, masculine,
physical, and degraded) and hence one group of women (white women)
from another (black women).

The stereotypical image of the African American domestic worker was
that of the mammy—an image that had its origins in the slave South. The

mammy was commonly portrayed as overweight and very physical, natural-ly designed for arduous domestic labor. Earthy and dark with accentuated African features, she was characteristically represented as an unsuitable part-ner for white males (Collins 1990). The mammy was seen to be obedient and loyal to her mistress, yet strong and aggressive with other African Americans, especially men. While clearly possessing a nonsexualized and uncivilized body, she was good with babies and children—but only able to nurture in a physical sense. Though full of inner contradictions and excesses, the mammy stereotype functioned to maintain the unstable and tenuous demarcation between white and black femininity, sexuality and mothering.

As new gender identities were socially constructed in the United States in the latter half of the nineteenth century, the differentiation of women's do-mestic work into unpaid and paid domestic labor played a crucial role in de-marcating and legitimizing boundaries between white and black women within a highly racialized code. The memory of slavery and its implication in all systems of social meaning served to naturalize these socially construct-ed differences. The power of the discursive and emotive remnants of slavery over the meaning of paid domestic labor, and the struggles of African Ameri-can women to eradicate these remembered aspects of exploitation and op-pression from the practice of domestic service, remain invisible to most ana-lysts of the transformation of domestic labor in the United States. In the next section of this chapter I explore some of the reasons for this invisibility.

Representations of the Transformation of Paid Domestic Labor

> Domestic service is a disappearing occupation or rivals the weather as a major controversial subject. (Stigler 1946, 1)

Changes in the meaning of race, gender, and domestic work during the late nineteenth century were accompanied by changes in the material practice of housework. The literature on the transformation of paid domestic work is differentiated by a preoccupation with its decline or disappearance or with its continued ability to produce and reproduce oppression.[9] All analyses tend to marginalize, and sometimes even eliminate, paid domestic work as a productive site of opportunity and resistance.

Modernization discourse depicts paid domestic labor as a declining occu-pation—a casualty of an evolving capitalism with its liberating labor mar-kets, increased commodification, and technological innovation in home production. Paid household work is theorized as both prior to and super-seded by capitalist development. In both its demand and supply side variants, modernization discourse implies that paid domestic work, to the extent that it continues to exist, functions as a gateway occupation through which unskilled labor passes into the mainstream.[10] A common discursive feature is the construction and authorization of domestic service as an occupational bridge for those who are marked as inferior or unskilled (Coser 1974; Stigler 1946; Katzman 1978).

In contrast to modernization discourse, which stresses the elevating consequences of capitalism, traditional Marxian discourse exposes the exploitation and immiseration of workers under capitalism. Marxian discourse usually theorizes paid domestic work as unproductive labor within a capitalist mode of production, and thus still subject to the dynamic of capital accumulation.[11] The immutable laws of capitalist development dictate that capital accumulation will penetrate the household, demonstrating "capital's increasing domination of all facets of life" (Strasser 1987, 54). "Pre-capitalist" domestic work is transformed as housework is mechanized and capitalist industry produces more household goods and services.

Neither of these discourses of paid domestic labor attend to the specificities of this work or to the subjects who performed it and were produced by it. The spotlight of analysis is securely focused on what is seen as the dominant economic process of capitalist industrialization. The production, appropriation, and distribution of domestic labor in a noncapitalist class process is problematized only as it becomes obliterated by or penetrated by capitalism.[12] In effect, what occurs is a discursive marginalization and subordination of the economic experiences of both women and people of color who have historically performed domestic labor and been denied access to capitalist class relations.[13]

Multiple oppressions theory departs sharply from modernization and traditional Marxian analyses by explicitly incorporating racial and gender oppression in analyses of paid domestic work. Emphasizing the interaction of race and class in demarcating salient differences among women, multiple oppressions discourse produces an analysis of paid household work as a highly devalued occupation assigned to the most oppressed groups in society. Highlighting the psychological oppression of African American domestic workers, multiple oppressions theory points to the ways in which white domination and privilege have been secured. African American women are portrayed as providing white families with "self-enhancing satisfactions" of superiority, thus reinforcing the privilege that comes from being white (Rollins 1985, 156). White women are represented as highly motivated by status and concerned to redefine their role in the domestic sphere as household managers of domestic workers and as social and emotional workers: seeing

to their husbands' comfort; developing the social, moral, and intellectual ca-
pacities of their children; and undertaking volunteer work to assist the less
fortunate (Dill 1994). These new household roles mark affluent white women
as "gentle women" with refined sensibilities, whose privilege rests upon the
delegation of the most physical and dirty work of the home to domestic
workers (Palmer 1989).

Multiple oppressions discourse depicts paid domestic work as a site of
inherent victimization—a constructed job space to which the most dis-
advantaged groups are consigned and out of which they must move in
order to become fully empowered or equal. In those cases where resistance
and struggle against the oppressive conditions of domestic service are noted,
they are most often theorized within the context of individual characteristics or personality traits of particular domestic workers. Dill, for example, argues that domestic workers struggled to make a socially devalued occupation
personally rewarding as captured in domestic worker Queenie Watkins'
phrase "make your job good yourself" (Dill 1994, 84).

The discourse of multiple oppressions shifts the explanation for changes
in paid domestic labor away from a sole focus on capitalism, adding to the
theoretical frame the mutually interacting structures of racism and sexism.
But rather than freeing us to focus on the specificities of paid domestic
work for African American women, the discourse produces an analytical
stranglehold that eliminates the possibilities of seeing this labor as a productive site of resistance and potentiality.[14] The focus on structural power and
privilege leads us to dismiss or discount the ways in which paid household
workers actively engaged in the re-classing, re-racializing, and re-gendering
of domestic work. The token recognition of individual acts of resistance
tends to leave untheorized the collective impact these personal actions may
have had on the economic conditions of domestic work. The powerful representation of structural oppressions as determining the interpersonal dynamics of domestic work renders all interactions that attempt to transcend
these structures either nonexistent, ineffectual, or inconsequential.[15] This
produces a tension in which personal struggles of domestic workers are not
recognized as having important economic or social consequences.

One important political implication of this discourse is that only struggles
that take place through collective, large-scale, or institutional mechanisms
are seen as effectively changing the oppressive and exploitative conditions of
paid domestic work. My concern is that such theoretical priors place limits
on our capacity to recognize and value the significance of workplace resistance among African Americans, many of whom have been historically denied access to traditional capitalist institutions (Hogan 1984; Kelley 1994).[16]

While multiple oppressions discourse emphasizes the privileged positions of certain women relative to others, the analysis of privilege often ends there without any self-consciousness of the power embedded in representational strategy itself. Traditional representations of domestic service tend to discursively devalue African American women's activism. Like others, I would like to abandon this devaluation and break free from the capitalocentrism, victimhood, and structural determinism privileged by the dominant discourses on domestic labor. My aim is to employ a different discursive framework that represents paid domestic work as a site of productive potentiality.

Class Analysis and a Revaluing of Paid Domestic Labor

Black feminist theory has long advanced the mutual effectivity of race, class, and gender identities, arguing that these identities should not be seen as fixed and intractable but rather as dynamic (hooks 1981; Collins 1990; Brewer 1993; Guy-Sheftall 1995; Higginbotham 1995). Black racial identity, for example, often shifts between a racial identity imposed by others and a racial identity one claims as one's own through struggle (Marable 1992). To be able to incorporate complexly constituted and changing identities, an analysis must allow for the simultaneity of oppression and opportunity (Brewer 1993). This simultaneity is compatible with an understanding of the embeddedness and relationality of paid domestic work: it is a space of possibilities and potentiality as well as oppression and exploitation.

The overdeterminist epistemology and anti-essentialist class analysis developed by Resnick and Wolff (1987) offers a set of representational strategies that allow me to revalue paid domestic work as a site of political potential and opportunity and to rethink the process of its transformation with African American women at the center of an affirming narrative. An anti-essentialist notion of class sees the process of producing, appropriating, and distributing surplus labor and the struggles around this social process as constituted by a host of material and discursive overdeterminants. This approach has been creatively used to explore the connections between the material conditions of class processes and the cultural politics of identity and personal empowerment,[17] and I am interested in employing it to develop a broader understanding of class struggle—one that can incorporate the effectivity of race and gender, historical and cultural narratives, personal style and dignity.

This form of class analysis allows me to detach paid domestic work from any central or determining economic dynamic, such as the force of capitalist industrialization. As a labor process, paid domestic work can be seen as influenced by a range of economic and noneconomic processes; so, for example, the capitalist commodification of household goods has no more inherent power to determine this work than do the cultural and emotional vestiges of slavery. My analysis also breaks from a teleological, uniform, and stage-like vision of economic transition, allowing a more complex picture of economic difference and change that emphasizes both the multiplicity of coexisting class processes in society and household labor's relative autonomy from capitalism. It allows me to look for class processes in discursively privatized spaces like the household, and to reveal economic relations that are foreclosed or obscured by previous explanatory endeavors.[18] Lastly, an anti-essentialist class analysis helps me to show how African American women were not simply passive victims of a racialized division of labor. Through this analysis I have become aware of the myriad ways that African American women struggled to redefine the conditions under which paid domestic labor was performed. Domestic workers fought against the continued association of their race with slavery and provided themselves with a new positive class identity as independent producers and sellers of domestic services. Over time, individual and collective acts of resistance helped to redefine domestic work and limit the memories and practices associated with slave exploitation, as well as shape new racial and gender identities.

From "They Job" to "My Job":
Class and the Transformation of Paid Domestic Labor

> When I say "my job" I mean a job I got and I'd keep if they acted decent. Now that is always by the day. Nobody trying to work me to death. "They" job is for them. A job you did and did more and more. (Clark-Lewis 1994, 162)

Paid domestic work for African American women in the postbellum period was "they job," a "job you did and did more and more and more" (1994, 162). The distinction between this form of work and that of domestic labor under slavery was, for many, not clearly marked. While not legally owned by their employers, domestic servants lived in and were at the beck and call of the household day and night. When not in uniforms they were clothed in their masters' and mistresses' castoffs. They were often restricted to entering a household through the back door (Clark-Lewis 1994). It was the custom for time off to be limited to Thursday evenings and every other Sunday. They were employed doing dirty or demeaning work—asked to polish banisters, doorknobs, scrub floors, and continually maintain and demarcate the boundary between dirt and purity (Palmer 1989).[19] Often the way tasks got delegated and performed revealed the connections between race, servitude, physical work, dirt, and domesticity. Long after the invention of the mop, for example, African American women were still expected to scrub the floors on hands and knees (Rollins 1985). In return for their labor, domestic workers were paid in kind in the form of room and board, with a small monetary allowance. The amount of this wage was unregulated, as was the quality of the lodgings and food, and varied according to region and by family or household.[20] As under slavery, some paid domestic workers were well treated and remunerated and others were not.

Although denied access to more desirable class transitional paths from slavery for several decades, African American domestic workers rarely thought of themselves as powerless individuals and continued to resist the memory of slavery that permeated their domestic work. In this section I explore how they struggled to redefine their work, making "they job" into "my job"—refusing to be simply suppliers of undifferentiated labor power, willing to perform every household task under any circumstance as if they were still slaves or general girls for hire. Over time, African American domestic workers demanded more money and eventually established contractual relationships, including use of prespecified verbal or written agreements which limited hours and tasks. They moved out of the master's house and redefined domestic labor as day work. They also worked through both formal and informal channels to establish industry standards for what constituted domestic work. In the process they forged new racial and gender identities that challenged the white supremacist ideals of femininity, race, women's work, and home that dominated cultural representation.

This transformation can be understood as an attempt by domestic workers to establish themselves as independent producers and sellers of domestic services.[21] The struggle to become a seller of specified domestic services can be seen as a fight for dignity and independence and for the right to control the amount of surplus labor produced, as well as who was to appropriate and distribute it. As a seller of unregulated and undifferentiated labor power to the master or mistress of the household in return for room, board, and an allowance, the paid domestic worker had no control over what work she did, how much and for whom, or over the level of subsistence at which she would live.

It is difficult to class the paid domestic laborer who labored under these conditions. She is not a capitalist wage laborer, with a defined portion of her labor designated necessary (the wage) and the rest appropriated by a capitalist as surplus value embedded in a capitalist commodity. She is more like a slave or feudal serf whose surplus labor is appropriated in kind by the master of the household in return for food, shelter, and perhaps a small amount of money. The task of analytically defining the class position of the seller of labor power in the household is a complicated one that will not be pursued here; my interest is in highlighting the class process that was constructed out of the murky social and economic relations associated with paid domestic labor.

As an independent producer and seller of specified domestic services—ironing, laundering, floor washing, etc.—the domestic worker became, in effect, an independent contractor producing use values in the form of tangible services sold in exchange for a specified amount of money. The worker was more likely to be able to determine how many services she would supply (that is, how much she would work), what the charge for each service was, and what her own subsistence level would be. She now had some power, albeit limited, over the movable boundary between necessary and surplus labor. Necessary labor was what she had to expend performing services that would produce enough income to live on, and surplus labor was all that was expended over and above this amount. As an independent commodity producer, the domestic worker could limit the amount of surplus labor expended as she was not required to work more than she needed to. And if she did decide to work more, the meager surplus produced could be appropriated by the worker herself. Or, if she scrimped on subsistence and redefined her necessary labor, the domestic worker could self-appropriate more surplus and decide how to distribute it.

Domestic workers did not have to own the means of production to be independent commodity producers. Their customers owned the means of production, including the actual place of work, the vacuum cleaners, washing machines, and other tools, as well as the cleaning agents and other inputs into production that domestic workers used. This class transformation did not require any initial investment—only a shift in the process of negotiating work and in the subjectivity of the worker. Moreover, any change in technology—the introduction of better cooking or cleaning equipment, for example—was paid for by the householder/customer. The independent producer was, therefore, not required to make a distribution out of appropriated surplus to secure these conditions of self-employment.

The emergence of a new type of domestic worker engaged in a self-appropriating class process did not, however, necessarily imply superior working conditions or a higher standard of living. This change took place gradually and under the extremely adverse, racist, and oppressive conditions that existed after slavery. Most African American women did not enjoy their labor as domestic workers—they continued to work long hours for little pay and under demanding conditions. As one former domestic worker interviewed by Clark-Lewis claimed: "Life for a colored woman didn't never get 'better.' The most it got was 'different'" (1994, 148). At the same time, this transition in the way that work was performed and surplus appropriated had important implications for the production of new gender and racial identities for African American women. In these areas of social life, what became different *was,* as I aim to point out, arguably "better."

Struggles to Transform Paid Domestic Labor

The transformation of paid domestic work involved a variety of strategies including individual and collective work actions, spatial segregation from work, migration from the South where slave memories were strongest, the development of support networks and community organizations, the protection of kindred relationships and familial sovereignty, and the pursuit of personal freedom, individual dignity, and cultural expression. The ability of African American domestic workers to collectively engage in class struggle through mainstream political and economic institutions was severely limited. Unions were known for their overt racism and exclusionary practices toward African Americans (Greene and Woodson 1930). In addition, domestic workers were never preferred candidates for traditional labor organizations (Van Raaphorst 1988). Unions were geared toward organizing permanent capitalist wage earners in skilled occupations. The domestic worker was generally considered a marginal member of the work force, a temporary worker in a devalued labor process. Consequently, not even the most important and comprehensive pieces of New Deal legislation covered domestic workers (Quadagno 1994).

Yet African American women in the early twentieth century pursued various avenues to overcome such obstacles. They organized within mainstream organizations whenever possible, though these efforts were seldom long-lasting or successful (Van Raaphorst 1988). They formed their own independent organizations and social clubs (Clark-Lewis 1994; Van Raaphorst 1988; The Workers Council Bulletin 1937).[22] They also attempted to work collaboratively with progressive housewives who were interested in improving the conditions of domestic work by taking leadership positions in such organizations as the National Committee on Household Employment.[23] The efficacy of working with housewives (commonly referred to as "the employer approach") was, however, strongly debated. One policy paper written explicitly for the Negro Council of Workers in New York City advocated a complete break from such collaborations and instead called for an autonomous and independent movement among African Americans to improve the conditions of domestic work (The Workers' Council Bulletin 1937).

When collective strategies proved problematic or inoperable, domestic workers engaged in various personal actions. It is very possible that African American women found these individualized actions more productive in dealing with their situations than traditional union organizing (Kelley 1994; Van Raaphorst 1988). Moreover, their individual acts often had a collective basis that had to remain hidden from others because of sanctions that might follow more overt actions.[24] In various regions and communities, for example, African American domestic workers developed a "common understanding" of their work and work standards (Van Raaphorst 1988, 211) and would identify and boycott households that refused to live up to such standards.

Changing positions was also a great lever in helping to forge more desirable working conditions. Turnover rates increased steadily after the turn of the century.[25] In periods of excess demand, domestic workers felt free to move as their circumstances dictated. Quitting became a way to control the pace of work, the kinds of work they would or would not do, and the amount of surplus they could self-appropriate. Many refused to take jobs that required ongoing personal services like picking up, dangerous tasks like washing windows, or demeaning tasks like scrubbing floors on hands and knees. Domestic workers avoided customers who stayed home simply to supervise.

An important condition of the transition to a self-appropriating class process was the way African American women transformed domestic work from a live-in occupation to day work or living out. Living out freed workers to decide how much of their labor was to be necessary and used to maintain a particular level of subsistence, and how much was to be surplus, to be self-appropriated and saved or distributed to the community in various ways.[26] Day work had a beginning and an end (Clark-Lewis 1994). More rigid time limits allowed household workers to increasingly dictate their own pace, set their own priorities for tasks, and complete assigned chores as they saw fit. Day work also helped to minimize contact with customers. For some, the most grievous aspect of domestic work was not the hard physical labor, but the potentially demeaning and racist relations with customers. Live-in domestic workers were expected to run around to suit the mistress's whims and to be at her beck and call (Clark-Lewis 1994). Limiting hours of contact decreased occasions for such abuse. Domestic workers demanded to be treated as vendors of a service and not as personal servants. As one African American woman says: "Answering bells is played out" (quoted in Hunter 1997, 4).

Household workers talked about the shift to day work in terms of choice and personal freedom. Day work allowed the prespecification of tasks, job control, and the servicing of more than one household. Domestic workers were no longer overly dependent on any one household and could readily quit if and when the situation warranted it. Day work also increased their ability to utilize free time for their own advancement, perhaps engaging in other forms of independent commodity production. For example, some day workers took in sewing or laundry or did catering on weekends (Clark-Lewis 1994).

A factor that facilitated the establishment of day work was northern migration to urban areas. Migration to the North was instrumental in shedding the memory of slavery and transforming African American work relations (Hogan 1984). African Americans migrated to secure better jobs and to escape racist violence in the South. Migration was a family regulated process and rarely an individual adventure.[27] Most Southern African American women migrated north to help kin with domestic chores or for specific job offers in paid domestic work. For domestic workers, migration resulted in a radical break from the Southern way of life and heightened a newfound sense of independence:

> The move brought the women increased earnings and fuller employment autonomy. It intensified their abhorrence of the servant role and led them to push back the limits of African American women's work. (Clark-Lewis 1994, 197–98)

Community-based relationships and institutions in both the North and South were also instrumental in pushing back some of these limits. Communal support networks and neighborhood organizations served to protect the interests of domestic workers as laborers and provided assistance when other mechanisms failed (Kelley 1994; Hunter 1997).[28] Community networks composed of friends, family, neighbors, and lovers provided resources, information, and positive self-affirmation. Such networks were used to form extended households, to pool income, to ease labor, and to exchange child care.[29] These networks fostered a sense of solidarity and community among domestic workers that directly challenged mainstream (white) representations of them as isolated individuals.[30] As washerwomen, for example, African American women worked as independent contractors, but often relied on communal networks for resources and to ease their labor (Hunter 1997).

The church was a key politicizing and socializing institution in African American communities. At the turn of the century, community churches held special Thursday evening services for domestic workers. Weekly church gatherings enabled domestic workers to immerse themselves in a community and to form relations beyond their immediate kin, including friendships with other domestic workers. Domestic workers often created and disseminated tricks of the trade by networking with other household workers. One trick of the trade included collectively identifying bad customers (Van Raaphorst 1988). The church also nurtured spiritual empowerment, a tried and true political weapon of resistance with boundless potential for community organizing.

Domestic workers found support and knowledge in their community role models. In particular, the laundress was an important contact in the North.[31] She was usually well respected and had a lot of contacts. She knew the market well and often helped a domestic worker land her first day job. The laundress was like a private vendor/contractor with regular clients (Clark-Lewis 1994). She was an entrepreneurial mentor, someone whom the paid household worker could emulate and turn to for advice. Other contemporary female entrepreneurs included seamstresses, hairdressers, and artisans who conducted modest businesses in their own homes and in the streets (Jones 1985).

Penny-saver clubs helped domestic workers deal with the uncertainty involved in independent production. As savings organizations, they served an important function because very small deposits were not accepted at local banks (Clark-Lewis 1994). Penny-saver clubs were motivated by ongoing financial need and the risks involved in independent commodity production. These clubs were modeled on extended family cooperatives; they functioned as mutual benefit associations that provided modest sickness and death benefits to domestic workers and sponsored important social and philanthropic activities in the community (Kelley 1994; Clark-Lewis 1994).

The transition to independent production/selling of domestic services also realigned domestic workers' most significant personal relations. They had more time for family obligations and increased participation in Sunday services, movie theaters, dance halls, and other social activities (Hunter 1997; Kelley 1994; Clark-Lewis 1994). Day work, for example, allowed household workers significantly more time and flexibility to be with their families:

> [Married black women] are accused of having no family feeling yet the fact remains that they will accept a lower wage and live under far less advantageous conditions for the sake of being free at night. That is why day work is so popular. (Jones 1985, 165)

A strategy to diffuse the social stigma of domestic work was to focus on its compatibility with family life. African American women emphasized the ways in which such work allowed them to make financial and emotional contributions to their families' well-being, thereby developing new class, race, and gender associations. African American women did not consider domestic work as fulfilling in and of itself or as a path of upward mobility. They saw it as work that was compatible with home life and that enabled them to concentrate on their children's advancement. The ongoing demand for domestic work and the flexibility of entering or exiting the market meant that they could use paid domestic work as a survival strategy when their husbands were laid off, on strike, unemployed, or underemployed; when there was a separation or a divorce; or when their children needed something extra like money for school or college (Dill 1994).[32] In addition, the flexibility of domestic work allowed mothers to adjust their hours around their familial responsibilities, such as an impending birth, an important community event, or a child's entrance into school.

Creating New Race and Gender Meanings

> Many women voiced their repugnance for their live-in situation with the much used phrase "they job." They described their time as live-in workers as being on they job or referred to a particular household by saying "when I worked at they job." In these phrases the women refused to own those jobs, to consider them extensions of themselves. (Clark-Lewis 1994, 125)

African American domestic workers were concerned with issues of dignity and autonomy as much as they were concerned to earn better wages and work fewer hours. They dreaded wearing uniforms that attempted to formalize a subservient status and often insisted on wearing their own clothes to work (Clark-Lewis 1994). They overwhelmingly rejected living in environments that would not allow them to be with their families or to go to church. Such restrictions were rejected because they were associated with slavery and servanthood, class positions they detested. In the process of reshaping the way they performed domestic labor, African American women forged new cultural meanings for black womanhood, removing the taints of slavery and racial and gender inferiority.

African American artists and writers reflected and represented these new meanings and identities, displacing negative stereotypes and confronting the dominant ideologies of race, class, and gender (Carby 1987; Harris 1982; Smith 1983).[33] Issues of dignity and its relation to domestic work appear frequently in the cultural production of African American women writers and the centrality of the domestic worker in the African American community is strongly reflected in their work. The evolving figure of the domestic worker in this literature is portrayed with increasing assertiveness and autonomy. Harris (1982), for example, traces three literary types of domestic workers— the mammy, the moderate, and the militant. Her reading supports my representation of a class transition among African American domestic workers.

The traditional "mammy" is exemplified by Pauline Breedlove in Toni Morrison's *The Bluest Eye*—a domestic worker who identifies with the mistress's family, upholding her employer's household as a model for moral and social emulation while rejecting and devaluing her own community. This representation of servility and inferiority exemplifies the internalized racism that slavery bred in African American people and the power it continued to wield over their work in the postslavery period. The representation of the more "moderate" or transitional figure of the domestic worker is offered by Lutie Johnson in Anne Petry's *The Street*. Lutie has a more developed political awareness and identifies with the black community, but wears a mask of deference inside white people's homes. She consciously uses phrases like "Yes'um" to mediate interactions with racist whites but sees her job as a means to a greater end—providing for her family (Harris 1982).

The more militant and assertive character of Alice Childress's Mildred from *Like One of the Family* (quoted at the start of this chapter) represents the kind of economic subjectivity associated with independent producers/sellers of domestic services. Mildred is strong and confident about her ability to do good work, and willing and able to refuse to do certain types of work. Her independent subjectivity is represented in a scene in which she discusses leaving notes as a way of tricking paid domestic workers into doing work without compensation. In this scene, a housewife leaves a note asking Mildred to take home some housedresses, wash and iron them, and return them in the morning. Mildred not only refuses to do this work, but also directly confronts the housewife by stating: "In the future, please don't leave me any notes making requests outside of our agreement." (Childress 1956, 155). Mildred is capable of protecting her class position as an independent producer/seller of domestic services.

As the working conditions of paid domestic labor changed, and a self-appropriating class process was established by African American women, the range of images or representations available to black women proliferated. African American women could now be seen as active mothers of their own children rather than as women who had abandoned children. They could be seen as offering emotional support and social leadership in their own viable households and strong communities rather than needing the emotional support and social guidance of their masters/employers. They could be seen as economically independent, living in their own homes, however humble, rather than dependent upon the food and resources of a white family. Importantly, they could be seen as politically militant and sexually empowered. Domestic workers, for example, would frequent dance halls to escape the confines of their work. The dances performed by these women was an important part of a unique blues aesthetic whose underlying principles were "irreverence, transcendence, social realism, self-empowerment and collective individualism" (Hunter 1997, 183). What it meant to be a black woman in the United States was irrevocably changed by the struggles of African American women to establish a self-appropriating class process in paid domestic work.

Conclusion

African American domestic workers found creative ways to profoundly change the nature of domestic work. They engaged in individual and collective actions that radically transformed paid domestic work, thereby changing its associated racial meanings, gender conventions, and class processes. Flexibility, autonomy, and compatibility with home life were not inherent attributes of domestic work, but rather outcomes of strategic choices made by African American women establishing themselves as independent producers/sellers of domestic services. The changing economic subjectivity and material conditions associated with this class transformation profoundly shaped other aspects of their lives; it altered their personal relationships through self-empowerment; encouraged the development of familial sovereignty; strengthened solidarity within the African American community through the use of communal networks and local organizations; heightened the women's sense of autonomy and dignity, resulting in new modes of expression, attitude, and style; and inspired new cultural representations.

By theorizing a transition from the position of sellers of labor power embedded in a social and economic milieu still strongly associated with slavery to a new class position as independent commodity producers (that is, sellers of domestic services) involved in a self-appropriating class process, I have cast African American paid domestic workers in a very different light than that shed by most other analyses of domestic work.[34] I have positioned them as active subjects in a history of change that is not centered upon capitalist development. I have represented them as overthrowing many of the potent slave-inflected meanings associated with domestic service and forging new, more dignified, and independent images of paid domestic work.

As self-appropriating independent contractors who distributed their meager surplus in distinctive ways within their families and communities, African American women can be seen as making an economic contribution to the process whereby standards of living and education levels for black Americans began to rise.

The rearticulation of domestic work as independent commodity production emphasizes the theoretical and political importance of class processes and other economic relationships.[35] By transforming the class processes that shaped their labor as domestic workers, African American women not only challenged and subverted previous racial and gender associations with such work, but also developed new meanings of what it was to be black and a woman. Attributes such as economic independence, autonomy, self-empowerment, spirituality, kin-keeping, communalism, and cooperation have become defining attributes of black womanhood. Such attributes were forged in the struggle to revolutionize the conditions of paid domestic work and break free from its continued association with slavery and servitude. As domestic workers, African American women were resilient and creative individuals who used the ambiguity of their position in white households for the survival and advancement of themselves, their families, and their communities.

Notes

I would like to thank John Bracey, Susan Feiner, Katherine Gibson, Julie Graham, Curtis Haynes, Shan Manikkalingam, Joe Medley, Stephen Resnick, Lucas Wilson, and Rick Wolff.

1. By 1900, 43 percent of all African American women workers were classified in private domestic service as either housekeepers, laundresses, or servants (Amott and Matthaei 1991, 158).

2. After emancipation, many African American women initially withdrew their labor from the fields and concentrated their efforts within the protection of their homes (Greene and Woodson 1930; Jones 1985). Eventually, however, the majority of African American women were politically or economically forced to work outside the home for pay (Jones 1985; Hunter 1995).

3. While a precise breakdown of the occupations of African Americans cannot be determined with accuracy before the 1890s, when the U.S. Census was first coded by race, Greene and Woodson (1930) document that domestic service became an increasingly important occupation for all African Americans after emancipation. Sharecropping was another dominant class-transitional path out of slavery

(Kayatekin 1990). African Americans were denied access to the capitalist class process as either producers or appropriators of surplus value until well into the 1900s (Hogan 1984).

4. African American women heavily populated domestic service until the post–World War II era. Approximately 54 percent of African American female workers were in private household service in 1930, declining to 39.3 percent by 1960 (Amott and Matthaei 1991, 158).

5. In contrast, it was considered unnatural, sometimes even criminal, for African American women to be full-time housewives (Higginbotham 1995; Hunter 1995).

6. Women's magazines from 1850 to the 1930s emphasized the virtue of cleanliness in the home, the exaltation of motherhood, the efficient management of the household, and the importance of beauty, personality, and romantic love (Dorenkamp et al. 1995).

7. It should also be remembered that immigrant groups including Irish, Europeans, and Jews were often identified as nonwhite or even black and set in contrast to the white ideal. In addition, women in these groups often performed paid domestic labor.

8. Dirt became strongly fetishized in popular culture and advertising, deeply implicated in policing social boundaries, especially those associated with race (Palmer 1989; McClintock 1995). A commonly advertised goal of cleaning was to be "whiter than white" (Hoy 1995, 151). See Higginbotham (1995) for an understanding of the power of race as a "global sign" or "metalanguage." See Frankenberg (1993) for an excellent discussion of the social construction of whiteness.

9. Paid domestic labor is represented variously as "residual and servile" (modernization theory); "unproductive and disappearing" (traditional Marxian theory) and "racialized and oppressive" (multiple oppressions theory). It is best, however, not to think of these discourses as completely distinct, but as occupying places on a continuum, with areas where different approaches overlap and influence each other.

10. There are two general approaches to positing the decline of domestic work within modernization discourses. In the supply side approach, domestic work is thought to be undermined by the egalitarianism and free labor ideology of capitalism (Coser 1974). The demand side approach depicts domestic work as a declining occupation because of a diminution in demand due to the smaller family size, increased availability of market substitutes, more equalized distribution of income, and the introduction of technological improvements that come with capitalist development (Stigler 1946).

11. Paid domestic work is categorized as unproductive labor in a capitalist society because it does not produce capitalist surplus value. See Marx (1976, 574–75; Braverman 1974, 411–12).

12. Gibson-Graham have called this theorizing of all forms of noncapitalist economic practice in relation to capitalism "capitalocentrism" (1996, 40–41).

13. Domestic labor is performed under a variety of noncapitalist class processes, but, as Gibson-Graham point out, most analyses of the household define it "as

space of capitalist consumption and reproduction rather than a space of noncapitalist production" (1996, 8).

14. Romero's (1992) analysis of paid domestic work calls into question the
elimination of these possibilities. Her work highlights the contemporary paradox of
domestic service as an occupation that is embarrassing and degrading, but one in
which the pay is higher and working conditions more autonomous and less alienating than in many other jobs. She argues that domestic work, in and of itself, is not
necessarily menial and degrading. Rather, it is the context in which the tasks are
carried out that makes them oppressive.

15. This tendency results in what is called deep structural analysis: "tightly
drawn correspondences between levels of development of practical capability and
particular institutional arrangements" (Unger 1987b, 1).

16. Kelley (1994) advocates a broader understanding of class struggle, one that
repositions the personal as political and economic. Such a repositioning could emphasize the ways that "safety, pleasure, cultural expression, sexuality, security, freedom of mobility, and other facets of daily lives" make important contributions to
worker resistance (Kelly 1994, 9).

17. Fraad et al. (1994) and Gibson-Graham (1996) have examined the intersection of class with gender and/or race in a postmodern framework.

18. In the introduction to Fraad et al. (1994), Spivak highlights the radical potential of this theoretical move: "there are ways in which the conceptualization, or
the thinking of economic reality, might change if class is unmoored from the public
sphere" (xiv).

19. As domestic space became more cluttered toward the end of the nineteenth
century, domestic work was increasingly disciplined by the obsessive tidying and ordering of ornaments and furniture (McClintock 1995).

20. Haynes (1923) documents regional differences in the types of services that
were included in general housework.

21. There is a growing body of work that attempts to rethink independent or
petty commodity production, especially in its more hybrid forms such as those that
rely on communal networks of support. See Gabriel (1990), Hotch (1994), and
Unger (1987b), all of whom attempt to theoretically and politically rescue independent commodity production from its sterile position within capitalocentric Marxian
discourse. Unger's notion of the "plasticity of social relationships," especially as it
relates to independent commodity production, emphasizes the radical potential of
the link between individual and collective empowerment and the formation or dis-
solution of social relations of labor (Unger 1987a; 1987b). Unger defines plasticity as:
"the facility with which work relations among people . . . can be constantly shifted in
order to suit the changing circumstances, resources and intentions. Plasticity is the
opportunity to innovate in the immediate organizational settings of production exchange . . . and to do so not just by occasional large-scale reforms but by an ongoing
cumulative flow of small scale innovations" (1987b, 153). Unger's theoretical work
emphasizes in particular the historical abundance and radical potential of coopera-

tivist varieties of what is often negatively labeled independent or petty commodity production (1987a, 342–47).

22. For example, a few African American women organized the National Association of Domestic Workers in Jackson, Mississippi, and the Domestic Workers of America in Philadelphia. One of the more assertive unions was the Domestic Workers Union, headed by African American Dora Jones, which was part of the Communist Trade Union Unity League. Some of these organizations developed creative alternatives to traditional union organizing, perhaps reflecting underlying class differences. One organization advocated for "a hostel and agency" (Van Raaphorst 1988, 328).

23. The National Committee on Household Employment (1933–1945) attempted to improve the conditions of domestic work through organizing, education, and research. The organization consulted with various "experts" and "policy makers" including scholars in home economics, leaders of organized labor, and representatives from the Women's Bureau.

24. To take an example from the previous century, the Atlanta washerwomen who went on strike in 1881 received heavy penalties. City landlords threatened to raise rents, and the city council passed legislation requiring all members of the union to pay a $25 per year license fee, the same rate as city businesses. See Van Raaphorst (1988).

25. Haynes (1923) reports that from 1906 to 1908 the modal length of service was six to eleven months; in 1930 it was three to six months.

26. Kelley (1994), Clark-Lewis (1994), and Jones (1985) underscore the importance of the shift to day work in breaking away from the slave-like attributes of paid domestic work.

27. Clark-Lewis (1994) states that occasionally African American men would "fall out," but by and large both women and men relied heavily on kinship networks in migrating north. Jones documents cases of women migrating north without traveling spouse or kin, but also concludes that migration was generally a "family affair" (1985, 157).

28. I do not want to imply a utopian or monolithic concept of community without intercommunity rival and conflicts. See Kelley (1994).

29. Although these extended family relationships are widely acknowledged as a positive resource, they could have produced added stress and responsibilities for African American women. See Scott (1991).

30. Domestic workers are commonly described as isolated individuals. This is at odds with many African American representations and traditions that look for the connections between individual empowerment and community rather than positioning them as polar opposites. See Barkley Brown (1990).

31. The work of a laundress was differentiated from that of a washerwoman, which was viewed as a traditional Southern occupation (Hunter 1997, Clark-Lewis 1994).

32. Many paid domestic workers were able to contribute to their children's education despite low income through hard work, thrift, and sacrifice.

33. Carby argues that African American women in novels are not just "passive representations of history" but "active influences within history," "cultural artifacts which shape the social conditions in which they enter" (1987, 95).

34. This break from the conventional analysis of domestic work is gaining favor among other scholars as well. Hunter (1997), for example, positions the majority of postbellum laundresses in Atlanta as independent contractors working within communal networks of mutual aid.

35. It is inconceivable that the society of that period would have discursively encoded African American domestic workers as independent contractors because such a signification would require whites to be viewed as their clients. This discursive foreclosure, however, does not rule out the historical capability to change the social relations of domestic labor initiated by African American women.

2

Domesticating Class:

Femininity, Heterosexuality, and Household Politics

Jenny Cameron

Within Western feminism it is generally understood that an unequal distribution of labor in households is symptomatic of women's overall subordinate position in western societies. As part of the struggle to improve women's social position, most feminists advocate a transition from the "traditional" household, where women are the primary domestic workers, to households where there is an equal sharing of tasks between women and men. These latter households are portrayed in much feminist literature as egalitarian and progressive.[1] The transition from a traditional to an egalitarian pattern of domestic work is a familiar vision of social change in which justice is believed to be achieved through equal measure—in this case, an equal measure or distribution of domestic work.[2] A feminism that equates equity with equalness has been described as an egalitarian feminism (Grosz 1990). The political goal of this version of feminism is to rid the social world of the mechanisms that privilege men and disadvantage women, to equalize women and men.

Against an egalitarian feminism a feminism of difference has developed alternative visions of justice. Wary that equality for women has too often meant that women must become the same as men, this feminism embraces and celebrates sexual difference. Here difference is understood as difference in and of itself without comparison or reference to men as the neutral standard (Grosz 1990). This approach does not essentialize difference—there is no figure of woman that is the counterpart to the figure of man—rather, it aims to open up the ways of living in a sexed body outside of masculinist representations of femininity.[3] A feminist politics of difference raises the possibility that justice for women might be achieved without renouncing sexual difference.

47

In the realm of social relations, particularly in terms of sex, gender, and desire, a feminist politics of difference has brought forth a multiplicity of ways of becoming.[4] When it comes to economic and labor relations, however, there appears to be more resistance to the envisioning of difference.[5] It seems that economic justice has only been conceptualized in terms of the economic independence of women in the formal economy and an equal sharing of labor in the domestic economy. In the economic realm, gender justice is to be achieved by neutralizing gender differences and securing economic equality, if not sameness, with men.[6]

In this chapter I suggest that both a feminism of difference and an egalitarian feminism link the unequal sharing of housework between men and women with conceptions of economic exploitation and gender oppression. Implicit in this alignment is a normative political vision of an equal distribution of housework in which domestic exploitation and oppression is overcome. In the light of the development of new forms of feminist politics inspired by poststructuralist theories of difference and strategies of queering, I examine this overlaying of concepts and their relationship to a liberal political vision. I ask what political opportunities for feminism are lost by the representation of domestic labor inequality, exploitation, and gender oppression as tightly and invariantly bound together. And how might the liberal vision of equality in the household possess its own oppressive effects on the differently gendered subjectivities and sexed bodies currently produced in and through domestic practices?

I have employed a number of different methods to help me explore these questions. The discussion draws its empirical inspiration from semistructured in-depth interviews conducted with women in Melbourne, Australia, in 1994. I use an anti-essentialist Marxian class analysis as a tool for prying apart the familiar feminist aggregate of unequal work, exploitation, and gender oppression, playing around with a variety of different class readings of the household of Fran, one of the twenty-two women interviewed. The objective here is to highlight what is at stake for feminism in any one representation of domestic economic politics. Toward the end of the chapter I employ a strategy of queering domestic labor and draw on the voices of Fran and others to illustrate the ways in which domestic labor practices are sites where gender and sexual differences proliferate.

Feminism and the Domestic Domain

Fran lives in what she describes as "a *normal* household with a husband and five children" (my emphasis). These five "children," aged between 17 and 25, all live at home. Fran says about herself that she is "a complete *stereotype*" (my emphasis) and someone who, like others in her own and previous generations, "look[s] on things in the *old-fashioned* way" (my emphasis). Certainly the overall pattern of housework in Fran's household appears to follow what might be called a traditional, or even a normal or stereotypical, pattern. Fran does the grocery shopping, the cooking and dishwashing, the laundry and ironing, and most of the cleaning of the house. Her husband is responsible for tasks associated with the masculine, primarily the maintenance of the cars and the garden and yard. The children help by cleaning their own rooms, occasionally washing dishes or ironing, and the daughters by cooking a meal if they are home on weekends. Fran does her domestic chores during the evenings, weekends, and Fridays, her one day off from her four-days-a-week job as an administrative assistant in a large public sector organization:

> Friday was the day when I put on the gloves and get really stuck into it. . . . I'd get stuck into the bathrooms, I mean not just a quick whizz round like I do everyday, I mean properly stuck into it. Stripping beds and doing all that sort of stuff, and I would finish maybe one, one-thirty, something like that. Oh, and I would have done the washing in there somewhere, and then I would start the ironing and maybe then cooking—a bit more cooking than . . . when I'm working.

In a feminist analysis that focuses on the overall distribution of tasks between household members, the pattern would clearly be seen as unequal, with Fran doing far more than her fair share of the work for other household members. Like so many other women who do a disproportionate amount of domestic work, Fran, it seems, is exploited by her family (Delphy and Leonard 1992; Folbre 1987; Walby 1990).

According to much feminist research, women's domestic exploitation takes place within the wider context of women's oppression.[7] The oppression of women may be attributed to a direct and immediate power that men are able to wield over women. For instance, Okin (1989) claims that in traditional households men "*do not want to* [do housework]*, and are able, to a large extent, to enforce their wills*" (her emphasis) (153). Or women's oppression may be attributed to more veiled and indirect expressions of power. Bittman and Lovejoy (1993) document the disproportionate amount of time Australian women spend on unpaid domestic work, despite a widespread belief that housework should be shared. They conclude that "[c]ontemporary patriarchy is about the subordination of women within the framework of equality" (319). This understanding of domestic labor anticipates that liberation from women's exploitation as primary domestic workers and from their more generalized exploitation and oppression within society will result from a society-wide transition to equalized power and economic relations between women and men:

> In a just society, the structure and practices of families must give women the same opportunities as men to develop their capacities, to participate in political power and influence social choices, and to be economically secure. (Okin 1989, 22)

Providing subsidized, high-quality child care, introducing family-friendly practices into workplaces, and distributing domestic work equally within families are some of the measures that Okin promotes so that the alignment of exploitation, oppression, and an unequal distribution of domestic work might be replaced by a second alignment—an equal distribution of domestic work, nonexploitation and nonoppression. In families characterized by this second alignment there would be "an equality of opportunity" (16). Thus women like Fran, no longer hampered by having primary responsibility for housework, would be able to devote more time to paid work and develop their careers. Along with their husbands they could be independent, with their sense of self derived not from serving the needs of their family but from their own activities outside the home.

Contained within this complex of representations of domestic labor, exploitation, and gender oppression is a disempowered and perhaps even falsely conscious subject. Fran is here pictured as exploited, oppressed, dependent, unrealized as a human, and a pawn in her husband's hands. In a desired future she would be liberated by limiting her performance of domestic labor, increasing her participation in the formal economy, and thereby gaining an equal measure of power that would allow her to act as an independent political being. It is worth considering the extent to which this familiar conception of economic and social justice and political independence for Fran is trapped within liberalism's formulation of equality.[8]

According to liberal discourse, equality is defined as the condition of human sameness, and to be truly human is to be equal to all other humans. Feminists such as Carol Pateman (1988) and Wendy Brown (1995) argue that the figure that parades as liberalism's universal human subject is an inherently masculinist one. Liberalism opposes and subordinates a (hyper)naturalized family to the more civilized realm of civil society. In doing so the figure of the feminine, which belongs to the familial sphere, is opposed and subordinated to the truly human subject—the rightful citizen of civil society, a masculine ideal. Feminist appeals to human sameness as the basis for equality and justice risk endorsing liberalism's masculinist subject and according with liberal discourse's naturalization and devaluation of the familial and feminine.

In light of this argument we may hear Okin's (1989, 17) call to "end the inequalities of gender, and to work in the direction of ending gender itself" as a call that sanctions human sameness over gender difference—that is, that repudiates the feminine and ratifies liberalism's masculinist human subject. Indeed the goal of establishing "an equality of opportunity" for women privileges and values civil society over the familial, the masculine over the feminine, and thereby instates, as the means for achieving justice for women, entry to civil society "on socially male terms" (Brown 1995, 184). Measures aimed at equalizing domestic relationships—like resocialization campaigns to promote an equal distribution of domestic work between women and men (Office of the Status of Women 1991)—are evidence of feminism's entrapment within liberal discourse and our difficulty of "think[ing] of justice for women in terms other than through our achieving equal measure with men" (Cornell 1991, 114).[9]

If we step outside the terms of liberal discourse, and the association of the feminine with the familial and the natural and the masculine with civil society and the civilized, we are free to question the assumption that economic justice for women (and the presumed elimination of exploitation and oppression) will be attainable in some transparent and knowable future by an equal measure of work in both the domestic and formal economies.[10] We are also free to explore the productive discordances where unequal domestic labor/exploitation/gender oppression do not produce economic sameness. That is, we are invited to unravel the rigid discursive clustering that implicitly underlies the liberal egalitarian feminist analysis of the household, that is the explicit focus of socialist feminist analyses of the household, and that lies unexamined within the corpus of feminist theories of difference.[11]

Class and the Possibility of Economic Difference

An analysis of the domestic arena put forward by Fraad, Resnick, and Wolff (1994) provides the tools for disassembling feminism's alignment of unequally shared housework with exploitation and gender oppression. They are interested in analyzing the various ways in which domestic surplus labor[12] is produced, appropriated, and distributed within the household, that is, in the different class processes taking place in the home. Their antiessentialist epistemology leads them to question any presumed determination or effectivity and to be open to the diverse array of processes and practices that constitute these class processes. For example, in a couple household where one partner appropriates the domestic surplus labor produced by the other, this exploitative domestic class process might have as one of its constitutive conditions an oppressive power relationship, which includes the exercise of physical violence by the exploiter against the exploited. In this household an unequal sharing of domestic work lines up with exploitation and oppression, and if the exploiter is male and the surplus labor producer female, we recognize the domestic scene that motivates many feminist political visions of the need for transformation. But in another household, oppressive power relations might be absent and the exploitative domestic class process partly secured by the physical disability of one partner or by a significant difference in the partners' hours of paid work. An anti-essentialist approach to the household does not specify invariant alignments or necessary, predetermined constituents of the different domestic class processes identified. Gender oppression may or may not be present as an immediate condition of an exploitative domestic class process. Instances of surplus labor production, appropriation, and distribution therefore need to be interrogated to determine which constituents can be theorized as at work and what type of class process we might want to represent as in place.

In her household Fran, through the work of cooking, cleaning, washing, ironing, and so on, is clearly the primary producer of domestic labor, and Fran's household appears to conform to a traditional pattern of domestic surplus labor production.[13] Yet at times there is a break in this traditional pattern:

FRAN: I've got a little regime that I follow where I—and I have been doing this for a lot of years—swim in the mornings. And so I leave home at about quarter to six, six o'clock, and I get home in time to literally throw clothes on, throw a piece of fruit down my throat, dry my hair, and go to work. And years ago my husband took over the whole breakfast thing. He gets up and prepares fruit for all the kids, still does, even at their ages. And, [whispers] I like the house to be vacuumed every day, so he does that, vacuums through the house every morning before he goes to work. So, he's really good with that.

JENNY: And that routine, was that just something that evolved because you were swimming?

FRAN: It was because when I had really little children I started doing that just after my last child was born. I don't swim every day, I swim some and walk others, but I'm not home, I'm out. My kids, especially my youngest, wouldn't know what it was like having me around in the morning. . . . And it did evolve, it was something I wanted to do for myself—being pregnant five times—and you just feel that you want to do something for yourself. My whole life was involved in these five children and the only way I could do it was while he was at home, and I was too tired at night so I had to do it early in the morning and that was really how it came about. But I'm still doing it.

JENNY: And he was happy to pick the breakfast and that up.

FRAN: Yes. It wasn't an issue. He's really good. . . . I never make our bed; he does that every day and that includes when the linen needs changing. Sounds like I do nothing, doesn't it?

Interrogating the class process at this moment of disruption of the apparently traditional pattern of surplus labor production reveals much about the politically interested task of designating a class process and identifying its conditions of existence. Either I can represent this practice of a man performing domestic labor as minimally important and no challenge to the designation of Fran as exploited and oppressed in the home, nor to the household as a site of economic uniformity, or I can open up my analysis and pursue a less restricted theoretical path by exploring the domestic labor practices of Fran's husband, their multiple conditions of existence, and the household as a site of economic diversity. Here is an example of economic difference that can be ignored or highlighted. I choose to do the latter.[14]

Every morning Fran's husband produces domestic surplus labor, preparing breakfast, vacuuming the house, and making their bed. To focus initially on his preparation of breakfast, the appropriation and distribution of this surplus labor could be interpreted in several ways. Perhaps the children appropriate the product of their father's surplus labor and exploit their father. Their exploitation might result from a socially condoned demand for students to have more time for study, perhaps so they can sleep later after a long night at the desk. Particularly toward the end of the year, when comprehensive exams are held, and at the start of the new year, the media abound with stories of the lengths that parents have to go to if they are to ensure that their children have the competitive advantage at school and university. In Fran's household, we could see the children as distributing their father's appropriated surplus labor to themselves to enable them to do well in their studies. By succeeding at university they reward their father for preparing their breakfast, ensuring that he will feel proud of them and continue to produce surplus labor for them. Here we have a representation of exploitation and unequal domestic labor that is clearly not overdetermined by oppression.

A second representation is that Fran's husband is self-appropriating—that is, he appropriates his own surplus labor and then distributes the products to his children.[15] A condition of existence of this class process might include the father's desire to express his parental affection for his children. He may find it difficult to express his affection in other ways, and by preparing their breakfast and eating with his children he gets to spend time with them. Perhaps Fran dominates family interactions when she is present, so he finds that breakfast is the time when he can interact with the children. By distributing the products of his surplus labor to the children, the father demonstrates his affection for his children. Presumably, so long as the children return this affection, the distributions of surplus labor to them will continue.[16] In this representation the domestic class process involves an unequal distribution of labor, self-appropriation (as opposed to exploitation), and again a lack of oppression.

Yet a third interpretation might picture Fran's husband's morning work as evidence of his exploitation and oppression by Fran. There may be constituents of the breakfast arrangement that are not specific to the relationship between the father and children but that emanate from specific aspects of Fran's marriage or from the wider culture. Fran's husband might prepare the children's breakfast, as well as vacuum the carpets and make their bed, *for her*. In other words, Fran's husband may be seen as producing surplus labor that Fran appropriates and distributes.

Fran's exploitation of her husband might be overdetermined by a cultural discourse that positions men as the henpecked husband at the beck and call of their wives in the domestic realm. Hilda Rumpole, the "she who must be obeyed" of *Rumpole of the Bailey;* Flo Capp, ready to deck Andy with the frying pan for any misdemeanor; and Hyacinth Bucket in *Keeping Up Appearances* remind us of the dominant role this discourse of home as the domain of the "missus" continues to play in popular culture.[17] A portion of the surplus labor that Fran appropriates from her husband could be seen as being distributed to secure the conditions of existence of her position as head of the household. The children, for example, might be represented as receiving a portion of the appropriated surplus labor from their mother in the form of their breakfast. In return for this distribution they might defer to their mother, reinforcing her position as boss and her capacity to appropriate domestic surplus labor produced by her husband.

A second possible overdeterminant of Fran's exploitation of her husband is one that is specific to the circumstances of this family. While Fran had been in paid employment before the children were born, it was both her expectation and her husband's that she would not reenter the paid work force while they were growing up. But when the children were young Fran had to return to full-time paid work to support the family through a financial crisis.

Both husband and wife found it difficult to accommodate Fran's paid work within their expectations of their own and each other's familial roles:

> My husband's got a very old-fashioned view about the whole thing. He would really prefer I wasn't working because he has this thing that he was unemployed and that was why I had to go to work. And he still can't seem to let that go. Even though I have told him I would work anyway now, and I like to work, that was the initial reason for me going to work.

Perhaps Fran's husband produces surplus labor for Fran as a way of vindicating his role in her return to paid employment. He works for Fran in her domestic domain because Fran had to work for him (or more precisely because of him) in his domain of the paid work force. In this interpretation we can see Fran distributing a portion of the surplus labor she appropriates to herself as a form of compensation for her time spent in paid work. For as long as Fran's husband feels guilt for his failure to provide for his wife and children, or for as long as Fran insists that there be recompense, he will produce domestic surplus labor for Fran.[18]

These speculations around the domestic work of Fran's husband illustrate that there is no one answer to the question of who is appropriating (or exploiting) and distributing his surplus labor. Each representation of the husband's domestic labor and of the possible appropriators and distributors of his surplus labor calls up different emotions, judgments, and political possibilities. The conditions that we highlight as constituting who appropriates (or exploits) and distributes are similarly shaped by our political commitments and desires. From the point of view of egalitarian feminism, for example, it would be easy to discount Fran's husband's production of surplus labor and to emphasize Fran's role as the primary producer of surplus labor, thus designating the husband as the appropriator/exploiter. And it would make sense to see women's oppression as one of the conditions of existence of this exploitative domestic class process. Such a formulation of the class process clearly accords with egalitarian feminism's alignment of exploitation, gender oppression, and nonshared housework and re-presents feminism's privileged account of domestic labor.

I raise what some might see as the absolute impossibility of Fran as an exploiter of her husband[19] to reflect on feminism's domestic politics. In order for feminist domestic discourses to establish their authority and clear the ground for feminism's emancipatory project, other representations of domestic practices and the experiences they give rise to have been silenced. Other accounts are seen as misleading, as obfuscating the truth, as not as real

as the privileged feminist account. My question is—what is lost by this standard representation?

One of the consequences of reading the unequal distribution of domestic
labor in this way is to render the household a site of economic sameness,
characterized by one set of power relations, labor relations, and inequalities.
Another consequence is to limit the political imaginary to a conceptualization of social transformation that is closely tied to liberal, masculinist visions
of equality defined as sameness or justice in equal measure. Both consequences limit the constitution of difference as a progressive force and a liberating representation. My interest is in breaking through the confines of these
limitations—in theorizing the household as a site of economic difference
and as a space in which many different political strategies for change might
be and are enacted. I return now after this long digression to Fran's labor as a
way of illustrating the potentiality of an analysis that breaks open the alignment between unequal domestic labor, exploitation, and gender oppression.

Activating the Domestic Feminine Subject

Poststructuralist feminism emphasizes the importance of language and representation in constituting subjectivity. Feminists like Brown (1995), Cornell
(1991), and Marcus (1992) have argued that defining women as sexually subordinate and vulnerable, for example, does not simply describe the reality of
women's sexuality and their sexual experiences but has the effect of producing women as sexually violable. Similarly, I would argue that the usual feminist representation of domesticated wives and mothers as dependent and
subservient, exploited and oppressed can be seen as having the effect of producing women as victims, as domestic subjects who are *acted upon*. Clearly
this representation of victimhood has historically played an important role
in politicizing and mobilizing many women, encouraging them to struggle
against the determining social structures that have been seen to force women
into positions of domestic dependency and subservience. My view is that
the politically enabling nature of this representation has, perhaps, run its
course.[20] It is time to consider why, despite a well developed and accessible
discourse of oppression and victimhood, women continue to perform unequal amounts of domestic labor. And it is important to consider the effect
of positioning all the women who continue to perform this labor as victims.

As we have already seen, the privileged feminist reading of Fran's domestic situation sees her as exploited, a victim of her husband's and society's
gender oppression. Yet Fran speaks in a voice that does not resonate with
this subject position. Is her voice to be listened to? Or is she speaking with a
false consciousness of her social and economic position?

For the moment I want to listen to Fran's voice, to its tone and content; and against the designation of Fran as an exploited domestic worker, I want to put forward the proposition that Fran produces, appropriates, and distributes domestic surplus labor within a self-appropriative domestic class process. In defining Fran as a self-appropriating domestic worker, I am listening to those qualities in her voice that suggest a worker who is independent and self-guided, organized and self-rewarding. If we pursue this representation, there is the potential to reconfigure Fran as an authoritative and *acting* domestic subject. Might this different representation signal a new, perhaps localized and partial, feminist and class politics of (domestic) difference?

Fran produces the surplus labor of cooking the family's evening meal, washing the family's clothes, and so on, and she appropriates the products of this surplus labor and distributes them as she sees fit. The discourse of the domesticated wife and mother partially constitutes this self-appropriative domestic class process. Fran distributes to her husband and children goods and services to satisfy their domestic needs and in the process is positioned as the "good" wife and mother who selflessly tends to her family. Although Fran has a paid job, her distributions of surplus labor to her family affirm that she is not like the undomesticated and "bad" wife and mother who selfishly puts her career first, her children in day care, packaged meals in the microwave, and pays for someone else to do *her* domestic work. The distribution of domestic products constructs Fran as a particular type of feminine domestic subject, and this gendered subjectivity helps ensure that domestic surplus labor is produced, appropriated, and distributed in a self-appropriative class process.

The discourse of home as the domain of the "missus," discussed earlier, can be seen as another condition of existence of the self-appropriative domestic class process. As the head of household, it is up to Fran to determine what household tasks are necessary and how and when these tasks are to be undertaken. A portion of Fran's surplus labor is distributed to help sustain this decision-making role. She prepares meals for her husband, for example, distributing to him a source of energy that enables him to perform his domestic chores, like the vacuuming of the house each morning, and allow her the time to exercise and clear the headspace she needs for household management. These tasks are done in a way that confirms Fran's domestic authority:

[A] lot of the things he does to help me, I know he . . . doesn't think they need doing, but he just knows I want them done, and he does them . . . you know, he really has been a very good support for me, really. That would be the only reason there haven't been any major bumpy patches [in the marriage], I would say.

Fran's husband helps even when it seems that he believes the tasks are nonessential. He subsumes his own ideas about domestic work and follows the directions of the "boss." (Of course, the demands of this boss are unlikely to be excessive, for they are curbed by the discourse of the domesticated wife and mother that says that Fran should be able to handle all domestic tasks herself). The help of the husband installs Fran as the head of domestic affairs, lending support to the discourse of home as the domain of the "missus." As she suggests in the statement above (and in her earlier discussion of swimming), these few hours ensure that her domestic responsibilities and the self-appropriative class process do not become overly burdensome.

The discourse of the independent worker is a third overdeterminant of the self-appropriative domestic class process. Whether involved in paid or unpaid work, independent workers are seen to go about their tasks with little or no assistance or input of ideas from others. In this household, Fran's children distance themselves from the production and appropriation of surplus labor—and seem almost unwilling participants in their role as recipients of a distribution of appropriated surplus labor. This is suggested in Fran's discussion of the organization of housework in the last few weeks when she has worked full-time, while her Friday replacement is away:

> Doing [the housework] on a weekend, they're all there, and they haven't got a clue, you know, they think I'm crazy. You know, "What are you cleaning the shower for? You just did it." And they don't know that I do all this because they're never there when I'm doing it and now all of a sudden they're starting to realize what I do. But instead of patting me on the back, and saying, "Gee, you're good, Mum," they think I'm just plain nuts. . . . They all think that everything I do is completely unnecessary, so "Why do I do it?" (laughs)

When Fran does the housework during the week, her surplus distributions are largely unnoticed by the children, but at the moment, when she does the housework on weekends, they witness the self-appropriative domestic class process. The children tell Fran that it is not necessary for her to produce domestic surplus labor, nor to make a distribution to them, and thus there is no reason for them to congratulate or thank their mother. They imply that, if their mother produces, appropriates, and distributes domestic surplus labor, she is doing it for herself, because she wants to do it, not because they require it. Yet Fran's surplus distributions are not rejected. The children eat the meals she distributes to them, sit in the clean rooms, shower in the clean bathrooms, wear the clean clothes. They do not leave home, nor increase their production of domestic labor, but remain dependent on Fran's surplus distributions. In the name of Fran's independence, her surplus distributions are received by the children to sustain and replenish themselves.

The three discourses that I have discussed as conditions of existence of the self-appropriative domestic class process have been presented as being smoothly reproduced by Fran's distributions of surplus labor. But the self-appropriative domestic class process that here has been rendered stable and steady can also be made to appear volatile and chancy. For example, the discourse of the independent domestic worker can at times conflict with the discourse of the "good" wife and mother. The children's dismissal of Fran's domestic work draws from Fran the response "Why do I do it?" In one reading, Fran queries why she continues to produce, appropriate, and distribute domestic surplus when this effort is not appreciated. In moments such as this, Fran's adherence to impeccable standards of work and a high rate of self-appropriation—that is, her interpellation as an independent domestic worker distributing a considerable amount of surplus labor—is thrown into question. The recognition of Fran as a "good" wife and mother and the gratitude she expects from her family—two things that draw her to this gendered subjectivity—are not forthcoming.

At these moments of tension between the constituents of a class process, a class transformation is possible, and it might be Fran, as an *acting* feminine domestic subject, who is responsible for the transformation. She may tell the children that if the work she does is unnecessary, then she is not going to bother doing it at all. In other words, Fran might go on strike—after all, Fran's gendered subjectivity is not being rewarded when she exerts herself to produce, appropriate, and distribute surplus labor, so why exert herself at all? The domestic strike might be resolved when the children, missing their prepared meals, clean clothes, clean family rooms, and so on, agree that Fran's domestic work is necessary. The self-appropriative domestic class process may then be reestablished with the children now willing to express appreciation for the domestic work that Fran does. Or perhaps Fran, having enjoyed time out from domestic work, insists that the children must now do some of the housework that they once thought was so unnecessary. Of course, Fran may keep silent and continue to produce, appropriate, and distribute domestic surplus labor in a self-appropriative domestic class process, but conflict and tension may be only temporarily suppressed, ready to erupt at any time in the future.[21]

The scenario of domestic class transformation laid out in such fine-grained terms may seem like a flight of fancy, but consider the transformations that have taken place in other households around the more familiar conflict between women's paid and unpaid work responsibilities.

ELIZABETH: I was working part-time when the children first went to school, and that was really awful because I was working half a day, five days a week. And you tend to think, "Right, I can do my paid work and then I can come home and do everything else." And I found that really hard. One of the mothers at school said to me, "I work full-time, and I say *'I can't do that!'*" And that stuck with me, it really did. . . . Then I had very long hours and a very responsible job. I was working from seven in the morning to seven at night. So everybody had to cook, clean, wash, and everything. . . . [I]f people wanted something done, they had to do it. It was four adults living independently in the one household. (her emphasis)

JUNE: I remember being thirty-eight years of age and suddenly feeling rather tired at the time, and just making an announcement to the boys—as I call the two men in my life, my husband and my son—"If you're not willing to participate in this household, then I will be giving up my job and you will miss out on the fruits of life that you rather enjoy, the overseas trips and things that we do that are part and parcel of our life." And I said "Righto, you want this kind of lifestyle, or you don't, and the choices are you help me and we retain it, or I continue doing what I'm doing and some of your lifestyle changes."

In these households the feminine domestic subject is the agent of change bringing about a transformation in domestic class processes—perhaps from an exploitative one to a communist one in June's household, and, in Elizabeth's household, to a multitude of self-appropriating ones. If domesticated wives and mothers can act and transform subjects at moments of conflict between paid and unpaid work, then the feminine domestic subject can enact change at other moments of conflict and contradiction. To represent women as acting political subjects rather than victims who are acted upon, and households as sites of a diverse range of class processes rather than just a single traditional class process, is to constitute fluidity in the economic and political terrain and to multiply the possibilities for transformation in the domestic situation.

Queering the Household—Multiple Femininities and Masculinities

Some of the clearest evidence of fluidity and transformation in the household is that associated with the negotiation of meaning around gender, and especially in the undermining of a naturalized connection between masculinity and particular domestic chores and femininity and other ones. Fran has described her household as "normal" and herself as "a complete stereotype" and even "old-fashioned." Yet Fran does no housework in the morning before she leaves for work. It is her husband who prepares the children's breakfast, vacuums the house, and makes their bed. As opposed to Fran's descriptions, the organization of housework, in the context of hegemonic notions of domesticated femininity and undomesticated masculinity, seems quite *abnormal* and *unstereotypical.* It is as if Fran is employing the language of normality as a regulatory fiction, to minimize the incoherencies of her own femininity and her husband's masculinity.[22] By representing herself as normal and stereotypical, Fran negates the possibility that leaving the house each morning and not being there for her children before school is contradictory to the discourse of a "good" wife and mother—someone who is unselfishly always there to care for husband and children.[23] This representation is perhaps particularly important for Fran given that she has had to also justify her absence after school when her children were younger and she was working full-time, a practice she has described as quite undesirable. Of course by representing the household as normal and herself as stereotypical, Fran's husband is also rendered normal. His masculinity remains intact despite the fact that doing housework is not a characteristic associated with hegemonic notions of masculinity. Their relationship is similarly rendered normal, that is, heterosexual.[24]

What is striking about Fran's description of her household is that she describes her own parents' household in much the same way, as a "*very traditional* upbringing, mother at home, father at work" (my emphasis). Yet when Fran discusses this household in detail, she explains that it was her father who taught her to iron men's shirts and, while her mother worked night shifts sorting mail during the Christmas period, it was her father who prepared the evening meals. Again these household practices exceed Fran's representation of this household as "very traditional."

Fran's use of the words "normal" and "traditional" works to conceal the ways in which housework is practiced differently in her and her parents' households. In a similar way we could see egalitarian feminism's division of households into two types—the traditional household where nonshared housework is aligned with exploitation and oppression, and an egalitarian or progressive household where shared housework, nonexploitation, and nonoppression are aligned—as suppressing the heterogeneity in household practices. Categorizing households into various types presupposes that each household is a uniform and consistent social site. Representing households as heterogeneous, however, makes inconsistencies, incoherencies, and moments of rupture in the household seem obvious and normal (Gibson-Graham 1996, vii–xi; Sedgwick 1993). One effect of rendering moments of inconsistency ordinary is to undermine the hegemonic narrative of binarized gender. Instances of men's nurturance and caregiving, and women's physical power and capacity, for example, might then seem commonplace rather than extraordinary.

A feminist representation of households as always already sites of difference has consequences for domestic practices. Fran herself points to the usefulness of such a discourse:

> FRAN: I quite enjoy mowing the lawn—this is just what I was going to say about men's and women's roles—but he has got this thing that he cannot stand me to mow the lawn. Absolutely ingrained from childhood, I think, that women don't mow lawns, which is so ridiculous, because I say, "You vacuum, you do heaps of things that would be considered women's work." He has got an attitude, a little bit, that he's doing it for me, that he's doing the vacuuming for me.

> JENNY: So he's not actually doing the work as such but he's helping you.

> FRAN: Yes, he's helping me in everything he does. And I have in some moments pointed that out to him—"I'm not going to say thank you; it's your carpet, you should vacuum it." Yes, so I'd say his sense of men's and women's roles are more set than mine because I'd be quite happy to mow the lawn and do those sorts of things, but he has this thing that that's not what women do, and I think it's just really from his childhood. And the period we grew up in . . . the woman in the house simply just didn't go to work, very rare cases where the woman did go to work. And I suppose he just can't get that out of his sight; it's in there for good.

Contrary to Fran's earlier representation of her household as normal, here she articulates the prohibitive, that her husband *does* women's work, that he is not simply helping out. Importantly, Fran's articulation of this prohibitive can be read as a purposeful, and perhaps defiant, action on her part. By stating that her husband does women's work, Fran both reinstates the idea that there is such a thing as women's work and destabilizes any presumed connection between femininity, masculinity, and particular household tasks. She creates the context to legitimately express ideas that seem inconsistent with her gendered becoming as a domesticated wife and mother; she can express a desire to do the "man's" work of mowing, inferring that she has responsibility for tasks outside the house just as, as she points out, her husband also has a responsibility for tasks inside the house. Whether or not Fran's accusation that her husband does women's work is successful in enabling her to mow the lawn—indeed this may not even be her specific purpose—her discussion nevertheless has consequences, as Butler (1995, 43–44) proposes:

> The actions instituted via [the] subject are part of a chain of actions that can no longer be understood as unilinear in direction or predictable in their outcomes . . . the effects of the instrumental action always have the power to proliferate beyond the subject's control, indeed, to challenge the rational transparency of the subject's intentionality and so to subvert the very definition of the subject itself.

Butler's proposal that one possible effect of the actions of a subject is to subvert the subject's very definition suggests that Fran's action of articulating the prohibitive not only has the effect of unsettling her husband's masculinity, but potentially has the effect of subverting her own gendered becoming as domesticated wife and mother and making possible her constitution as a subject gendered within other discourses.

The destabilization of Fran and her husband's current gendered subjectivity and the possibility of their reconstitution as subjects gendered differently brings with it in turn the potential for alternative housework practices and alternative domestic class processes in this household. For example, Fran's accusation that her husband does "women's work" might tempt him rather uncharacteristically to retort, "It's about time you did some men's work!" They may agree to divide up the household tasks not on the basis of what is expected of masculine and feminine subjects, but on the basis of the tasks that they enjoy doing. So Fran might mow the lawn and look after the gardens, and her husband vacuum the carpets, wash, and iron. This new division of work between Fran and her husband might result in two self-appropriative domestic class processes.[25] Alternatively, Fran may decide to take up her husband's challenge to do "men's work" and find permanent full-time employment so she becomes a full-time paid worker like her husband. She might then insist, like Elizabeth and June, that the whole family share the responsibility for household tasks, resulting in the shared familial production, appropriation, and distribution of domestic surplus labor, a communist domestic class process.

This chapter has focused on the one household, but the sorts of domestic discontinuities I've discussed here can be found in other households. For instance, Margaret's husband bakes biscuits and cakes that she takes to work, but she finds herself unable to "confess" to some friends and colleagues that it is her husband and not she who bakes. She enforces the regulatory fiction of domesticated femininity and undomesticated masculinity, suppressing both her husband's transgression (doing the domestic work of baking) and her own transgression (being a woman in a heterosexual couple who does not bake). In May's household, her husband vacuums and does the cooking and washing in a housework arrangement that May describes as "shared." But alongside these housework practices May says that she has "old-fashioned" ideas about housework, that she has the expectation that work inside the house is women's work and work outside is men's, and that she wants her husband to be hypermasculine:

> MAY: I'd rather let him be masculine than the other way, so like I don't mind. A lot of people don't like the macho male, but I don't mind—that's what a male's supposed to be. I mean, if he's not macho he's going to be the other way, and I'd much rather a macho male than the opposite.

The discourses that May employs of a gendered division of household labor and the hypermasculinized male can again be read as regulatory fictions. The actual housework practices and her husband's enactment of his gendered subjectivity exceed and transgress May's discourses.[26]

When housework practices and gendered becomings are represented as always already different from each other, it is possible to hear in these narratives of Fran, Margaret, and May the disruption of established notions as to what is normal and traditional, feminine and masculine (and even heterosexual and homosexual). And with the liberation of multiple meanings for these concepts comes the potential for a proliferation of discourses of alternative housework practices, class processes, and gendered becomings.

Conclusion

In this chapter, I have argued that the familiar feminist characterization of households as traditional, as opposed to progressive or egalitarian, obscures the way domestic labor and gendered becomings in households are always already instances of difference. This dichotomous representation relies on a polarized clustering of attributes—unequal labor practices, exploitation, and gender oppression at one end of the spectrum and equal labor practices, nonexploitation, and the absence of gender oppression at the other—and suggests that the feminist emancipatory project focus on moving households from the less desirable traditional end to its liberated opposite. One of the consequences of this analysis is that economic difference within households is ignored and the political possibilities that stem from this difference are unthought.

My work extends the poststructuralist theoretical insights developed by a feminism of difference into the economic and domestic realm. Using an anti-essentialist analysis of class processes in the household, I have explored the diversity of practices whereby domestic surplus labor is produced, appropriated, and distributed and questioned the ways in which these practices are represented. This exploration involved unlinking the tight connections often presumed between the unequal performance of domestic labor, exploitation, and gender oppression and raising the possibilities of representing men as exploited domestic subjects and women as self-appropriating domestic workers. This latter designation of a woman as a self-appropriating domestic worker was developed as a political strategy to represent the domesticated wife and mother as independent and authoritative, rather than dependent and victimized. The identification of a self-appropriating domestic worker associated with the performance of an unequal but nonexploitative measure of housework suggests that feminism need not reject out-of-hand the role of domesticated wife and mother as a tenable option for women. Of course, this is not a blanket endorsement of that role, nor of the host of other familiar gender differences that are currently manifest in households, but it is an invitation to consider the possibilities for difference in the domain of the domestic. I have attempted to subvert liberalism's devaluing and negation of the feminine and familial, and egalitarian feminism's disavowal and repudiation of the domestic as a realm that only constrains and encumbers women. This revaluation and refiguring of the domestic feminine subject raises important possibilities for feminist politics.

Combining a discourse of household heterogeneity with the understanding of the subject as constituted by discursive practices, like housework, offers a way of seeing housework, domestic class processes, and gendered becomings as never final or complete but always open to reconstitution. In this approach change comes not from judging and condemning an existing division of labor or class process or gendered becoming, but by theorizing the emancipatory possibilities that might already be contained within the current domestic order.

Notes

Thanks to Barb Dalton for talking me through the chapter, the editors for their comments and discussion, and the participants in the Workshop on Class, Amherst, Massachusetts, June 1996.

1. Studies that specifically identify households in which there is an unequal distribution of labor as traditional include Baber and Allen (1992), Baxter (1990), Bittman and Lovejoy (1993), Wheelock (1990), and Yeandle (1984). An equal sharing

of housework is described in various ways, for example: "innovative work patterns" (Goodnow 1989, 54; Goodnow and Bowles 1994, 181); "egalitarian domestic labor arrangements" (Baxter 1993, 5); "egalitarian arrangements" (Pina and Bengtson 1994, 902–3); and a "liberal" gendered division of labor (Wheelock 1990, 120). Wheelock (116) describes households that move from the liberal gendered division of labor to a more traditional pattern as "regressing."

2. As housework involves heterogeneous tasks, it is necessary to specify what equal measure might mean in the domestic context. For the purposes of this chapter, I will define equal measure as equal time spent doing household labor. While I recognize that different household tasks require varying levels of skill and are valued differently within our society, and that one could argue for alternative ways of assessing equality in the performance of domestic labor, I am choosing to proceed with this simpler definition.

3. These include masculinist representations of a black and white femininity, a working-class and middle-class femininity.

4. Within a feminist politics of difference, I would include projects such as Butler's (1990; 1993) on the uncoupling of sex, gender, and desire, Cornell's (1995) on the imaginary domain and the redefining of women's sexuality, and Sedgwick's (1993) on the dissolving of the lines that divide gender and sexual identities.

5. In a book that includes an incisive critique of feminism's reliance on ressentiment and victimhood as the moral grounds from which political claims are made, Wendy Brown (1995), for example, nevertheless portrays women as encumbered by their responsibility for domestic work, bound to perform unpaid domestic work for men, and, as a consequence, limited in their access to civil society.

6. The socialist ideal has, perhaps, at least until recently, been the preeminent example of the understanding that social equity is achieved through economic sameness and equality.

7. Perhaps the most developed theory of women's domestic exploitation and men's oppression of women is the domestic mode of production approach, associated with the work of Christine Delphy and Sylvia Walby, and the patriarchal mode of production approach developed by Nancy Folbre. I will not address this distinct body of work in this paper, but see Cameron (1996/1997) for a detailed discussion.

8. And, I could add, essentialist Marxism's location of work at the core of social life (man's species being) and "true" consciousness as necessary to political subjectivity.

9. The point is not to dismiss the importance of such campaigns, but simply to suggest that they are limited as feminist strategies of transformation.

10. I am not suggesting that it is possible to work completely outside of liberal discourse; any outside is likely to be temporary and partial.

11. This aporia with respect to the household and economic analysis within poststructuralist feminism is an interesting symptom of the rejection of more structuralist socialist feminist theories of gender. But by leaving unexamined the putative sameness of women's experience of domestic labor, we are potentially undermining the exploration and endorsement of difference in all other dimensions of sociality,

sexuality, and subjectivity. The proposed unraveling of the triad—unequal domestic work, exploitation, and gender oppression—owes much to Sedgwick's discussion of undoing the "Christmas effect" (1993, 5).

12. Surplus labor is here defined as labor that is over and above what is necessary for one's own self-maintenance.

13. Fraad, Resnick, and Wolff (1994) would name this pattern of domestic surplus labor production a "feudal" domestic class process.

14. The reader may, at this point, be amazed at the apparent silliness of this type of microclass analysis of the household. While I recognize and even share this response, it is useful also to reflect on it. Why is the detailed division of labor and power over certain jobs on a factory floor—the subject of union demarcation disputes and other such public attentions—seen as legitimate and serious, while the same issues in the household are seen as somehow trivial and silly? We are led back once again to the hold that liberal discourse, with its devaluing of the domestic, the familial, and the feminine, has over political and economic thinking.

15. This process could also be called self-exploitation. I prefer the term self-appropriation as it enables a thinking of nonshared housework in nonexploitative terms. In another political context, self-exploitation may be the more strategic concept.

16. If the children refuse to give their father affection, he may stop distributing surplus labor to them. Each child and the father may then prepare their own breakfast—in class terms they would each produce, appropriate, and distribute their own surplus labor, a self-appropriative domestic class process. Or an exploitative domestic class process may be established as the children demand that their father prepare their breakfast, telling him that they do not have the time or that it is his job as a parent to do it. Or the children and their father may sit down and decide to take turns, each on a different day of the week, preparing breakfast. This shared production, appropriation, and distribution of surplus labor would be a communist domestic class process.

17. Once familiar practices that were consistent with this discourse include the husband's handing of the paycheck in its entirety to the wife to manage, and, in Australia at any rate, the wife's banishing of the husband to the side room on the veranda as a means of regulating their sexual encounters. Or the husband, who after a late night out at the pub with his mates, comes home to a meal of "hot tongue and cold shoulder."

18. Once these circumstances change, the domestic class process is likely to be transformed, and a very different domestic class process may replace the old one. It is impossible to predict the result of a domestic class transformation such as this.

19. Perhaps because it is inconceivable that in a patriarchal society women might be able to exploit their husbands, or because women are assumed to have an essential or constructed inability to exploit another human being.

20. Within feminism the domestic labor debate has theoretically and politically foundered over this issue of victimhood. With rising numbers of women in the paid

work force as well as feminist mothers who are arguing for the right to stay at home, the domestic sphere has become a complex arena in which such a simplistic and categorical analysis seems inappropriate. While there is no doubt that the victim image still has the power to mobilize people around issues of domestic violence and rape, the value of this representation for women is being questioned by feminists such as Marcus (1992).

21. When there is explicit conflict between the discourses and practices that constitute a class process, other representations of a class process may resonate more strongly for acting subjects. At the moment that Fran asks "Why do I do it?" the naming of the domestic class process as self-exploitation may speak to Fran and enable her to conceive of alternative domestic class processes, while at other times this may be a representation in which Fran cannot recognize herself. A feminist politics that includes supposedly "competing [and contradictory] narratives" (hooks 1992, 44), rather than allowing only one to speak as the truth of women's experiences and circumstances, suggests a politics of potentiality whereby subjects might be constituted and reconstituted within different discourses (for an example of this form of feminist politics see Gibson-Graham's [1994] reflection on their research project with mining town women).

22. Butler (1990, 136) uses this phrase to describe how the assumed heterosexual coherence between sex and gender and desire—such that the female sex is assumed to cohere with the gender identity "woman" and desire for the body sexed male and gendered man, and the male sex is assumed to cohere with the gender identity "man" and desire for the body sexed female and gendered woman—conceals the already existing proliferation of different arrangements of sex and gender and desire.

23. Similarly, Fran's aside at the end of her discussion about the morning organization of housework, that it "sounds like I do nothing, doesn't it?," can be seen as working, not to make plausible what she suggests—that she does nothing—but as confirmation that indeed she does most things.

24. See Cameron (1996/1997) for a discussion about the construction of heterosexuality around housework.

25. Or perhaps Fran and her husband might have a communist class relationship.

26. It is noteworthy that May represents her husband as the "macho male" against the image of the limp-wristed, effeminate male homosexual invoked by the phrase "the other way." May aligns machismo and heterosexuality, and effeminacy and homosexuality, precluding the possibility that "macho man" can also be homosexual man. In Cameron (1997) I discuss how normative heterosexuality is haunted by its constitutive others—homosexuality and deviant heterosexuality.

3

Exploitation in the Labor of Love

Harriet Fraad

In his last and longest work Louis Althusser returned with urgency to the family in the conviction that he had profoundly underestimated its importance:

> [H]ow long will even the most informed and intelligent people allow themselves to be deluded by something even more blind and blinding than that dreadful deaf fish of the unconscious, which Freud trawled up from the very depths of the seas in his long net? How much longer will they fail to recognise the blinding evidence of the true nature of the Family as an ideological State apparatus? Does one now have to point out that, in addition to the three great narcissistic wounds inflicted on Humanity (that of Galileo, that of Darwin, and that of the unconscious), there is a fourth and even graver one which no one wishes to have revealed (since from time immemorial the family has been the very site of the *sacred* and therefore of *power* and *religion*)? It is an irrefutable fact that the Family is the most powerful ideological State apparatus. (Althusser, 1993, 104–5)

Althusser considered the family a key site where children suffer narcissistic wounds, assaults on their very sense of self and basic dignity. He focused on those wounds using his own particular person as a case in point.

Althusser's concentration on the pain of childhood offers a field of new insights beyond those gleaned by other Marxists who have exposed the family as a basis for authoritarian personality formation (Adorno 1950) and as an institution that shifts the cost of reproducing the next generation of workers from capital to the workers themselves. His attention to the injuries of childhood reveals the family as a site of deep humiliation, teaching lessons of self-abnegation in the face of powerlessness. In its enforcement of emotional servitude, childhood is a training ground preparing the individual for the accumulating set of ideological and official subjections that together constitute the adult world of contemporary capitalism.

Althusser examined his own childhood to illustrate how he was subjugated and how his lifelong struggle to overcome the emotional servitude in his family influenced every aspect of his career, political activity, and painful intimate relationships. Much of his autobiography is devoted to an analysis and demonstration of the family as a "child's private circle of hell" (1993, 135). He chronicles his daily anguished labors of producing the emotional services that his mother required:

> Even though I grumbled inwardly at what she said, I always went along with it. I existed only through my mother's desires, never my own, which remained inaccessible. . . . I was torn, but helpless in the face of my mother's desire and my own inner conflict. I did everything she wished. (Althusser 1993, 58)

What is striking in Althusser's autobiography is not only the intense pain of his childhood, but his association of that pain with the continual and enforced expenditure of emotional labor in service to his mother. Ultimately, it appears that his story is one of extreme emotional exploitation of the child by the parent. In the language of exploitation theory, the child who was Althusser produced not only his own necessary emotional labor, but also surplus emotional labor that was demanded and appropriated by his mother.

In the story of Althusser's childhood, we encounter the possibility that the Marxian theory of exploitation (conceptualized as the appropriation of surplus labor by those who are not performers of that labor) might fruitfully be extended to a new frontier, the intimate world of childhood. It is that possibility that I wish to develop in this chapter, in which I begin to investigate the emotional labor of children in U.S. families and to explore familial exploitation as one of the key sources of emotional pain and adult mental illness.

The chapter begins with a discussion of emotional labor and its unique product, emotional services. This discussion serves as the background and underpinning for the theory of emotional exploitation. Using this theory of exploitation as a tool of illumination, I explore some examples of mental illness derived from my experiences as a psychotherapist. At the end of the paper, I suggest possibilities for nonexploitative families and how they might function to produce and distribute emotional services.

Emotional Labor/Services

While feminists have developed notions of emotional labor (see, for example, Hochschild 1983, 1997; Chapkis 1997) and while Marxists have developed the theory of class exploitation as surplus labor appropriation,[1] the aim of this chapter is to integrate these two major contributions: to introduce a concept of emotional labor and relate it to the class process of exploitation within the family. The chapter attempts to reveal the particular emotional labor of children as well as its systematic exploitation.

Within the Marxist tradition, surplus labor has often been understood to be produced and appropriated solely in the production of goods. As services have become more important economically, struggles within Marxism have led to the recognition that surplus labor analysis can and should be applied to the production of services as well. Similarly there have been battles among Marxists to recognize that surplus labor analysis can illuminate not only commodified but also noncommodified production. In other words, surplus labor analysis may apply to products that never pass through a market on the way to their consumers.

Recently Marxists have ventured to bring a class analysis of surplus labor into the nonmarket arena of the household (Fraad et al. 1989, 1994; Gibson 1992; Cameron 1996/97). This paper builds on that work, theorizing the class dimension in the production, appropriation, and distribution of one kind of service, emotional service, in family-based households.

Women's labor in the production of emotional services has been a focus of feminist scholarship from the early works of Gilman (1966, 1972) and Kollontai (1971) to the more recent theories of Chodorow (1978, 1989, 1994), Nakano et al. (1994), and Ruddick (1995). Studies of emotional labor in the context of particular service industries range from the work of Chapkis (1997) and van der Veen (this volume) on the sex industry to the countless discussions of women's labor in the nursing profession (Benner and Wrubel 1989; Burr 1996; Deckard et al. 1988; Fagin and Diers 1983; Harmer and Henderson 1960; Streety 1990). Hochschild pioneered the discussion of emotional labor as a component of such traditionally female jobs as that of flight attendant. Her book, *The Managed Heart* (1983), traces the way that emotional behavior is part of both what she refers to as "straight" and also "improvised" work rules and expectations (77–86). The rule that a flight attendant must smile at and thank departing customers is a "straight" work rule. The requirement that a flight attendant return customer surliness with friendly availability is an "improvised" work rule requiring the flight attendant to improvise a response according to a rule that she be pleasant.

Emotional services often require exhausting human labor. Trying to understand and empathize with another's psychological needs and to satisfy those needs requires full awareness and the strain of focusing one's senses, intellect, and musculature toward another. Everyone has at some time experienced the feeling of physical exhaustion that follows a session in which another person or a group needed one's mobilized psychic attention and affection, that is, one's emotional labor power. To use Marx's terminology, emotional labor is a concrete kind of labor that produces a concrete use value called emotional services. Extending the classic Marxian definition, we can now define labor as the expenditure of brain, muscle, and emotion over time.[2]

Psychological nurturing work is already widely recognized as a component of jobs such as nursing, teaching young children, and psychotherapy, which yield emotional services that people want and need to consume. Yet it can also be argued that most workers producing a particular service (serving a meal, selling a stove, cleaning a wound, cutting hair, etc.) produce, as a joint product, the emotional service of pleasing the consumer. Service personnel may deny their customers the satisfaction of emotional service. They may attend customers with an emotional indifference and boredom bordering on hostility. In such circumstances the customer may well experience the denial of that emotional joint product she or he counted on consuming. The practice of tipping is a kind of recognition of the special care of which emotional service is a component. Supervisors oversee service workers in part in order to command the emotional attention that is a component of service work well done.

The extent of emotional service rendered is generally related to the amount of money spent. The expensive boutique delivers service and emotional care along with its apparel, whereas the discount chain does not. Restaurants that cater to the wealthy usually deliver more service and emotional regard than does McDonald's. Even at McDonald's, however, servers must be polite and friendly, thanking customers and wishing them a good day.

Emotional services are distributed partly through the market. As a crucial component of human survival from infancy on, they account for the disbursal of billions of dollars. The therapy industry, an industry built on providing emotional services for money,[3] is burgeoning in the United States. The publishing industry produces a huge output of explicit and subtle literature on self-care and the care of others in the form of books, audiotapes, and videos helping to perform every emotional service from reducing stress to curbing destructive tendencies and even replacing them with emotional self-nurturance. The entertainment industries provide people with emotional services ranging from fun to catharsis.

Television purveys a range of models for giving and receiving the entire spectrum of emotional services from understanding and compassion, to emotional support, to vicarious expressions of rage and aggression, to challenge, excitement, and passion. The Internet provides access to emotional services through chat rooms and groups sharing common fantasies and reassuring people that they are not alone in their particular proclivities. Religious organizations make millions giving and receiving emotional care in ways that range from support groups to absolution.

Although words like family and home have powerful emotional referents, when we think of home and family it is rarely the production and distribution of emotional services that comes to mind. Yet families are above all where emotional needs are expressed, formed, and deformed, and where emotional services are produced, appropriated, and distributed. The surplus labor dimension of this process of service production has not been explicitly examined under the lens of Marxian class analysis, which offers a field of potential insights into emotional deprivation and the travail and pain that is associated with it in the family and outside it.

Emotional Services and Class Processes

Just as we may be concerned with class processes and how they operate within relationships involved in the production of cars or security services, we may also be interested in how class processes operate within emotional relationships between people. Is surplus labor being produced, appropriated, and distributed, and if so how? Are the class relations in which emotional labor is performed feudal, independent, capitalist, communist, or any combination of these?

When assembly line workers apply themselves to the job with a passion, that emotion may be seen as an aspect of their job performance that affects the production of surplus labor but is not part of the capitalist class process in itself. Because it is not a feature of the commodity being produced, the emotional quality of the work experience for the assembly-line worker is not included in the accounting of the production, appropriation, and distribution of surplus labor.

For a nurse in a private, for-profit hospital, who is required to nurture her (or his) charges, emotional labor is a part of her production not only of service but also of surplus. The for-profit hospital for which she labors sells a commodity, health care. Her emotional service production is required as a component of that commodity. She provides a service, nursing, which is both physical and emotional. She performs such physical services as administering medication and dressing wounds and, as a joint product of her labors, the emotional services of listening, soothing, demonstrating concern, and so on.

Her capitalist employer appropriates surplus labor from her in the form of surplus value. Her emotional output is a fundamental element of the nursing services she delivers.

Of course, the nurse need not be employed in a capitalist enterprise in order to produce necessary and surplus labor in the form of emotional and physical services. If she labors in a communal health facility owned and operated by health-care providers who produce, appropriate, and distribute their own surplus, then she produces her physical and emotional nursing services within the communal class process. If she is self-employed as an independent contractor, she provides physical and emotional nursing services and appropriates and distributes her own surplus within an independent class process.

What class process would be involved if our nurse were at home nursing a sick partner or child? To answer that question, we would need to explore the class processes of use-value production in the household. Very possibly the nurse's household and her emotional production is organized along what have been identified as "feudal" class lines (see Fraad et al. 1994). In the sentimentalized household of right-wing nostalgia,[4] for example, the wife labors in a home with means of production (stove, vacuum cleaner, etc.) provided by her husband. She performs necessary labor (cooking, cleaning, etc.) for herself and surplus labor (cooking, cleaning, etc.) for her husband (Fraad et al. 1989, 1994). In addition, she tries to please the lord of the manor with sexual and emotional services. Like a feudal serf, she produces surplus labor for and also declares her love for the lord while the lord pledges her his love and protection. Within the ideology that helps to perpetuate this kind of family, the wife's cooking, cleaning, and emotional service is not viewed as labor but rather "nest-making" or expressing love as part of a genetic-emotional destiny in a way that parallels the religious destiny that converted the labor of the medieval serf into a natural mission ordained by God. The knowledges and skills the wife acquires through housework and caring intimately for her family are unspoken, unrecognized, and unpaid. The disguise of the homemaker's labor as a genetic or divine mission facilitates her exploitation just as the designation of serfs' labor as a sanctified destiny facilitated their exploitation.

Parents and Children in Feudal Emotional Relationships

In households in which there are largely feudal processes of domestic surplus labor production, children may also sometimes function as serfs, producing domestic surplus for one or both parents.[5] Many children in the contemporary United States, for example, are also expected to "serve" their parents with a servitude that is primarily emotional.[6] Parents may want and need their children to be whatever it is that they themselves need rather than what may be best for the children. Such parents unconsciously school their children in emotional servitude and parental needs. They rear their children within their own neurotic limitations while they provide some physical safety, some support, some protection from outsiders, some form of love, and some concern for what they feel lies in the child's best interests.

Children cannot help but try to be what their parents need. Their survival depends on pleasing the adults in charge, or they come to feel that it does. Children strive to be the desire of their parents (Lacan 1968, 294–95; Mitchell and Rose 1982, 38). Often they feel that the desire of their parents is to have created the parents they wished they had instead of children who require their care and attention. Toiling to satisfy the contradictory and changing needs of parents, children may spend a lifetime straining to compensate their parents for the burdensome crime of being children.

Many children toil to produce happiness for their parents while they sustain their own happiness alone. Their pressing emotional concerns may be ignored. Their hard emotional labor may go unrecognized in the same way that their mother's domestic labor may be unacknowledged. They are reported to be as congenitally "happy" as the happy housewives in 1950s television commercials. In Marxian terminology, many children perform emotional necessary labor whose product is emotional service that is necessary for their own psychological survival. However, they also produce hours of emotional labor above and beyond that which is necessary; the product of this surplus labor is emotional services appropriated by their parents. Neither the children nor their parents may be conscious of this process. It may seem as normal and natural as women's performing household labor in the 1950s seemed before it was problematized by second wave feminists.

Part of what makes children's emotional servitude seem natural is a culture of childhood feudalism. Although this is changing, the media, children's literature, and many parents and parenting manuals (Greven 1992)—especially those associated with right-wing fundamentalism—present the "good" boy or girl as helping his or her parents in every way possible without a thought to her or himself.[7] Religious child-rearing manuals may instruct parents specifically on "breaking the child's will" in order to achieve unquestioning obedience to parental demands (Greven 1992).

Children are legally tied to their parents. If they run away, those that shelter them may be prosecuted for harboring runaways. When runaway children are found they are returned unless they are legally "emancipated." It is telling that the legal release of children from parental custody is expressed in the legal vocabulary for freeing slaves.

Many child-parent emotional arrangements resemble the classic feudal obligations between serfs and lords. Just as lords usually protected their serfs from other lords, leaving the serfs little protection against their ostensible protectors, many parents protect their children from the predations of strangers. However, the children have little protection from the parents themselves. Yet parents are the overwhelming culprits violating children.[8] Parents and children are bound by mutual obligations, but the power to enforce these is overwhelmingly in the hands of the parents. Although there are some legal protections against child abuse, child murder, sexual abuse, and incest, the legal system is not directly available to children.

Children's lack of other civil rights as well as access to the legal system leaves them dependent on the law of their parents. In the United States they are also largely dependent on their parents' economic fortunes and generosity for access to opportunities ranging from quality child care and food to computers to such cultural enrichments as music, art, or dance lessons (Children's Defense Fund 1997, 10–11, 17–18).[9] These are a few of the political, economic, and cultural conditions that shape children's feudal status.

Emotional Labor and Exploitation, Emotional Pain and Illness

In *The Managed Heart* (1983, 187) Hochschild outlines three stances that emotional laborers take toward their work. The first is a complete and wholehearted identification of the self with the job. This, she warns, is most likely to lead to what she calls "burn out" and what is in Marxian terms a depletion of emotional necessary labor. The second stance toward emotional labor is a conscious but guilty separation of aspects of the self from the emotional role one must play. The guilt stems from a rule that if one does not give one's all, one is culpable for duplicity. This second stance is possible for some adolescents who are separating themselves from the usually unspoken rule that parents' emotional needs come first. The third stance toward emotional labor is a positive separation from some aspects of the emotional role assigned, gratified by the emotional mastery such distance requires.

Young children are emotional laborers who cannot separate their own needs and desires from those of their parents and other caregivers. Their fate is complete, wholehearted identification with parental demands that may leave them emotionally depleted. The self-gratifying stance toward emotional labor is not available to children who are neither intellectually nor emotionally capable of separating their emotions from those their parents wish to recognize. Thus very young children may be trapped in the most depleting stance toward emotional labor.

If a child labors to fulfill the psychological needs of parents while the child's personal emotional needs are invisible to those parents, the invisibility of the child's needs means that they cannot be acknowledged, let alone met.[10] When that child produces emotional services to meet the emotional needs of a parent without reciprocity, the child provides her or his own emotional necessary labor and turns much of the surplus into work to please the parent. The child in a relationship to a parent in which emotional services are appropriated and distributed by the parent without parity may need to cut back on producing emotional necessary labor in order to produce the surplus emotional labor required by the parents. When a child's surplus labor and its product of emotional surplus for a parent is extremely large and the child's necessary labor and its product of emotional service is meager, the child may not have sufficient necessary labor for psychological survival. If her or his necessary labor is not augmented by distributions of emotional surplus from siblings, other relatives, or anyone else, the child will not develop adequately physically, mentally, or emotionally and in extreme cases may literally "fail to thrive"[11] or become mentally ill.

To further complicate the matter, intense anger is often generated by the sacrifices children make in order to please their parents. Each child will express anger in ways that fit his or her unique personality and circumstances. These include direct rebellions such as disobedience and tantrums and indirect revolts in violence or cruelty to siblings, playmates, or themselves. Below I offer a few examples drawn from my psychotherapy practice of child emotional exploitation and the illness and violence that results.[12]

Daisy

Daisy suffers crippling panic attacks. She cannot breathe. Her heart races. She must run to stop the nameless terror. Her panic attacks strike unpredictably . . . at home with her young children, in the car in traffic jams, at work in the small back office.

Daisy was trapped with her uncle and her father in the attic where they sexually abused her. She could not afford to feel the emotions triggered by her ostensible protectors. The feelings reemerge many years later in terrifying panic attacks.

Daisy expends considerable emotional labor time repressing the rage, shame, and betrayal she feels as the victim of her uncle's and her father's sexual abuses. As a child she could not break powerful unspoken family rules. She could not betray her father and uncle's secret even though they betrayed her trust. Her emotional life was not a consideration in her family.

She understood that to betray her uncle and father's secret would mean that she, and not they, would be abandoned by the family.[13] She provided the emotional service to her parents of concealing her rage and pain, devoting much of the labor that she needed to sustain herself to the task of providing emotional services to her parents. The self-deprivation that this entailed (and continues to entail) is now manifest as paralyzing panic attacks.

As a child Daisy's emotional labors were augmented by the kindness and care she received from others. Her grandmother and her younger sisters demonstrated their devotion in the emotional services they performed for her. These helped Daisy to live.[14]

Daisy needed to produce vast quantities of emotional labor to withstand her father and uncle's abuse, suppress the pain and outrage it caused her, and pretend that she did not require the solace that she was taught she could not demand. Many adults whose childhood emotional life required self-suffocation no longer have the capacity to provide themselves with the emotional services they need. They carry vituperative rage at their own needs that they may vent on a convenient target. Who could be more convenient than one's children? Repressed adults may transmit the cruelty and exploitation of their own emotional service production to their children, who pass it to their own children, and so on.

Daisy has a daughter. When Daisy's little girl expresses her needs for kindness, comfort, and sympathy, Daisy becomes enraged. She cannot allow herself to have compassion for her child because she learned from her own mother that a child's pain is to be silenced and condemned. The more Daisy identifies with her child, the less she can allow her child to express the threatening feelings that she herself suppressed. Daisy expresses her hatred of the feelings and needs she had as a child that her parents taught her were unspeakably bad. She rages at her daughter's demands for just the kind of protection and solace that she herself never had. Like many adults who seal off as "other" their emotional experiences of childhood, she fears confronting her own emotions through her child. She needs to crush the threatening feelings through crushing her daughter's needs by any means necessary, including abuse.

Sarah

Sarah is a highly successful inner-city school administrator. She is lauded for her unflappable composure in a crisis atmosphere. At home, alone, Sarah cuts herself. She is so relieved to bleed. Her blood reassures her that she is alive. She is not the perfect, bloodless, robot-child her parents needed.

Sarah's survival in her parents' household depended on pleasing her parents by imposing no emotional burdens on their strained lives. The literally unspeakable painful emotions she felt as a child now emerge in bleeding cuts.

In order to mobilize herself to perform the emotional tasks needed by her acutely stressed and volatile parents, the young Sarah needed to deny her own emotional need for care. She spent her efforts on producing emotional surplus labor for her parents at the expense of the labor necessary for her own happiness and self-care. In the process she grew to despise her needs as much as her parents despised her for having them. Her buried necessities erupt with a punishment for needing. She cuts herself until she bleeds. She cannot feel the wounds when she inflicts them but is reassured by the flow of her blood. She is alive even though she cannot feel. The pain of the cuts the day after they are inflicted fills her with the pain she felt as a needy child. Her destructive symptoms enact the unspoken tragedy that she is not permitted to articulate. Lacking the emotional capacity to free herself from her painful legacy, Sarah repeats that legacy through a ritual of self-cutting.

James

James is a talented, successful writer. He is not nearly as productive as he could be. His hands cramp until he must stop writing. He has run the gauntlet of medical practitioners and alternative health specialists. There is no discernible physical reason for his crippling disability. James's hands are enforcing the family law that he is not to out-compete his disabled brother and his unemployed father. He is being the "good" boy his parents wanted. James's cramped hands enact family rules that he does not have the strength to dispute or countermand. As a child he exhausted himself in the performance of emotional labor, balancing what have literally become crippling demands on him and at the same time concealing those demands as an emotional service to his parents.

In each of these cases the children produced emotional surplus labor to sustain their parents, hide their personal pain, and maintain secrecy about the exhausting effort it took to do so. In denying their parents' indifference and abuse, Daisy, Sarah, and James expended the particular psychic exertion necessary for maintaining secrets. Such exertion involves colluding with one's exploiters to deny one's painful reality.[15] Self-denial in the service of their parents was a particularly taxing psychic toil, draining Daisy's, Sarah's, and James's emotional energies. In all three cases their necessary labor and its product, emotional service, became inadequately small partly because surplus labor and its product of emotional service to parents became very large. The depletion of the emotional labor necessary to sustain these three people was a powerful factor in producing their mental illness. In other words, their mental illness was shaped by their exploitation as emotional laborers performing psychological services for their parents. Daisy, Sarah, and James were suffering from a high rate of feudal emotional exploitation. In seeking therapy as adults, they are obtaining commodified emotional services. These services help them become the fully functioning adults they could have already been, had their families or others offered them sufficient emotional services in childhood and had they not been forced to cut back on their own necessary labor in order to produce surplus emotional labor for their parents.

Communal Relationships between Parents and Children

Some parents' greatest desire is to see their children become independent, fulfilled people. These parents strive to provide encompassing support to their children. They labor to recognize and appreciate their children as separate people. In this case the children may try to fulfill the desires of their parents by working to achieve independence, self-acknowledgment, and happiness for themselves. In such families both parents and children may labor emotionally to provide fulfillment of their own and each other's affective needs. No one is mostly alone creating emotional surplus for another who appropriates it. Instead, all work communally for themselves and each other. This type of family may participate in a kind of communal class process in which family members jointly produce and together appropriate and distribute emotional services.

The formal allocation of emotional labor is dependent on children's acquisition of language and some consciousness of their own emotions and needs. This process may begin as early as six years of age. Communal families may have conferences in which family members air what bothers them and explain what they need from each other. They may also have informal meetings around particular issues that spontaneously arise. These issues have to be presented in ways that are accessible to children, ways that will change as children mature.

Communal allocations of familial emotional work are remarkably achievable. The extensive literature of family therapy abounds with examples of families who entered counseling with a profound inability to communicate with each other who then learn to negotiate their needs and problems in a communal emotional fashion. As a therapist who has worked with families, I am impressed by the possibilities for a communal allocation of emotional labor.

The ability to communicate one's own emotional needs and to communally produce, appropriate, and distribute emotional labor within a family is dependent on creating a communal culture that provides an ideological condition of existence for communal allocations of psychological work. Just as children within a family characterized by feudal conditions of emotional labor learn to give without demanding in return, to hide their needs for the emotional labor of others, and to give without thinking of their own needs, children in a family characterized by communal conditions of emotional labor learn to do the opposite.[16] This learning may be reinforced by media experiences, children's literature, early child-care experiences, and after-school reinforcements that help to create a communal culture for the performance of emotional labor. By the time a child is ready to attend public school, these communal practices may be so well learned that a child can sustain them at home while learning to submit, at least to some extent, to what are often noncommunal emotional requirements at school.

In a family characterized by communal parent-child relationships, a parent would not sexually abuse a child as Daisy's relatives did because they would imagine the impact of such abuse on the child who is considered a feeling person. Similarly, a parent could not demand developmentally inappropriate caretaking as did Sarah's and James's parents.

Parents whose relationships to their children are characterized by the communal class process will, of course, make mistakes in understanding what is best for their children. However, they empower their children to challenge their decisions and reveal their mistakes. They struggle to change and better their relationships and discuss ways to do so. Their children do not suffer from a requirement to repress their emotional needs and neither do they need to keep the secret of their own abuse. Their reserves of emotional labor are replenished by parents' emotional services.

In families in which emotional services are produced communally, there are still many problems. All parents are contradictory, problem-ridden people. Power relations between parents and children are starkly unequal. Children's survival is still largely dependent on their parents. They have virtually no direct access to civic protections. However, in families in which emotional services are communal, no one is emotionally exploited, producing surplus labor that is appropriated by others. Families in which emotional labor is produced communally develop many differing strategies for producing and distributing emotional labor in nonexploitative ways.

Conclusion

Children's psychological exploitation has been explored in the literature of psychoanalysis from Freud onward and has been continuously portrayed in fiction from Dickens, Hugo, and Brontë in the nineteenth century to Canfield and Allison in the twentieth.[17] Child anguish is disclosed in work such as Alice Miller's (1982, 1984, 1990) on parental insensitivity to child emotional realities and the literature revealing the extent and the psychological toll of child sexual abuse.[18] Similar studies have exposed prevalent child battery.[19]

In the United States today millions of people are mobilized around their personal pain, sharing their emotional damage at the hands of their families. Alcoholics Anonymous, Al-Anon, Al-A-Teen, Adult Children of Alcoholics, Narcotics Anonymous, Cocaine Anonymous, Overeaters Anonymous, Anorexics Anonymous, Bulimics Anonymous, Co-Dependents Anonymous, Sex Abuse Anonymous, Relationships Anonymous, etc. offer an analysis of childhood and family oppression and a program for liberation that organizes millions of Americans into vital though generally apolitical groups. The enormous range of therapies and organizations that address the experience of pain in family upbringing speak to the problematic condition of the family as the principal social site of child rearing and nurturing.

As Althusser's autobiography and the stories of Daisy, Sarah, and James so movingly attest, great possibilities of happiness and fulfillment are lost due to the psychological damage inflicted by families. In this paper, I have tried to make sense of some of that damage by acknowledging the emotional labor of children, often invisibly performed in response to parental demands. By recognizing the laboring role that children play in delivering emotional services within the family, we also come to recognize the possibility of child exploitation in U.S. families today. The concepts of necessary and surplus labor central to the Marxian theory of class exploitation enable us, in more than a metaphorical way, to describe and understand the extraordinary sense of emotional depletion and pain that characterize the experience of so many adults.

In spite of some powerful Marxian work on the family (for example, Engels [1972], Kollontai [1971, 1977a, 1977b], Adorno [1950], and Althusser [1993]), the class dimensions of childhood and parenting have not been explored. The utopian visions and hopes that most parents have when they have a baby and that children have until they can no longer sustain their illusions are at present captured only in sentimentalized right-wing family ideology and religious visions of a holy family. Marxian understandings and utopian possibilities of social parenting and collectivity are currently undeveloped and unknown.[20] Nevertheless, the politicized personal issues that are center stage in the United States at the moment can be seen to revolve around whether to provide the social conditions of existence for feudal or for communal families. Issues such as abortion rights, welfare for indigent parents and children, benefits for families with damaged children, social supports for working families, child care, after-school care, and guaranteed health insurance for children are clearly conditions of existence for communal families. Families most likely to be able to sustain emotional communality are planned families with wanted children. They are families who get help, freed from the overwhelming and total responsibility for their children. Parents with extensive support in day care and after-school programs have more opportunities for fulfilling lives of their own with time to relax, find satisfying work, and still engage in creating communal practices of communicating emotional needs and sharing in family emotional labor.[21] At the same time, each extra-familial resource that is provided for children gives those children an additional life support outside of the total and exclusive control of their parents.

In this chapter I have explored a new way of connecting the realm of Freud with that of Marx, emotional labor with physical labor, and intimate exploitation in the family with documented exploitation in the workplace. My purpose in developing these links is to help liberate children from the family that is the primary site of their emotional exploitation.

Marxists have exposed the exploitation of workers' physical and intellectual labor as a prerequisite to ending their exploitation. It is my hope that a class analysis of children's entrapment within exploitative emotional labor will help to expose those conditions and transform them. A class analysis offers one way to bridge the hitherto daunting gap between concerns with life outside the intimate arena of the family and the masses of people searching, often desperately, for relief from their personal pain. The liberation of adults from exploitation outside the home needs to be joined by the emancipation of children from emotional exploitation in the home. This may allow us to take one more step toward freeing the child outside as well as within us.

Notes

This chapter is indebted to Richard Wolff, Stephen Resnick, Julie Graham, and Katherine Gibson for their careful reading of previous versions.

1. See, for example, Resnick and Wolff (1987, 1988), Amariglio (1984), Gabriel (1989), Fraad et al. (1994), and Gibson-Graham (1996).

2. The phenomenon of burnout that is widely discussed in the literature of the

nursing profession and other helping professions suggests the level of physical, intellectual, and emotional effort required to provide emotional services.

3. In some schools of psychotherapy, emotional caring is an explicit component of the service, while in others any emotional expression is thought to interfere with the transference.

4. This household in its idealized form never existed for the mass of people. Even during its ostensible height in the Victorian period, countless mothers and children of the poor had to abandon their own families to work as domestic servants in the households of the wealthy. However, it was not only the labor of poor U.S. women and children that contradicted the Victorian patriarchal family romance. Rampant child and wife abuse of all kinds, child labor, and the Victorian penchant for child sexual abuse belied the family ideology of that period. Then as now, strongly posited and sentimentalized ideologies of benevolent families concealed relationships of exploitation (Fraad 1995, 375). For an excellent description of the contrasting ideology of the family and family realities of the 1950s to the 1980s, see Coontz (1992).

5. There is evidence that children help to produce domestic surplus more readily than do their fathers (Fraad et al. 1994, 31, n41).

6. This differentiates U.S. children from children in poorer countries who may be expected to deliver not only their emotional labor but also their industrial labor (or the wages of that labor) to their parents.

7. Television programs such as *Roseanne* have had significant impacts in breaking down feudal family culture. Roseanne Barr is an outspoken critic of children's feudal servitude. Her book, *My Lives,* and her address to the 1991 convention of the Survivors United Network expose her painful emotional and sexual exploitation as a child.

8. Children's most dangerous predators are their parents. Across the United States every year an estimated 2,000 to 5,000 children die from child abuse (Curtis et al. 1995, 4). Every three hours a U.S. child is murdered (Children's Defense Fund 1992, 136). These murders result from the abandonment of children to their families. Most of the murders were committed by parents (Chira 1994, 9). Approximately three million children a year are physically abused by parents striking their children with objects (Lewin 1995, 16). This figure does not include either emotional abuse or neglect. Fully 80 percent of reported child abuse is perpetrated by parents. All authorities agree that most abuse is never reported. It is interesting to note that child-care providers outside of the home are responsible for only 1 percent of child abuse (Curtis et al. 1995, 5). The case of missing children is yet another example of parental predations. Ubiquitous photos of missing children convey the dangers of which we have all been warned: marauding, stranger-kidnappers may abduct our children. However, every year between 200 and 300 children are abducted by strangers, while 350,000 are abducted by family members. Another 127,000, usually referred to as "throw-aways," are evicted annually from their homes by parents who provide their children with no alternative care. Almost a half million children run

away from homes. The majority of these runaways flee from parents who abuse them (Forst and Blomquist 1991; Lee 1993).

9. This is not true for children in other wealthy industrialized nations. Although numerous children in other industrialized nations are born into poverty, these nations allot benefits that help reduce child poverty and deprivation.

10. Parents will often try to stop a child's tears or screams. However, interrupting a child's disturbing emotional expression is often a service to relieve the parent. It is not the same as working to analyze what motivated the child's emotional upset and how to relieve the child of the source of the pain.

11. Children who do not receive emotional care may have such severe developmental lags that they cannot grow. They remain physically stunted as well as developmentally retarded (Spitz 1945, 53–74; 1946a, 113–17; 1946b, 313–42). The physician's report on a three-year-old client of mine showed that she was developmentally lagged in every area from toilet training to speech production as a result of severe parental emotional neglect. Those lags were eliminated after her mother, with parenting help and supervision, interacted with my client, communicating warm emotion during two twenty-minute periods a day for three months.

12. Names and some details have been altered to maintain patient confidentiality.

13. Indeed when she finally revealed her abuse, she, like the majority of incest survivors who "tell," was cast out of the family. For descriptions of this phenomenon, see Fraad (1996/1997), Barron (1995), Sleeth and Barnsley (1989), McNaron and Morgan (1982).

14. Daisy is an incest survivor who has managed to provide enough emotional necessary labor to survive. However, incest is highly correlated with suicide. The results of studies of daughters who survived father-daughter incest indicate that 38 percent of incest survivors attempt suicide, 20 percent become alcohol or drug dependent, and 60 percent suffer from major depression in adult life (Herman 1981, 99; Blume 1990, 182–190; Barron 1995). It is relevant that people who have suffered incest are referred to as "survivors."

15. This, of course, is not a phenomenon exclusive to family life. Anyone who has tried to organize workers to recognize their exploitation on the job may encounter similar resistance.

16. A friend of mine who is working on creating communal distributions of familial emotional labor described the following informal family meeting with her three-year-old, her eight-year-old, her husband, and herself at dinner. It began when her three year old picked up her macaroni with her hands. The child's father said angrily, "Put that down and use a fork or spoon." To which the three-year-old responded, "Tell me nicely; I won't listen till you tell me nicely." The father then asked politely, and the daughter began eating with utensils. A discussion followed about how people feel frightened if someone has an angry voice, but they can listen if they are addressed nicely. The discussion covered how each of them felt when they heard an angry loud command versus a polite request, how each needs kindness in order to learn and how to try to give that to each other. Here, a basic condition of existence of

communality was being established. Skills in accepting and articulating emotional need were discussed and learned.

17. For an excellent discussion of children in literature, see Kuhn (1982, 65–106). In addition see the classic French example of the emotionally exploited child, *Poil de Carotte* by Renard (1893, English translation 1967).

18. This is a vast literature of which Rush (1980) wrote the first important classic work. For a review of the literature see Fraad (1996/1997).

19. The description of the battered child syndrome in 1962 (Kempe et al.) initiated an awareness of child physical abuse. Psychohistorians beginning with Lloyd deMause (1975) have described continuous routine child abuse and molestation throughout human history. However, they address neither issues of emotional labor nor its systematic exploitation.

20. Visions of communal alternatives to isolated nuclear families were, it seems, a greater part of left consciousness in the nineteenth century than they are today. For a good overview of those communistic alternatives to the nuclear family see Nordhoff (1966) and Levitas (1990).

21. The total dependence of children on their parents creates crushing emotional and financial burdens on parents. The extent of those burdens may well increase parents' rage and frustration at their children and reduce their ability to treat their children with the consideration and respect required for emotionally communal family relationships. Social supports for children have a remarkably successful record in preventing child abuse (Frenza 1993; McFarland and Fanton 1997; Brown and Jenski 1997). It is relevant that child abuse drops drastically after age six when children are required to attend school and are therefore away from their homes for several hours a day, both relieving their parents and giving the children opportunities to find extra-familial supports.

4

Spring Flowers

Susan Jahoda

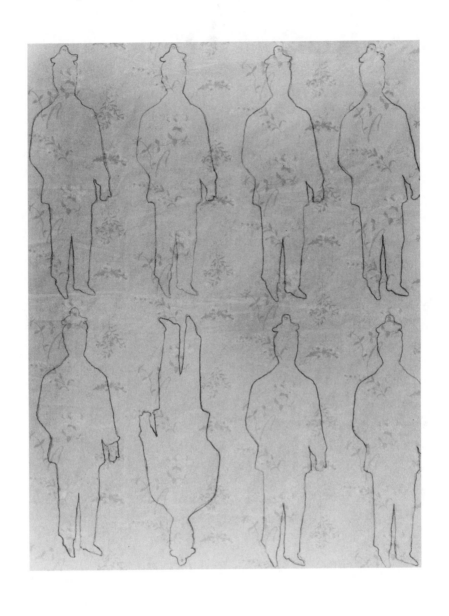

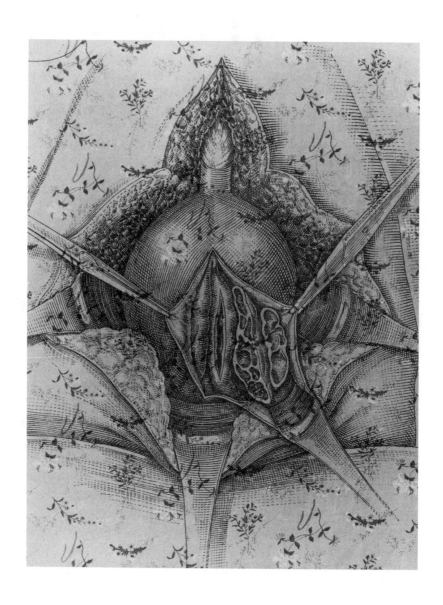

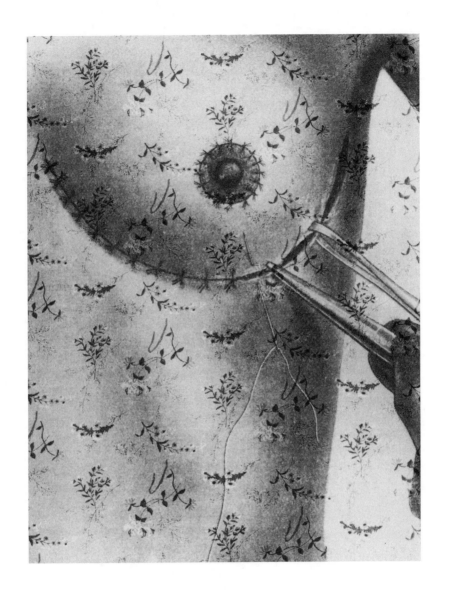

productions

Lately Josephine's routines had become haphazard. Beds were made a few hours prior to their reoccupation and dinner mostly consisted of Thai and Chinese take-out. Henry didn't get home from work until nine and Lillian put in an appearance sometime after that. Josephine sensed she was coming down with a cold. She wondered, while carefully placing bulbs in window boxes, whether plants were susceptible to contracting human viruses. At the first signs of mucus her birth mother had strung halved onions around her neck and applied eucalyptus compresses to her chest. Josephine responded to an itch below her right eye as three stretch limos pulled up in front of an adjacent building. Carelessly, she dusted the ledges. From the window she could see people ascending and descending the steps of the Metropolitan Museum.

She closed her eyes, but an image lingered. It had been cold and raw on the day before Lillian's vaginoplasty. The only trace of Henry, a note left for Josephine on the kitchen table: "Feed plants and stalk Lilly at comfortable distance, if and when she goes out." As usual, Lillian had departed at noon. Josephine followed five minutes later, giving her charge adequate time to vanish. Then, having nowhere in particular to go, she fixed on a different specter—the museum's new installation of Oceanic and African art. Entering the capacious rooms, she walked past two guards whispering at a volume calculated to attract her attention: "Hey man, look at her. She's come to the right place. Like she's part of the show. Stepped right out of the cases." They laughed, tapping their feet. Josephine clenched her jaw, narrowed her eyes and began to sweat an angry heat, a poisonous substance seeping through the porous envelope of her body. She turned and spat in the direction of the guards, then quickly escaped the exhibit.

circulations

It was recess on her first day of school in Marabone, Arizona. Josephine, en-circled by children, was being prodded by the spiky branches of an ocotillo cactus. Children scattered as a teacher's hand grabbed the back of her neck. A gesture motivated by a secondary intention to lead the wounded child toward a first-aid station. Josephine recalled the look of disgust on the woman's face as she wiped her palm, wet from perspiration, on the side of her floral, polyester skirt. There had been no escape. Josephine's adoptive father Billy had uprooted his doubtful wife Rosie and the child born of another mother, and reestablished his family in a ghost town, east of the Purpleseed Mountains. Billy worked as a guard at the state prison.

Josephine's imagination flourished like an adapting weed, fighting to stay alive in an inhospitable environment. And as the phenomenon of her presence weighed heavily on her frame, she grew crooked and strange, to others and to her-self. Josephine became a spectacle in a community that fed incestuously on its iso-lation. Her appearance was a sign, intuited as confirmation of the inhabitants' own perpetuation and wholeness. For ten years she zigzagged between rundown trailer homes and flat-roofed shacks, three churches, and two spirit houses.

One day Josephine stole two thousand dollars from under Rosie and Billy's mattress, packed a small suitcase, and headed in the direction of the truck stop. There she exchanged her virginity for a ride to New York City with a bisexual trucker hauling pecans. For five days and nights her blood navigated the mal-nourished places in her body with a drunken delirium. And like a witness to an infant's first smile, she responded to herself with triumph and relief.

All the bulbs in place and watered, Josephine went into the kitchen to wash her hands and run the dishwasher. She found some old shallots, halved and threaded them together and placed them around her neck. As she lay down on the sunlit portion of the living room floor, the odor of onions filled the air. Peacefully, she drifted into a deep sleep. Lillian, returning from a shopping spree, stepped over the body and quietly entered Josephine's bedroom. There she laid out a set of votives, gifts for Josephine, at the foot of her bed.

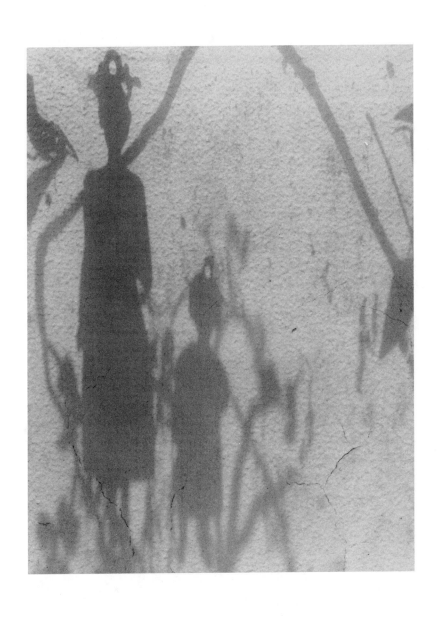

reproduction(s)

After arriving home one evening, Henry wandered onto his enclosed roof garden. He pulled yellowing leaves off random plants, preoccupied by a phone conversation he'd had earlier in the day with Ruby, his octogenarian mother. Their weekly conversations and occasional dinner engagements sustained their troubled connection, while satisfying illusions of fulfilled obligations. Today he had suggested Sunday lunch. Would she mind if he brought Lillian along? Rubbing the bloom of an African violet between his thumb and index finger, he recalled her greeting: "How's my little chameleon this week?"

Henry feared his mother's disapproval. It left him bewildered and raw; incapable of insight. Indeed, her acute critical edge was so effective that he never suspected it was a ruse, a thin blanket over complex fields of envy, ambivalent entanglement, and pride. The less he revealed about himself the more she assumed.

"Is she one of us, Henry?"

"What do you mean, one of us?" he responded, knowing very well what she meant.

"Henry, I mean is she black?"

"Lillian's Jewish, mother."

"Well, I suppose I ought to be thankful she's a woman," Ruby said with unintended irony. What shall I bring in, bagels and lox or fried chicken and watermelon. A bit of both?"

"Whatever strikes your fancy, mother. Would you like me to call a caterer? Perhaps you'd prefer to eat at a restaurant?" His tone was formal.

"No, bring her here, to my place."

Examining the window boxes and flower beds, he wondered why no shoots had emerged from the spring bulbs he had brought home for Josephine to plant.

exchange value

It was Friday, noon. Lillian stepped into the mirrored elevator, checked her make-up and, within two minutes, was heading directly east toward the bank. She avoided upper Madison Avenue, a playground for private-school kids in search of distraction, food, and other gratifications. Although the last skin graft had given her a more authentic female appearance, she was reluctant to subject herself to derisive inspection, especially by those who believed themselves exclusively permitted the pleasures of transgression. At the bank Lillian withdrew an extra hundred dollars from her lover's account to deposit into Josephine's savings; this was a Friday ritual to supplement their housekeeper's wages.

Her thoughts drifted to an exchange with Henry. She had jokingly argued that he undervalued all forms of domestic labor, particularly when related to the maintenance of his daily needs. "When was the last time you made a bed?" she said, lovingly cupping her palms over his well-tempered buttocks. "I thought that was one of the reasons you moved in with me, you know, to make beds and then lie in them," he said, drawing her closer. "Anyway, you don't even make the beds, Josephine does."

"I think you have a perception of yourself as genetically predisposed to maid service," Lillian responded, her manicured nails indenting his polished skin.

"Lilly, honey, don't lay that on me. Josie spends more time as your companion than she does keeping house." Kissing her on the forehead he continued. "Have I mentioned recently it appears we no longer have a housekeeper? I consider myself generous under the circumstances. And, sugar," he said, shifting the focus of his gaze, "you can't imagine how complicated the circumstances are." Lillian, afraid to question his last remark, wondered whether he was referring to Josephine's additional payment.

The machine disgorged its receipt; the transaction was complete. Had Henry investigated the destination of the missing funds? It was unlikely. Was he aware of her indiscretion? She wondered whether Josephine's lapses as a housekeeper were related to her own urges to displace her. Henry's enjoyment of candlelight dinners, so artfully presented, and his subsequent amorous advances provided her with interchangeable moments of pleasure; perverse longings to envision herself as sole attendant to her man's symbolic incompetence. Was the hundred dollars, indirectly, an illicit payment to her evolving self? These thoughts generated panic. Lillian's legs folded and she found herself in a heap beneath the automatic teller.

Collecting herself and a few scattered bills, Lillian wandered into a neighboring coffee shop. Over tea she evaluated her fortune in having met Henry, a man endowed with both imagination and material wealth, a man willing to collaborate in stitching together the biography of a woman with a boy's history. When Henry insisted that she move in with him she had agreed, under two conditions. Josephine was to be employed as their live-in housekeeper, and Henry would have to cover all the expenses associated with a complete sex change. Prior to their living together, Henry's housekeepers came through an agency contracting white girls from the Netherlands. Although Henry protested his parents' refusal to employ black domestics he found himself adhering to the same ethic. It was simpler to avoid scenarios provoking the unbearable rising of his mother's voices within. Voices that questioned his sense of duty and racial authenticity. Lillian managed to assuage his guilt that, under sensual pressure, temporarily dissipated. Henry reluctantly engaged Josephine and she started work the following week.

Lillian paid for her tea and left a generous tip. She felt uneasy. Why was she gambling with irreversible transformation?

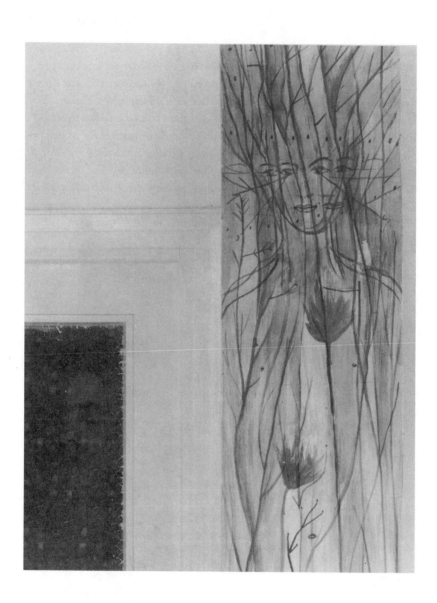

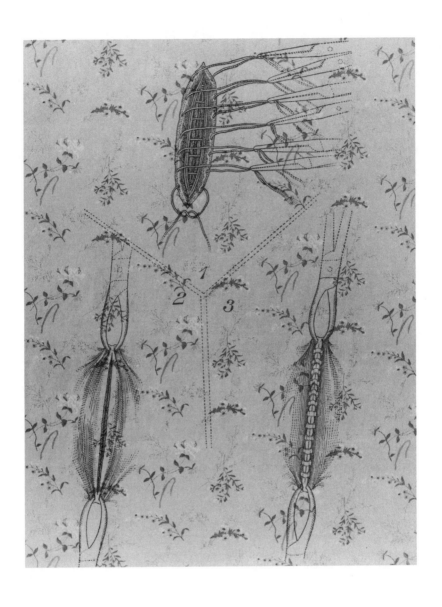

1

2   3

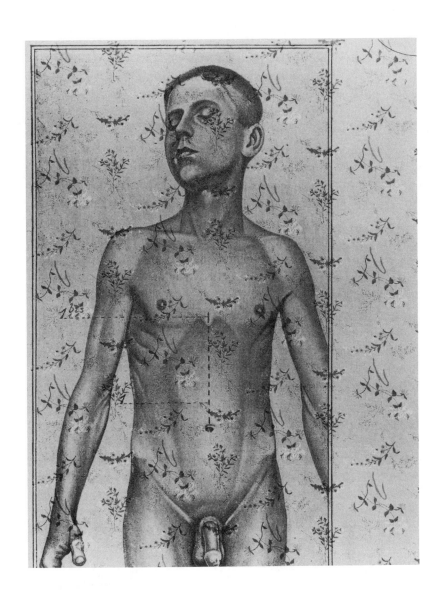

piecework

Pearl, a woman with an unreliable income, had always encouraged Leslie's love of ballroom dancing. Twirling, wall-to-wall, in their two-room apartment, he stepped lightly, always careful to avoid a slip of the needle on the old gramophone. Leslie's theatricality amused his mother. He was a solitary child who spent hours preoccupied with the contents of her wardrobe. His pleasure, to invent himself as her female companion. Appreciative of these attentions, Pearl began to rely on his excellent eye for combining stylish castoffs. On Saturday afternoons she followed his instincts, as they combed uptown thrift shops in search of bargains.

Leslie's discriminating taste proved useful. On social occasions Pearl could mingle, able to perform a class above her income. Invested in his mother's fragile social status, Leslie understood the relationship between her cultural capital and his own ease in passing into a suspicious world. In turn, Pearl protected and nurtured his transgendered inclinations. Occasionally Leslie wore something of hers when they appeared together in public: a stroll over to the lower East Side for a blintz and coke. Sometimes, arriving before dark, they would deliver finished portions of the garments Pearl sewed for a living. Her employer, a bloated man with a half smile, might indulge his fantasies and invite them into the hallway. Scrutinizing Pearl and the fruits of her labor, he would pull money lecherously from his trouser pockets, count the bills in slow motion, and pay her—sometimes less and sometimes more than she deserved. The exchange complete, mother and son would divide the new workload and carry the unfinished garments back to their apartment.

Memory traces were precious. They had survived a calculated amnesia, necessary to the transition from Leslie to Lillian. Other memories were undergoing erasure or reinvention in a blind and endless process of editing.

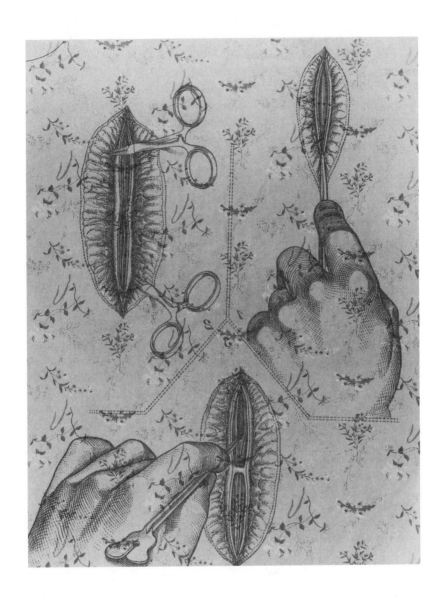

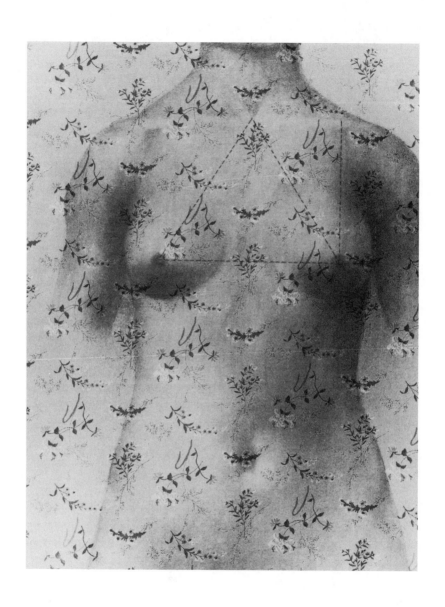

necessary labor

Leslie, impeccably dressed in Pearl's clothing, was delighted by Henry's decla-ration that although he wasn't really sexually interested in women, he could per-haps learn to be. Henry had materialized at every one of Leslie's six shifts. He sat at the bar, left of center, tipping Leslie generously for a series of whisky and sodas. Leslie was venturing to possess. Henry was intoxicated and determined to conquer, even though he wasn't exactly sure what he was pursuing. It didn't matter. When Henry wanted something he settled the details at a later date.

A week passed. Leslie, sensing relief from his fiscal situation, agreed to quit his job bartending and work for Henry as a buyer's consultant. Unqualified and uninterested in what such a job might entail, he arrived to work for a man almost old enough to be his father. Promises of an erotic adventure served only as partial motivation. Unfortunately Pearl's death had left him both metaphori-cally and potentially homeless. He was insolvent. Her labors, which barely sus-tained their daily needs, had guaranteed nothing beyond survival.

Leslie was given an extravagant salary and a luxurious apartment on the eighth floor of one of Henry's department stores. Within a month he had paid off Pearl's debts, put their belongings in storage, and sublet the only two rooms he had ever inhabited to a pair of drag queens. His sinecure required a written re-port on the status of each unit, from cosmetics to pet furniture, in all six stores, suggesting potential improvements. Henry, a generous lover, transported Leslie to places he had previously only envisioned. The food and drink, new to Leslie's palate, sweetened his receptivity to Henry's aging, well-preserved body.

surplus labor

By the age of forty, Randolph, a self-taught jazz musician, was a successful entrepreneur in the recording industry. His third marriage was to Ruby, an opera singer. Juggling her career with the subsequent birth of their twin boys eventually weakened what had once been a flawless soprano voice, renowned for sustaining an unwavering succession of high Cs.

Henry was David's eyes. The blind boy would cup his palms around his identical brother's face, drawing their bodies together. Together, in playful ceremony they whispered, "You are the eye of myself, you are the eye of myself," their breath emanating, it appeared, from a single source.

Randolph was present only in the luxuries he provided, though he made an effort to materialize at holiday and birthday celebrations. Ruby favored her sightless son. Henry learned to get what he needed through David. David was Henry's voice. One day, in a freak accident, David was hit by a swerving yellow cab competing with another for his fare.

It was the fifteenth anniversary of David's death. Leslie placed his lover's head between his breasts. Wrapping his legs around Henry's hips he locked him in a maternal embrace. Henry began to suck. Leslie's breasts were full, wet, and milky. "This morning I wanted to be your mother."

"You were," Henry said.

trans-actions

Josephine's traveling companion dropped her off at the mouth of the Lincoln Tunnel. Her instructions, to call his cousin and take a subway up to 86th and Lexington. Eventually she located the Convent of the Sacred Heart, a bed and breakfast run by an order of nuns. On the basis of her connection, Josephine was invited to remain at a reduced rate. There would be a few light duties, the sisters were incurious, her room was spacious, and breakfast was edible. However, she was unable to abide by the requirements of a celibacy she had recently abandoned.

After a month she found a studio apartment and a job as a ladies' room attendant at Henry's midtown branch. In a pink cavern located on the ground floor near cosmetics, Josephine worked eight-hour shifts sanitizing surfaces. The defilers were women with urges to distinguish themselves through primitive acts of revenge and exchange, women seduced into acquiring beauty at inflated prices and profits.

By restricting his intake of fluids, Leslie was able to avoid restrooms during working hours. Although he was now a transsexual, with a distinct feminine demeanor, he harbored insecurities about providing the right signals. Urinating in the gendered location of one's choice was, to Leslie, the definitive test. What else did people have to do except examine each other, and themselves, while waiting in line? His initial encounter with Josephine coincided with his first appearance in a public bathroom.

The only person present, she was pouring liquid into the inner liners of soap dispensers. He was overcompensating. He commented on the pleasant aroma. One foot was placed too far forward, giving his appearance an exaggerated asymmetry. Josephine said the odor had become too familiar to detect, but he would be entirely convincing if he could shift his body weight to his back leg. She placed the out-of-order sign on the door and demonstrated how he could align the middle of his shoulders with the middle of his hips.

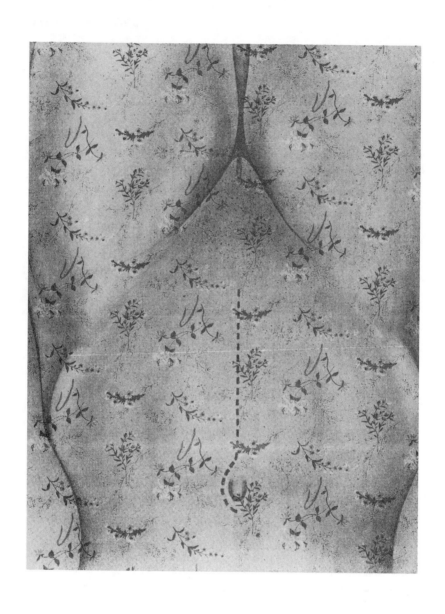

unequal exchange

Henry mourned the financial and erotic losses incurred in the transitions his lover endured, from male to female. Hormone therapies and reassignment surgeries were depleting his play money. He was also reluctant to part with the vestiges of Leslie's male body that afforded homoerotic pleasures in the privacy of his bedroom yet heterosexual visibility in public arenas. Leslie believed he was clever enough to appeal to Henry's obsession with the unique and to the displaced allure of bringing forth inheriting offspring. If he represented his metamorphosis as an investment and miracle of birth, for which Henry was entirely responsible, Leslie could succeed in fully becoming Lillian.

Henry silently humored his beautiful young lover, forgiving the transparencies of his manipulations. For Leslie had brought a myriad of possibilities into his middle passage, with promises of rare and endless fields of perversion: penectomy, orchidectomy, castration, vaginoplasty, breast augmentation, face lifts, eye lifts, removal of the Adam's apple, electrolysis . . .

Mostly indulgent and sometimes irritable, Henry spent longer hours at his various offices, took business vacations, and tended his beloved garden. The earth in the window boxes remained mysteriously undisturbed.

investments

Following each procedure Lillian remained at home, confined horizontally for periods of time. When in their bed, Henry craved sexual attention, which Lillian was in no state to provide. She suggested he temporarily satisfy his needs elsewhere; a strategy devised to produce an opposing response, for Henry disliked inclusionary practices. He would wait for the prize, ultimately more desirable.

Eventually Lillian occupied her own bedroom. It was then that she became aware of Josephine's night crying. Occurring always at the same hour, its tenor was sacramental. Josephine cried to open the pathways of her longing into consciousness. Crying aerated the recesses of her dreams, where she visited her places of origin. And once in that state her body revived. Her spirit rebelled against her location, and her anatomy celebrated night as light and winter sun as tropical warmth. She remembered her ambitions, symbolically enacted by the gesture of her plantings. "Mama, mama, mama, hold me in your eyes. I will find you."

distributions

When Josephine didn't seem to be recovering from pneumonia, Kora faced losing the child through death or social intervention. Visiting a doctor inevitably led her caseworker to diagnose neglect and justify separation. Penicillin cured Josephine's infection, but one month later the child was removed from her mother. Kora's connection to life and her dreaming were abruptly severed.

As soon as it was confirmed that conception could never take place, Billy and Rosie considered it their moral obligation to adopt. God would look on them kindly. The couple visited the orphanage once a week. Having little else to do on Sunday afternoons, they took pleasure in this duty. Kora was barred from seeing Josephine. The four-year-old was informed that her mother loved her but couldn't afford to support her. Soon she would have new parents, white-skinned and hard-working.

Billy, a policeman, took the night shift. Rosie worked part-time in her uncle's grocery. Having long ago submitted to the rote practicalities of subsistence, she was prematurely aged, her body striated with the markings of deep and enduring distress. Rosie lived in fear of Billy's aspirations to preside over the incarcerated. He kept a watchful eye on listings for prison jobs, insisting that he would go anywhere when the right one appeared. When offered the job in Arizona, he accepted immediately, saying that the change would be good for all of them. At first Rosie refused to go. But Billy was very persuasive. He convinced her that the child would be taken away from her. As an unskilled, single parent, her earnings couldn't sustain them both. She relented.

Billy and Rosie were churchgoing people, well-respected, and blindly schooled in crafting devotions under the required circumstances. They were incapable of intimacy; their love appeared cruel. Josephine had never known such poverty.

communal appropriations

One night Lillian crawled into Josephine's bed. They lay, still and undisturbed, two permeable forms, collaborating in a subversive gathering of strength drawn from all that had defined them as aberrant. Knotted together, they felt secure, their bodies damp and salty from intermittent tears.

Henry's sleep was interrupted by a full bladder and the subsequent discovery of an erection. He masturbated, urinated, and then wandered into the kitchen to get a seltzer. Josephine's door was slightly ajar. Widening the crack, unobserved, he watched. In general, Henry controlled all visible exchanges between his investments. In this case he avoided intervention, his curiosity and jealousy tempered by empathic lust.

gifts

After the vaginoplasty, Lillian was afraid to let Josephine out of her sight, as if being alone substantiated her nonexistence. She desired only the company of women. A newborn adult, she needed to concentrate her energies on charting semblances of femininity. Josephine became her beloved paradigm. Domestic life fell into disarray as energies centered on the shifting relations between an unstable cast of characters. The winter passed slowly.

Endless streams of beauticians, speech therapists, and herbalists drifted through their physical space. Josephine stopped answering the phone and cleaning the bathrooms. April approached. Lillian, having created a paper trail of social and legal documents fully identifying her as a woman, was waiting to hear whether she'd been accepted into college. Josephine, gratified by the substantial funds in her savings account, was also making plans.

In need of a different venture, Henry proposed marriage to Lillian. The thought of an early summer wedding gave the household direction, a sense of temporary resolution. One evening Henry, in a mood both amorous and generous, arrived home with reservations for a week in Paris. He had successfully opened three new stores on the West Coast, a task far simpler than reestablishing a domestic hierarchy at home. Sensing Josephine needed time alone, and feeling confident that she could survive without her, Lillian agreed to go.

When the couple returned, the apartment was unoccupied. On the roof garden they discovered a note. Complete with map, it was pinned to a window box. A line was drawn marking a route from New York to Mississippi. The note said "I have flown in the direction of the spring flowers, never to bloom in your garden." Henry smiled. He dug into the earth, his fingers searching out the inverted bulbs.

5

Beyond Slavery and Capitalism:

Producing Class Difference in the Sex Industry

Marjolein van der Veen

"Madonna exploits her sexuality on her own terms."

"What does it mean to exploit your sexuality on your own terms?"

"It means *you* name the price."

"The representation of female sexuality that she offers is of strength and self-determination."

"Is there a difference between exploiting your own body for profit, and having someone else exploit it for you?"

"Everyone is involved with exploitation: a person whose body it is, the salesperson, and the audience it's entertaining."

"The significant distinction is: who earns more money, the exploited body, or the salesperson? And what about the audience?"

"Exploitation of sexuality has achieved a new respectability, because some of those women whose bodies have been exploited have gained control over that exploitation. They earn more money. They call the shots."

"They are not thought of as victims."

"If they earn most of the money, no. They probably don't think of themselves as victims either."

"What about the audience?"

"What about them?"[1]

As a type of sex work,[2] prostitution evokes strong and divergent judgments, ranging from its validation as an empowering activity to its condemnation as a form of violation and victimization. Among those who condemn prostitution are radical feminists who regard it as a form of sexual slavery and

Marxist feminists who tend to see it as an exploitative activity that prolifer-
ates with the dislocating effects of capitalism. Radical and Marxist feminist
discourses typically focus on women in prostitution (and exclude the male
prostitute) and produce certain characteristic representations: prostitutes
are female objects of male power who become commodities exchanged in
the market, or are coerced into prostitution by pimps and traffickers or by
the economic forces of capitalism.[3] Emanating from these feminist discourses is a political vision of rescue and eradication, in which victimized
women are freed from the evils of prostitution through its total elimination.

For all its moral clarity and confidence, this eradicationist vision is quite
embattled, and not simply because of its tendency to create an unholy alliance between feminists who oppose prostitution and the new right that
supports "family values." Those who would wish to ban prostitution confront a vocal prostitutes' rights movement and the innovative sex radical
discourse that supports it. Sex radicals and prostitutes' rights advocates call
for the decriminalization of prostitution and—not seeing it as immoral or
exploitative per se—oppose the efforts to criminalize and eradicate it. They
highlight the actual and potential empowerment of women in the industry.
Women tend to earn more in the sex industry than in other industries; they
can be independent of both male partners and capitalist employers; often
they are able to call the shots when it comes to sex, setting the terms of the
sexual contract. Rather than being victimized by the sex industry, women
are in a position to enjoy its benefits and to transform it to their advantage.

In this confrontation of visions, moralities, and wills, relations of political antagonism are founded on a straightforward discursive reversal. What
is an evil for one side is a good thing for the other. What is enslaved, exploited, and degraded within one discourse is held up in the other as free, self-
sufficient, and engaged in self-realization. Whereas radical and Marxist
feminists find themselves allied with conservatives of the family values sort,
sex radicals tend to find themselves allied with conservatives of an entirely
different stripe—libertarians who oppose interventions in the market, restrictions on commodification, or limitations on speech/action.[4]

Each of these discourses and political positions could be seen as embracing
an economic analysis of sorts. Given the widespread use of terms like "capitalism" and "slavery," for example, it is clear that notions of economy and
class are not entirely absent from radical and Marxist feminist discourses on
prostitution. However, the economic representations of prostitution that
circulate in these discourses tend to be both totalizing and monolithic—
prostitution is either all (sexual) slavery, or it is all capitalist or caused by
and functional to capitalism. On the sex radical side, the economy tends to

appear (often implicitly) as the generic and universal "market" of liberal discourse. Within this zone of ostensible freedom, few distinctions are made between types of class relations. This makes it difficult to problematize or even to perceive the substantial class differences that may exist between, say, a worker in a brothel who is paid a wage by the owners, a worker who supports herself by streetwalking, and a collective of workers who sell sex in their apartment and pool their incomes to buy protections of the sexual and legal sort.

I would like to suggest that the sex radical and prostitutes' rights dicourses that attempt to contribute to the improvement of prostitutes' positions could be broadened to include a diverse range of economic possibilities, and that recognizing a diversity of options (in the form of class relations) could contribute to transformative projects not yet envisioned—beyond slavery, capitalism, and even beyond independent commodity production. Producing a discourse of class difference in the sex industry, in which capitalist, independent, slave, feudal, and communal relations can be seen to coexist and interact, could foster a politics of economic innovation and empowerment.[5]

The sex industry in general, and its class relations in particular, are partially constituted by the discourses that circulate within and around it. The discourses that universally condemn prostitution as inherently exploitative, degrading, or threatening and call for its regulation, criminalization, and/or eradication have had a profound role in shaping the difficult conditions of prostitution. A consideration of different class possibilities in the sex industry disrupts the making of universal moral judgments and calls for closer attention to the specific class relations in which sex work is performed.[6] Such a class discourse neither condemns nor valorizes prostitution per se, but begins to construct a new morality around the different exploitative and nonexploitative class relations that exist in the industry. Like the sex radical project, an anti-essentialist class analysis of prostitution opens the political terrain to new possibilities and alliances.

Class and Regulation

In any particular social setting, an entire discursive apparatus encompassing moral judgments, laws, social policies, court decisions, enforcement standards, informal policing practices, and industry self-regulation operates to constrain and shape the sex industry and to foster particular kinds of class relations at the expense of others. This regulatory apparatus, while complexly constituted, is thoroughly infused with the largely negative valuations of prostitutes and/or prostitution that circulate in the United States. Sex radicals and prostitutes' rights advocates have therefore found it important to undermine and displace prevalent representations of prostitutes/prostitution. This strategy of critique and displacement is also useful in attempting to address the (hidden) class consequences of these regulatory formations and to open up the possibility of class difference and class empowerment within the industry as a whole.

In what follows I begin with the representations associated with what I have called "Victorian morality" and then consider representations circulating within feminism today. Each of these can be seen to have participated in constituting exploitative class relations of prostitution. I conclude this discussion with an exploration of representations emanating from contemporary sex radicalism and a speculative assessment of their potentially different class implications.

Victorian Morality and the Class Politics of Surveillance

In finding commodified sex objectionable and assigning virtue to non-commodified sex, the Marxist and radical feminist discourses bear the traces of a conventional, heterosexual Victorian morality. This morality valorized women as wives and mothers whose duty it was to practice monogamy and sexual restraint and to carry out the productive and reproductive functions of the heterosexual household. A hierarchical dichotomy among women (sometimes characterized as madonna/whore) stigmatized women who transgressed social boundaries and deviated from the norm— unwed mothers, lesbians, prostitutes, and women with active sexual desires were considered unproductive, degraded, or deviant. The madonna/ whore dichotomy also served to maintain hierarchical distinctions between women and men. Women (at least the majority of "normal" women) were "naturally" passive and submissive, the *objects* of desire, while men were "naturally" active and desiring *subjects*. Sullivan illustrates how sexual difference was (and still is) commonly represented:

> In our culture sexual difference is usually talked about via notions of (men's) bodily integrity and (women's) bodily submission. Women's bodies are marked out as vulnerable, violable, and possessable. In heterosexual intercourse, women's bodies are said to be "entered" or "penetrated" by men's bodies. Young women are said to "lose" their virginity while prostitutes are seen to "sell themselves." (1995, 195)

Whereas men who purchased sexual services were largely exempt from stigmatization, female prostitutes who "sold themselves" were considered damaged and violated, and were represented as dirty, contaminated, and criminal.[7] They were thought to threaten the social order and bring ruin to society, whether by spreading disease and contagion, corrupting public morality, or threatening male prosperity through charging for services men otherwise received for free (Corbin 1987, 209).[8]

Victorian England was at the same time restrictive and permissive with regard to prostitution. While on the one hand Victorians saw prostitution as a threat to society, on the other they saw it as a necessary evil. The activities of prostitutes were seen to preserve the moral purity and integrity of "good" women by providing an outlet for men's baser desires (Matlock 1994; Bell 1994; Corbin 1987). Given its necessary function, prostitution was to be tolerated, isolated, and regulated rather than eradicated altogether.

The moral vision of women's proper role in society, and the associated stigmatization of prostitution, were instrumental in the construction and implementation of social and legal policies that transformed the class relations in which prostitution occurred, encouraging prostitution within brothels (often capitalist) and under the control of pimps (perhaps in slave or feudal class relations), while restricting independent forms in which prostitutes appropriated their own surplus labor. For example, the 1860s Contagious Disease Acts and the 1880s Criminal Law Amendment Acts in England isolated prostitution by removing prostitutes from their neighborhoods and geographically confining them to red light districts. This confinement made it much more difficult for prostitutes to engage in independent forms of sex work, and instead encouraged the more institutionalized forms of prostitution under the control of pimps who provided protection against legal authorities (Walkowitz 1980, 128). Prostitution was tolerated when it was contained in certain districts or conducted in clandestine spaces, such as the brothel, whereas it was repressed and persecuted when conducted in casual and independent forms on streets and residential neighborhoods.[9]

Contemporary Regulatory Representations: Prostitution as Sexual Slavery

The Victorian representation of prostitutes as threatening and dangerous and associated practices of surveillance and regulation were challenged by social reformers, feminists, and socialists, who had come to view prostitutes as *victims* forced into the sex industry.[10] In the 1970s and 1980s, radical feminists similarly focused on the "traffic in women" as exemplary of the victimization of, and violence against, women perpetrated by male domination and patriarchal institutions. Kathleen Barry defined prostitution as "sexual slavery" and highlighted the kidnapping and forcing of women into prostitution connected with international trafficking networks and organized crime (1979, 1984).[11]

Radical feminist discourses have produced a representation in which *all* prostitution is sexual slavery. But in constructing such a universal representation, these discourses not only obscure existing differences among prostitutes, but foreclose the political possibility of creating new ones. I would prefer to argue that no one social relation characterizes prostitution, though there are probably many instances of prostitution that entail enslavement. If the prostitute is kidnapped or sold and becomes the property of another (an agent, pimp, madame, or trafficker) for an extended period of time, the relationship could be characterized as one of slavery. The slave owner may have the prostitute work in a slave class process in which the slave owner sets the terms of the work, appropriates and distributes all of the surplus labor, and spends an amount just large enough to cover the slave's subsistence.[12] Forcibly kept in this situation, any prostitute who attempts to escape may be punished by the slave owner or the owner's agents. Close supervision may also be needed to force the prostitute to produce a certain value for the owner. The owner's surplus will be distributed in various ways to safeguard and maintain this slave process, perhaps by hiring helpers and guards, paying off police, judges, etc.

What is important for my analysis, however, is the performative implication of the radical feminist representation of prostitution as a site of universal slavery. Those who see prostitutes as victims (as opposed to sexual deviants) tend to advocate an end to state toleration and regulation of prostitution and instead support the criminalization and/or eradication of the institution.[13] But the stigmatization and criminalization of prostitution may actually render (and, I would argue, has rendered) sex workers more vulnerable and more dependent on slave owners, agents, or traffickers while denying them the legal or political rights that might assist them in escaping from a slave arrangement.[14] In this sense radical feminist discourses may have fostered the coming into being or continuation of slavery and slave exploitation as opposed to their elimination.

Prostitution as Marked by Capitalism

Not every prostitute is engaged in a slave class process, nor is everyone who crosses a national border to work in the sex industry being trafficked into slavery. Marxist and socialist feminists argue that women are being "trafficked" out of the home by the forces of industrial capitalism rather than simply by sexual slave traders and traffickers. These economic forces include the rise of private property (Engels 1978) and the forces of capital accumulation, which lead to the destruction of peasant economies, rising rates of urbanization, proletarianization, the immiseration of the working class, and increasing displacement of people into the lumpen proletariat (Marx 1987, Lenin 1975, Goldman 1970, Kollontai 1977c). In these structuralist analyses, prostitution is caused by, or functional to, the underlying laws of the capitalist system. Economic factors drive or determine prostitution as a social phenomenon. The capitalist economy has its own inner logic, a globalization of capitalist production based on the laws of capital accumulation, which is responsible for the proliferation of prostitution.

Recent analyses of sex tourism, particularly in certain developing countries, have also focused on the logic of accumulation, highlighting the growth and extent of capitalist penetration (Truong 1990; Lee 1991; Chant and McIlwaine 1995). With the leisure/tourism industry becoming a new terrain for capital investment, accumulation is now taking place from the surplus value extracted from exploited labor in prostitution. Not only does the dynamic of capital accumulation cause prostitution, but the institution of prostitution itself becomes a source of capital accumulation.

In humanist Marxian discourses, the critique of prostitution focuses on the commodification of sex. While all forms of market relations are tainted, the selling of sex is considered to be especially alienating and dehumanizing (Overall 1992). Here the tendency to view markets and commodification as essentially capitalist identifies prostitution as a phenomenon of capitalism.[15]

Marxist and socialist feminist analyses tend to represent all forms of prostitution as marked by capitalism. Prostitution may be caused by capitalism or may be a specific site of capitalist exploitation or may be a violation of human dignity in the form of commodification. Like the radical feminists, Marxists and Marxist feminists have produced a totalizing vision, one that offers no space of class possibility outside of capitalist relations. The economy takes on a fully capitalist identity, and noncapitalist economic identities are denied a place in the economic imaginary (Gibson-Graham 1996).

My goal is to break apart this monolithic economy and recognize a diversity of class relations, while recognizing that the activity of prostitution is often conducted within a capitalist class process. In this process a third party (an employer) buys the labor power of the sex worker (employee) and consumes it in the process of producing and selling a commodity to others (clients). The employer pays the employee a wage equal to only a portion of the total value the worker contributes to the enterprise and appropriates and distributes the surplus. Workers may be free to sell their labor power in exchange for a wage[16] and free of feudal or slave obligations to work for any one particular person. But workers may also be subject to supervision and managerial control, may have little control over decision making (e.g., regarding prices and earnings), may be vulnerable to speedups (attending to more clients in a shorter period of time) and an intensification of duties (e.g., offering more services to the employer or clients) (Chapkis 1997).

Capitalist forms of sex work do seem to be flourishing, if measured by their depiction in a host of films, from Spike Lee's *Girl 6* to Atom Egoyan's *Exotica,* or by the growth of sex tourism enterprises, escort agencies, and phone sex businesses.[17] In some cases, capitalist forms of sex work have been fostered by the intensification of legal regulations and public attitudes against prostitution. In Boston, for example, prostitutes are being pushed off the streets by police and neighbors and are increasingly finding employment in capitalist escort services (Flint 1996). In Australia, the legislature of Victoria recently legalized brothels (which tend to be capitalist) while leaving street work and independent work in residences illegal, thus fostering capitalist over other kinds of class relations. The legislature of New South Wales legalized prostitution as such, creating a more open and permissive set of class possibilities.

Toward Alternative Regulatory Practices: Producing New Cultural Representations

In order to counter the dominant discourses that portray prostitutes as victims forced into inherently exploitative situations, sex radicals and prostitutes' rights advocates have tended to represent prostitutes as independent and have valorized the entrepreneurial aspects of prostitution. They are also rearticulating sex work as a laboring activity, as a form of work like any other, and call for the improvement of the rights and working conditions of sex workers (Alexander 1997; Bell 1987; Bell 1994, 1995; Chapkis 1995; Delacoste and Alexander 1987; Jenness 1993; Nagle 1997; Pheterson 1989, 1996). Sex radicals and prostitutes' rights groups (such as Coyote, Pony, and the Red Thread) have been particularly attentive to the dominant cultural representations and moral codes surrounding prostitution that stigmatize sex workers as deviants and victims. Gayle Rubin, for example, shifted her position after being criticized by sex workers for her rhetorical use of prostitution (see Rubin 1975) to invoke moral outrage at women's oppression. The sex workers argued that this rhetorical tactic maintained and intensified the stigmas encountered by women who performed sex work (Rubin 1994).[18]

Rubin and other sex radicals have criticized the valorization and maintenance of the dominant heterosexual standard and the stigmatization, marginalization, and regulation of other sexual practices considered abnormal or deviant. They advocate the legitimation and celebration of an array of different sexual subject positions, including that of commercial sex. In place of representations of prostitution as inherently victimizing, they are producing more empowering alternative representations of sex workers, for example, as experimenters and (safer) sex educators with valuable knowledge and experience to convey to others. Sex workers, like massage therapists or psychotherapists, can be regarded as healers or can gain recognition as entertainers and performance artists.[19] That the life of a sex worker can be exciting and glamorous is recognized by the Prostitution Anonymous groups that have sprung up to deal with addiction to prostitution. According to Charlotte Davis Kasl, author of *Women, Sex, and Addiction*:

> The addictive part is the ritual of getting dressed, putting on makeup, fantasizing about the hunt, and the moment of capture, "to know that you could go out there and they would come running. What power! Men would actually pay for sex." . . . For women in prostitution . . . that feeling of power, along with the excitement of living on the edge, is one of the hardest things to give up. (Quoted in Bell 1994, 133)

At the moment, however, sex radical discourse confronts a well developed and developing regulatory system. All fifty states in the United States (except for a few counties in Nevada) currently prohibit soliciting and engaging in prostitution, living off the earnings of a prostitute (pimping), and running a business (pandering and procuring). In recent years, many states in the United States have intensified laws and legal actions against prostitution. By 1994, twenty-one states in the United States had passed laws requiring mandatory testing for HIV, and eleven of these states made prostitution a felony for those arrested after testing positive (Alexander 1996, 226).

In most cases prostitution is a criminal offense, but the laws may or may not be strictly enforced, producing different levels of regulation. The police have considerable power, often targeting those visibly engaged in prostitution, particularly street prostitutes, rather than the more clandestine forms in brothels or escort services. Thus, different levels of enforcement may work against independent commodity producers. According to one sex worker:

> I've worked on the streets and in the casinos in Nevada. But I don't work the streets anymore. What I do now is really not prostitution, it's domination. I still charge for it and I still like doing it. If I could work on the streets I would, but the police make it too dangerous. They arrest you a lot so that you have to

spend all your earnings to get out of jail. And then, they make you work in dark corners; you can't work out in the open for any amount of time . . . but I think if the police didn't bother me and if it was legal, I'd be working the street still. It's much easier and you don't have to play the boyfriend-girlfriend routine, you know, and it's quicker! (Quoted in Delacoste and Alexander 1987, 166)

The ability of the police to arrest and fine prostitutes may make sex workers more dependent on agents for protection from bad clients and police and for access to money to pay off police or pay their fines when arrested.[20] Efforts to hide from police may encourage more hidden and transient forms of prostitution—sex workers may move around from city to city, making it harder to rely on sex work as a casual form of work to supplement income from a regular job and also making it harder for sex workers to organize in some form of collective fashion to control the process of their labor.

Despite their representations of sex work (including prostitution) as a locus of independent, entrepreneurial, and empowering activity, sex radicals and prostitutes' rights advocates confront a regulatory apparatus that discourages independent forms of prostitution and encourages institutionalized and exploitative forms under the control of agents. This situation has prompted a growing movement against criminalization. In order to foster the sort of independence among prostitutes that they portray in their representations, sex radicals and prostitutes' rights advocates demand that the industry be decriminalized and subject to the same regulations as other independent contractors and employers (Bell 1994, 116).[21]

Beyond Slavery and Capitalism:
Feudal, Independent Commodity Producer and Communal Class Processes

Radical and Marxist feminist discourses coalesce around views of prostitution as degrading, victimizing, or exploitative, views that have been articulated by an anti-prostitution politics that seeks to regulate, criminalize, or eradicate prostitution. The idea that prostitution could be anything other than exploitative and victimizing is absent from these discourses. Not only do they ignore alternative possibilities in the sex industry, but they also seem to ignore their own performative effects as cultural and political practices that overdetermine other processes in society, including the class processes in sex work. By universally condemning prostitution, they may be implicated in fostering the development of slave, capitalist, and other exploitative class relations through the punitive regulatory regimes they are in part responsible for engendering.

Each of these discourses constitutes prostitution as a universal evil. This leaves us with one emancipatory possibility—a world free of prostitution.[22] I am interested in the alternative sex radical discourse that has a different view of emancipation, one not so heavily burdened with rescue and replacement, one in which the "emancipatory future" of sex work is already present—if only in certain segments of the industry—and the goal of politics is to create conditions in which more prostitutes are empowered and fulfilled. Sex radicals have produced a discourse of prostitution that is less universalizing (or less extremely so). This discourse makes it possible to talk about difference in the sex industry—with some workers seen to be in difficult and degrading circumstances and others working under more independent, empowered, and pleasurable conditions. I would like to add to this vision of present difference and (implied) future possibility a discourse of economic possibility, one founded in a view of the sex industry as always already economically differentiated along class lines. This vision, I believe, can contribute some new and positive options to the sex radical and prostitutes' rights agenda, options for transforming the economic and class conditions of prostitution. It is with this goal in mind that I want to elaborate some class possibilities in addition to the class positions already discussed.[23]

Feudal Class Relations

Slave and capitalist class processes are not the only exploitative class relations within which prostitution can take place. A sex worker may be indebted and under some sort of obligation, oath, or fealty to an agent (or pimp) for a period of time, a situation which may characterize a feudal arrangement. The bonds of obligation may be formed by familial or love commitments, debt obligations, or a status of illegality.[24] The feudal agent sets the terms of the contract, allowing the sex worker to keep a portion of her earnings while the remaining portion is appropriated by the agent. The agent may then distribute some of the surplus for various services to secure the performance of work, such as rent, payoffs to police, and protection for women. Again, cultural stigmas and the criminalization of prostitution may cement the bonds of obligation to, and place more power in the hands of, the agent, preventing movement into other employment. The plight of the young Eréndira in Garcia-Marquez's movie, for example, may exemplify a feudal relation. After mistakenly burning down her grandmother's house, Eréndira must pay back her debt obligation by selling her sexual services, which grows into a vast business coordinated by the grandmother who advertises and solicits the clients.

Prostitution is popularly associated with the existence of pimps, as depicted in movies such as *Taxi Driver* or *Mighty Aphrodite*. However, the existence of a pimp does not necessarily signify a feudal class relation. The legal definition of pimping is "living off the avails of prostitution," which could apply to anyone (a partner, parent, child, etc.) who is receiving financial support from a prostitute. If the prostitute is self-employed and producing, appropriating, and distributing the surplus himself or herself, what is actually occurring is independent commodity production. Here, the independent commodity producer is the first receiver of surplus, setting the terms of his or her labor. Some portion of the labor time goes to meet subsistence needs and the excess is surplus labor. The producer may distribute the surplus in various ways, to support partners or family members (who become, by legal definition, pimps), to hire someone to help solicit clients, to pay for rent, or for personal consumption. Thus the "pimp" relation may be associated with either a feudal or an independent commodity producer relation, depending on who is appropriating and distributing the surplus.

Independent Commodity Production

Independent commodity production, often referred to as self-employment, involves a class process in which the individual worker both produces and appropriates his or her own surplus labor. This class process is associated in the popular imagination with being a small businessperson and having control over all aspects of the production and sale of the commodity. The independence, control, and significantly higher earnings often obtained in sex work are among the salient reasons given for engagement in prostitution. As one sex worker declares:

> The fact is, there's a livable wage to be made in the sex business, and we decide when, where and with whom we'll do what. Money talks, bullshit walks, and we don't have to put up with anything we don't want. (Quoted in Delacoste and Alexander 1987, 25)[25]

With independent commodity production, it appears that the producer of the commodity is determining the terms of the prostitute/client relation— what is provided, when, where, with whom, how, and at what price. For the prostitute, economic self-determination is associated with control over one's sexuality. Herein lies the glamor of Madonna, who for many exemplifies a strong, self-determining agent who exploits her sexuality "on her own terms." For Hal Hartley, this means that she names the price, earns a lot of money, and calls the shots.

According to Hartley, the significant distinction between exploiting your own body for profit and having someone else exploit it for you is "who earns more money." In the class terms deployed in this essay, however, the significant distinction is who produces, appropriates, and distributes the surplus. The class process is distinct from, yet overdetermined by, other processes such as market exchange ("who names the price"), power ("who is calling the shots," who is in control, or who is managing the business), income ("who is earning more money"), or cultural meanings ("who is thought of as victimized"). While these processes might influence each other, their relation is nonetheless contingent. There is no necessary correlation between independent commodity production and control over price, calling the shots, or earning more money. One could imagine a scenario in which a sex worker is producing, appropriating, and distributing the surplus independently, but decides to delegate power to a manager, or to distribute a larger amount of money to an agent or salesperson, who is now earning more money than the sex worker.[26] The nature of independent commodity production will be contingent on the context in which it occurs.

The valorization of independent forms of sex work by sex radicals and prostitutes' rights advocates may thus obscure the more deleterious aspects of prostitution as a form of independent commodity production. Working alone, for example, may lead to loneliness and long hours of work for the independent producer who struggles independently to earn a subsistence income. The independence and control associated with independent production may be largely illusory. The self-employed businessperson does not have complete control over prices, as she or he is still subject to the competitive prices and conditions of the marketplace. An increase in competition may force the producer to lower prices or to redistribute some of the surplus to secure a market position, for example by spending some on self-promotional advertising. Particularly in markets where sexual services are exchanged for drugs, the demands of addiction can contribute to a lowering of prices or increase in services. Prices may fall so low that the sex worker may not even be able to secure her or his necessary labor, the amount needed for survival. The sex worker may succumb to competitive pressures by other sex workers who are willing to offer the same service at a lower price, or willing to offer more or "better" services for the same price (e.g., sex without condoms). Such incentives to offer unsafe sexual services leaves sex workers more vulnerable to STDs and HIV transmission.[27] The independent commodity producer is sometimes said to be engaged in self-exploitation and may actually be in a very precarious economic position (Gabriel 1990).[28]

Furthermore, the provision of protection and security, which under a feudal or capitalist class relation is usually provided by an agent or employer, is now the responsibility of the self-employed producer. In Spike Lee's *Girl 6,* Judy (a.k.a. "Lovely") takes a job in a clean and modern office that produces phone sex. The employer distributes the surplus to ensure a safe, clean office with security guards and managers who monitor and screen the calls for safety purposes. Upon reaching burnout, Judy takes a leave of absence from the office and takes up the same work in her home, but must now provide her own security, getting an unlisted number, and a second phone. Unfortunately, this is inadequate, as she has already violated procedures by giving out her phone number to a crazy client who finds out where she lives and threatens to kill her, leaving her with no option but to leave town and leave the phone sex business behind.

This discussion of independent commodity production illustrates how the same class relation may at times yield prosperity and freedom and at other times danger and repression for its participants, depending on the context. Some independent commodity producers may flourish, accumulate, or even move into another class relation, for example, becoming an agent, madame, or pimp who appropriates the surplus of others. (The story of Heidi Fleiss exemplifies the transition from sex worker to madame; Fleiss, as the notorious "Hollywood madame," made hundreds of thousands of dollars in the years prior to her arrest.) Other independent commodity producers may suffer from the effects of competition, the lowering of prices and earnings, deteriorating working conditions, and constant physical danger.

Communal Class Relations

Another alternative is for prostitutes to organize and work communally (in a communal class process of producing, appropriating, and distributing surplus labor) or collectively (through unions or other collective associations). Would communal class processes (or collective associations) ameliorate the conditions of prostitution? Not necessarily, of course. One can certainly imagine a barbaric commune. But possibly. When the surplus is appropriated by the producers themselves, perhaps they would distribute it among themselves and see an increase in earnings. Perhaps higher earnings would allow sex workers to move in and out of the industry more freely. Or they could use the surpluses to purchase their own buildings and establishments, thereby eliminating exorbitant rental payments to landlords. Since there would be no third party (employer or agent) appropriating the producers' surplus, the pressures of speedups and intensification of work by such third parties may be eliminated. Collective associations could share information (e.g., about clients) and maintain industry standards that protect prostitutes from falling prices and pressures to perform dangerous or degrading services. In other words, a transformation in the class process or other social relations may transform and improve the nature of the work, the service, or commodity that is produced and sold, the earnings that are obtained, and thus the lives of the participants in the industry.

Nonetheless, as with other class processes, there is no necessity that a communal class process will bring about such changes. Sex workers engaged in communal relations may still be subject to outside pressures from other individuals and groups (e.g., the state) who may exercise power over how the communal surplus is distributed. Surpluses may be squeezed through the setting of high prices for inputs (e.g., rents) and low prices for services sold to the client. The communal appropriators may opt for self-management, but they may still subject themselves to speedups and an intensification of work and services, perhaps to increase surpluses. There may also be incentives or pressures for individual members to work independently and to privately appropriate surpluses, for instance, to help support family members or to build up a pool of private savings to support themselves after they leave the industry. Thus, there may be pressures to leave a communal arrangement for another class relation. Finally, a communal class arrangement is still subject to moral codes, stigmas, cultural representations, laws, and social policies that may overdetermine it in adverse ways.[29] In short, there is no guarantee that a communal class process will improve the lives of its participants. It depends on the context.

What strikes me, however, is that the hostile regulatory context that presents itself to prostitutes in the United States actually makes the communal enterprise a practical economic alternative. Prostitutes have already begun to organize collectively in this country; it takes only a short leap of the imagination to extend the idea of collectivization to the economic or class dimension. If criminalization and police harassment have driven independent prostitutes to seek agents, or forced them into more institutionalized (read capitalist) forms of sex work, might not prostitutes be better served by their own institutions or agencies, ones in which they may also communally appropriate the considerable surplus they produce? In communal enterprises they might obtain physical protection from both clients and the police (safety in numbers) and be able to use the surplus to secure legal and other protections (for example, through bribes). They could also use it to purchase health insurance, set up retirement plans, or contribute to a political fund for decriminalizing prostitution. In the process of working together and making these kinds of decisions and distributions, they might generate an additional and novel representation of the prostitute—not just as an independent and self-sufficient professional who is sexually and personally empowered, but as a worker whose labor process is communal and whose wealth is generated within and distributed by a community. This emergent communal identity might disrupt the images of venality, deviance, and outsiderness that are associated with prostitution and make it visible as a site of economic, as well as social and sexual, innovation and excitement. Prostitution could thus become a conduit of desires not just for sex but also for community.

I understand that this is a fantasy produced by a Marxist feminist situated in academia, and it is not necessarily shared by prostitutes. But the ability to distribute and control the social wealth they generate is something that many prostitutes may desire. In keeping with my own somewhat minimalist understanding of emancipatory futures as present and familiar (if only as possibilities) rather than as distant and radically new, I have found both hope and inspiration for this communal vision in the collectivization of prostitutes that is taking place in a number of settings. I am thinking here of the formation of organizations such as Coyote ("Call off your old tired ethics") in San Francisco, Los Angeles, Boston, and Seattle, Pony (Prostitute Organization of New York), the Red Thread in Amsterdam, Maggies in Toronto, the Vancouver Sex Work Alliance, the Prostitutes Collective of Victoria in Australia, and the Network of Sex Work Projects in England. In Australia, the first sex worker union was organized in 1995 under the umbrella of the Australian Liquor, Hospitality, and Miscellaneous Workers Union. The union is fighting against unfair dismissals and mistreatment, and is also trying to obtain holiday and sickness benefits, annual and maternity leave, occupational health and safety provisions, overtime, pension benefits, and meal breaks (Walsh 1996). Many other organizing efforts in the 1970s and early 1980s were directed toward decriminalization, but recently the focus has been more on HIV education and outreach (Jenness 1993). While some outreach projects aim to provide safe sex education to sex workers, others highlight the fact that sex workers themselves have the greatest knowledge of sexual safety and can provide important safe sex education to the general public. Prostitutes' collectives are thus trying to change the image of sex workers as victims and spreaders of disease to that of producers of health, guarantors of protection, and providers of other forms of sexual knowledge. As sites where collective projects and fantasies are promulgated and sometimes realized, these types of collective initiatives form both the imaginative and practical ground for projects of communal class transformation.

Conclusion

Representations of prostitution have a profound effect on laws, policies, and social practices, and hence also on the nature of class relations within the sex industry. In particular, the discourses and policies that attempt to eradicate prostitution, even if not successful, play a significant role in fashioning the nature of sex work, sustaining slave, feudal, or capitalist class processes and making the survival of independent or communal forms more difficult or embattled. A class analysis of the sort I have attempted here, with its own "morality" centered on exploitation, can contribute an understanding of economic difference and elicit the multiple class processes within the sex industry, including those that have been marginalized or suppressed in the dominant discourses on prostitution. Rather than viewing prostitution only in terms of slavery or capitalism, this analysis opens up space to imagine and potentiate alternative, nonexploitative class possibilities in the sex industry. Discourses and policies that recognize sexual and economic difference, and promote nonexploitative class relations, may help to generate higher earnings, economic independence, and better working conditions for sex workers, and may even contribute to emancipatory visions of a society founded on (or at least open to) communal class relations.

Notes

I would like to thank Laura Agustin, Jack Amariglio, Becky Forest, Eric Glynn, and Yahya Madra for their generous and insightful comments on earlier drafts of this essay. But special thanks and gratitude go to the editors Katherine Gibson, Steve Resnick, Rick Wolff, and especially Julie Graham, for their support and involvement in the evolution of this paper to its present state and for their hard work and guiding vision in bringing this book project to fruition.

1. Excerpts from *Simple Men* produced by H. Hartley and T. Hope, Fine Line Features.

2. In this essay I define sex work as the laboring activity of providing sexual services of any kind, and prostitution as a type of sex work which involves an exchange of sexual services for money or other goods or services. By my definition, prostitution would include certain forms of sex work (including pornographic modeling and stripping) not typically thought to fall under the label of "prostitution." See Bell (1994, 108) for the rationale behind the International Committee on Prostitutes' Rights broad definition of prostitution.

3. Prostitution is often used as a metaphor for the exploitation and oppression of women under capitalism and patriarchy. Consider the following statements made

by Marxists and radical feminists: "Prostitution in the ordinary sense is only a specific expression of the general prostitution of the laborer" (Marx 1988, 100). "What is the cause of the trade in women? . . . Exploitation of course; the merciless moloch of capitalism that fattens on underpaid labor, thus driving thousands of women and girls into prostitution . . ." (Goldman 1970, 20). "Prostitution is a crime committed against women by men in its most traditional form. It is nothing less than the commercialization of the sexual abuse and inequality that women suffer in the traditional family and can be nothing more. . . . Dismantling the institution of prostitution is the most formidable task facing contemporary feminism" (Giobbe 1990, 80). "Female sexual slavery is the underpinning of the institution of prostitution as well as marriage" (Barry 1979, 12). "The prostitution exchange is the most systematic institutionalized reduction of woman to sex. It is the foundation of all sexual exploitation of women" (Barry 1995, 65).

4. As debates about prostitution and pornography unfolded through the 1980s and 1990s, radical feminists found themselves associated with conservatives, both taking antiprostitution and antipornography positions and supporting censorship and restrictions on these markets. On the other side are sex radicals, who are allied with liberals (and libertarians) in opposing censorship and intervention in these markets. Marxist feminists who oppose pornography and prostitution on the basis of commodification and exploitation tend to ally with the former. For comprehensive reviews of these various theoretical and political positions, see Jagger (1980), Shrage (1994), and Zatz (1997).

5. The concept of class employed here refers to the processes of production, appropriation, and distribution of surplus labor. Class analysis as I understand it involves examining the overdetermination of class and nonclass processes that constitute an activity such as prostitution, pulling it in different and contradictory directions, and subjecting it to continual change and transformation (Resnick and Wolff 1987).

6. Class is just one entry point through which to examine differences in the sex industry. Alternative entry points—race and ethnicity, gender, age, nation, income groups, etc.—are equally important but beyond the scope of this paper.

7. McClintock describes how the iconography of dirt was used in marking, controlling, and policing social boundaries: "Dirty sex—masturbation, prostitution, lesbian and gay sexuality, the host of Victorian 'perversions'—transgressed the libidinal economy of male-controlled, heterosexual reproduction within monogamous marital relations (clean sex that has value). Likewise, 'dirty' money—associated with prostitutes, Jews, gamblers, thieves—transgressed the fiscal economy of the male-dominated, market exchange (clean money that has value)" (1995, 154).

8. Opinions as to the causes of prostitution varied. Some traced prostitution to the containment of male release, while others attributed it to poverty, mental illness, deviancy, or the proclivity of prostitutes for idleness, pleasure, dress, drink, and excitement (Bell 1994, 54).

9. According to Roberts, the French regulation system developed in the nine-

teenth century severely restricted both independent whores and working-class women. A single anonymous denunciation was all that was required for a woman to be investigated by the morals squad. Any woman found without a man to vouch for her was a target for the police, and any woman who lived alone and received one or more lovers could be picked up by the police and designated as an official prostitute (1993, 204).

10. The social purity crusade of 1870–1918 demanded the repeal of the state regulations, the Contagious Disease Acts in England, that had been implemented in the preceding decades. Out of this crusade emerged the campaigns against the "traffic in women," or "white slavery," which highlighted the issue of involuntary and forced prostitution (Walkowitz 1980, 127). These campaigns came at a time when there was considerable anxiety about young single women leaving the home, entering the wage labor force, and the weakening of moral codes and increase in casual sex outside marriage (Peiss 1989). The "traffic in women" discourse of the early 1900s was ultimately addressed in international law with the passing of the 1949 UN Convention for Suppression of Traffic in Persons and of Exploitation of Prostitution of Others, at which time many UN member nations criminalized prostitution.

11. The slave connotations of prostitution in this discourse are also manifest in the understanding of the prostitution commodity—prostitution entails the selling of a body and self (i.e, the self becomes the commodity) and not merely the sale of a service as with any other commodity (Pateman 1990, 1988; Barry 1995).

12. Alternatively, the slave owner may have the slave work in a non-slave class process. For example, the slave owner may force the prostitute to sell labor power for a wage in a capitalist class process.

13. The differences in the debates over prostitution and the trafficking of women crystallized at the 1995 Beijing conference. One position, put forward by the Coalition against the Traffic in Women (supported by Kathleen Barry and Andrea Dworkin, among others), wanted to criminalize prostitution, including the activities of traffickers, pimps, and clients, although not prostitutes, in an effort to eradicate prostitution. The other position, put forth by the Global Alliance against the Trafficking in Women, avoided focusing on prostitution per se, and instead defined "trafficking" as any illicit and/or forced transport, and forced labor in general. According to this position, what is problematic is not the sale of sex itself, but only the forced or coerced sale of sex, which then becomes an issue of basic human rights. This latter position was adopted for the Beijing Women's Conference platform for action, which called for the eradication of forced prostitution but exempted prostitution in general. Instead, the platform calls for the decriminalization of prostitution as a means to strengthen the human rights, bargaining position, and labor conditions of sex workers. It is this latter coalition that has gained the support of sex workers themselves.

14. The illegal status of foreign migrant sex workers may also sustain slave class processes. In some cases, amnesty is granted to migrant sex workers who come forward to the police with a claim of having been trafficked, on the condition that they

refrain from prostitution (*New York Times,* 9 July 1997, A4; Hofman and van Zoggel 1995). However, the prohibition against women continuing to practice sex work and the threat of deportation may prevent some from leaving the slave class relation.

15. Gibson-Graham (1996) note that commodification is often invoked as a metonym for capitalism. The mere existence of a market exchange process, however, does not necessitate the existence of capitalist class processes. Commodities are produced by slaves, for example, or by independent producers who are not engaged in capitalist employment relations.

16. However, with the criminalization of prostitution, the "freedom" to sell labor power to a capitalist employer is itself circumscribed.

17. The latter have so exhausted the phone-exchange systems in the Caribbean that new area codes have been established (*New York Times,* 26 May 1996, section 4, 2:2).

18. Rubin's later work draws on Foucault to critique the imposition of dominant Victorian moralities that construct regulatory norms around sexual practices that are heterosexual, marital, monogamous, reproductive, noncommercial, same generational, and occurring at home (Rubin 1984).

19. For such alternative representations of sex work, see Bell (1994) or the winter 1993 issue of *Social Text* (volume 37).

20. Sex workers also highlight the hypocrisy in laws that on the one hand allow police to arrest those engaged in prostitution, but on the other hand do nothing when a prostitute has been raped or robbed. As one prostitute said, "First of all, arresting johns is bad for business. Secondly, it pushes us further underground where we're more vulnerable. And thirdly it misses the point: if they're interested in justice, why don't they take our charges seriously when we make them. They arrest men for paying us but not for raping us. Yeah, a whore can get raped—anytime a trick takes sex without negotiating it, he's guilty of rape!" (quoted in Pheterson 1996, 44).

21. Prostitutes' rights advocates support the decriminalization of prostitution, but not its legalization by the state (as in Nevada), where the state regulates, licenses, taxes, and controls which forms of prostitution are allowed in which areas. Such forms of state control promote "state pimping," in which the state decides what sexual commodity or sexual service is to be produced and where. Rather, prostitutes' rights groups want freedom from state regulation as prostitutes, and instead ask to be subject to the same state regulation as all other workers and business owners (Bell 1994, 116).

22. See Laclau (1996) on the limits of traditional discourses of emancipation.

23. While this exercise may seem trivial, the proliferation of categories is also the proliferation of possibilities—of seeing and enactment.

24. The agent may be involved in a lending process with the sex worker, who may be obligated to distribute some of her or his earnings to pay off debts. For example, a trafficker may have paid for a sex worker's voyage and obtained marriage certificates or other documentation, for which the sex worker has incurred some debt and is then in a debt-peonage relationship.

25. According to Singer, sex workers may even "be in a better position than most women, especially wives, to determine the time, circumstances, and conditions under which the [sexual] encounter will take place, as well as to be in charge of establishing its limits, temporally and substantively. What she will and won't do is much more subject to explicit bargaining" (1993, 54).

26. Likewise, one could imagine a scenario in which a third party is exploiting a sex worker, appropriating the surplus produced, but has set up the enterprise in such a way that the sex worker is earning more money than the entrepreneur. Moreover, a capitalist enterprise may democratize power in the workplace and introduce self-management, but still be involved in exploitation, appropriating the surplus of its workers.

27. HIV prevention efforts are made more difficult by laws criminalizing prostitution. In Massachusetts, laws against "common nightwalking" allow police to arrest women who are caught with condoms in their possession while walking in the "wrong" neighborhoods and using the condoms as evidence against them.

28. Whether or not independent commodity production entails self-exploitation is a contested issue. On the one hand, the direct producer of surplus labor is also the appropriator and distributor of that surplus. There is no other person who is appropriating surplus labor and thus no exploitation. On the other hand, the notion of a fully constituted individual and autonomous "self" whose preferences and interests are unified and consistent may be seen to be a construct of the Enlightenment. An alternative conceptualization of a decentered subject, constituted by multiple and conflicting aims, interests, and activities, might allow for a different conception of the class relations of independent commodity production. Thus a person may have certain interests in the role of a direct producer of surplus labor, but may have different and conflicting interests in the role of an appropriator of her or his own surplus. In this view one part of the "self" may be involved in exploiting another part of the "self," and it is in this sense that the independent commodity producer may be thought to be engaged in "self-exploitation." Furthermore, while the independent commodity producer may be both producing and appropriating surplus labor (a process that, as discussed above, can be considered either nonexploitative or self-exploitative), the producer may be socially embedded in an environment that is very economically competitive, and may feel compelled to distribute her or his surplus to others in particular ways or even to cut back on necessary labor (for subsistence) in order to continue as an independent producer (see Gabriel 1990).

29. In France during the 1970s, for example, the more stringent enforcement of laws against soliciting and procuring led to prostitutes increasingly working together in their own premises. In response to these communal forms of work and the rise of prostitute activism and organizing (in 1975 prostitutes occupied a church in Lyon for a week, and others followed suit in other cities throughout France) the state passed a law that made it possible for prostitutes working in the same apartment to be found guilty of mutual procuring (Corbin 1990, 359).

6

Classing the Self-Employed:

New Possibilities of Power and Collectivity

Janet Hotch

The "Problem" of Self-Employment

For some workers being self-employed means having flexibility in the hours they work and how they work, but for many it means working many more hours than the average wageworker. For some workers it means that they can choose to work at a particular job (and quit) without having their identity tied to that job; for others it means entrapment within a low-paying job from which there appears to be no escape. For some workers it means that they can decide to turn down work that a client offers or not work at all for a couple of days or even months; for others it means continually searching for jobs and needing more than they can find. In the light of these ambiguities, self-employment can carry connotations of independence, agency, and self-fulfillment, despite the hardships it may entail; or it can mean drudgery and uncertainty.

The question of what it means to be self-employed is related to another perennial question: who can be considered self-employed? Management consultants, doctors, and home day-care providers have all been considered self-employed. The diversity of occupations, skill levels, socioeconomic status, and work experiences among the self-employed make generalizations about this class of worker almost meaningless.[1] Efforts to gain an accurate count of workers engaged in self-employment are fraught with difficulty,[2] and considerable debate surrounds the supposed rise in self-employment in the United States over the past two decades.[3] These debates about definitions and numbers bear directly on the organizational strategies of the labor movement if it tries to respond to and reposition itself in the contemporary labor market. The questions of who is self-employed and who is a wageworker speaks to worries over who the labor movement should represent and how it should augment its declining base through organizational reform and experimentation. Labor analysts want to promote certain policies and political initiatives vis-à-vis the self-employed, based on their interpretation of the data, and they interpret the data in accord with their theoretical, political, and policy concerns.[4]

Responding to the unprotected status of many self-employed workers who enjoy neither employer-paid benefits nor job security, labor lawyer Marc Linder, for example, stresses the fact that many so-called self-employed workers are underpaid, overworked, and not truly independent from capitalist exploitation. For Linder, it is important to discredit the statistical evidence of a rise in self-employment because such a phenomenon is typically associated with an increase in entrepreneurialism and conjures up false images of self-sufficiency and independence (1992). He advocates a class analysis that separates out the "true" self-employed (a dying, if not already dead, breed) from the "pseudo self-employed" and from capitalist employers.[5] Only in this way, he believes, can we obtain for the "nominally" self-employed the protections afforded wage laborers.

Linder's views are consonant with the familiar narrative that attributes the rise in self-employment to the changing behavior of large corporations. In this narrative, companies' response to the need for flexibility has created two tiers of workers: core and peripheral. Core employees work under typical (Fordist) employment contracts, with "permanent" jobs that pay both wages and benefits, while peripheral workers enjoy neither job security nor benefits packages and their jobs are seen as precarious (Gertler 1988; Christopherson 1989; Rodgers and Rodgers 1989). Self-employed workers fall into the category of peripheral workers. The theoretical focus is on the capitalists who choose to hire the self-employed instead of standard employees, sometimes even rehiring their own laid-off workers as independent contractors to do the same jobs they had done for wages as employees. Clearly the emphasis in this narrative is on points of commonality between the self-employed and the precariously employed and away from points that differentiate the self-employed from employees.[6] A similar emphasis is visible in Linder's attempt to deny the very existence of self-employment and maintain that what is called self-employment is simply another form of capitalist employment. By stressing the underlying commonality between superficially different types of workers, Linder hopes to facilitate the emergence of a unified working class.

In this chapter, I want to pursue the opposite tack and argue that maintaining the distinction between the self-employed and wage laborers may not be a hindrance to the organizing strategies of the labor movement and to other movements for economic change. I would like to suggest that such a distinction might actually help in formulating different organizational modes, offering new directions for the labor movement.

Grouping the self-employed with other flexible workers (e.g., part-time and temporary) ignores the unique features of self-employment and the special challenges and opportunities presented to those who want to be involved in organizing them. Seeing all workers, self-employed or not, as coming under the aegis of capitalism obscures the possibilities of noncapitalist development that organizations of self-employed workers might pursue. My interest in this essay is to explore the specificities of self-employment from the perspective of class and then to speculate on the range of possibilities for organizing self-employed workers. I will also suggest ways in which self-employed workers could join together to create noncapitalist, communal sites of production as a path toward security and growth (thereby opening up the possibility for divergence from the expected trajectory of "success," in which the self-employed move into a small capitalist business). Both are strategic directions for organization that are unimaginable when all forms of work are theorized as just so many forms of capitalist employment.

A Class Analysis of Self-Employment

The following examination of self-employment is grounded in an anti-essentialist epistemology with a focus on class as its theoretical entry point. Unlike other types of class analysis, I do not wish to construct a class structure from which one can determine class interests, nor to show that certain workers, objectively or subjectively, belong to the same class. In the approach used here, class is not defined as a social grouping but as the economic process of producing, appropriating, and distributing surplus labor. Self-employment is understood as generally involving a particular type of class process characterized by the *individual* production and appropriation of surplus labor.

Most productive workers (self-employed or otherwise) produce both necessary and surplus labor. Necessary labor is usually defined as the amount of labor a worker must perform to satisfy her or his culturally determined basic living needs. Surplus labor is that which is produced over and above necessary labor (Marx 1977).

The Marxian tradition has generated an open-ended typology of class processes including capitalist, feudal, slave, communal/communist, and ancient/independent. The capitalist class process can be characterized as a specific interaction between laborers and nonlaborers, in which wage-workers produce a surplus, and capitalists appropriate that surplus (in the form of surplus value) and then distribute it to satisfy the conditions of existence for capitalist production, among other things. The communal class process, on the other hand, is characterized by the collective production, appropriation, and distribution of surplus labor. Self-employment is generally equated with the ancient or independent class process, or "mode of production,"[7] in which the individual producer appropriates and distributes her or his own surplus labor.

One of the elements of the capitalist class process that distinguishes it from independent and communal class processes is exploitation. The term "exploitation" is defined here to refer to the act of nonlaborers appropriating the surplus of laborers (Resnick and Wolff 1987, 20). While the capitalist class process is exploitative (as are feudal and slave processes), the communal and independent class processes are not (although they may be oppressive). Workers involved in these latter two class processes are self-appropriating rather than exploited.[8]

Though it is easy to make a theoretical distinction between necessary and surplus labor, applying this distinction to actual cases of self-employment is more problematic. Because the self-employed's reproduction as an individual worker is intrinsically related to her or his reproduction as self-employer/producer, there is no clear boundary between necessary and surplus labor for the self-employed. Not only does the rate of self-appropriation,[9] defined as the ratio of surplus to necessary labor, vary from one self-employed worker to another, but the ease with which the two processes of necessary and surplus labor production are distinguished varies with the particular conditions of each self-employed worker.

Imagine, for example, a self-employed independent contractor who has made little investment in equipment (i.e., does not own any means of production), works at the client site, and relies on word-of-mouth to obtain customers. This worker appears to distribute (and therefore appropriate) little or no surplus, because there are few if any expenses uniquely associated with being self-employed. Consider the difference between this situation and that of a self-employed independent contractor who maintains an office, has purchased equipment with the help of a sizable bank loan, has incorporated to protect personal assets in case of a liability claim, and is a member of a variety of business associations to help expand her or his client base and "network" with other self-employed workers. The labor expended to secure these particular conditions of existence is surplus labor. On the other hand, the labor expended to feed, clothe, and shelter that worker (and perhaps her or his family) is necessary labor.

The self-employed (by my definition) are usually engaged in some surplus labor production and appropriation, straining to allocate expenses to a particular category—subsistence needs (i.e., necessary labor) versus other expenses (i.e., surplus labor). What is interesting is that the line of differentiation between necessary and surplus labor not only varies among self-employed workers but is also continually being repositioned for any given worker. This is not a problem for our analysis, however; it is actually a feature. The conceptualization of a variable rate of self-appropriation (which may approach zero) allows us to recognize and discuss the particular experiences of self-employed workers vis-à-vis the production of surplus labor.

The rate of self-appropriation for a given worker is constantly changing. For example, an increase in the amount of necessary labor required for the reproduction of the laborer, due to either inflation or an increasing cost of living, may reduce the amount of surplus labor the worker can produce. This in turn may result in an effort to reduce the number of surplus distributions. For example, the worker may resign from membership in associations deemed to be discretionary. In this way, looking at the ratio between necessary and surplus labor is one way to understand a person's particular self-employment situation.

One could also consider ways in which demands on surplus overdetermine the quality of life a worker might enjoy. Conditions of existence for self-employment that were once free or unnecessary may suddenly become expensive or unavoidable and thereby increase the self-employed's rate of self-appropriation. For example, new licensure requirements, changes in tax law, or increased competition may result in more labor being committed to the production of surplus. In such cases, a worker might work more hours or reduce the allocation to necessary labor, thus lowering her or his standard of living. This reduction in standard of living may, in turn, reduce the ability to perform work. Such conditions may cause a crisis for the self-employed worker (Gabriel 1989, chapter 4).

On the other hand, the same factors that may undermine self-employment for some workers may help to secure it for others. For example, licensure may protect some workers in a particular field against competition and establish legitimacy for their particular occupation, resulting in their ability to raise rates and add to their surplus. Thus, licensure can be seen to have potentially contradictory effects: reducing competition for some self-employed workers while rendering others unemployed.

What is the point of making the necessary/surplus labor distinction? Clearly, the distinction is a theoretical construct that has no currency among workers or those involved in organizing them. Nonetheless, this theoretical construction allows us to articulate an area of difference among the self-employed. It helps us to better understand why self-employed workers may not share the same needs and goals.

Beyond a Class Analysis of Self-Employment

While it is important to describe the independent class process in order to highlight the differences between it and other class processes, this elaboration in and of itself will not be sufficient to the task of classing the self-employed. To say that a self-employed worker is one who is engaged in a unique class process associated with self-employment, i.e., the independent class process of self-appropriation of surplus, is problematic on two levels: (1) most self-employed workers, like all workers, are engaged in multiple class processes at any given time or over time, and (2) not all workers who call themselves self-employed (or are so-called by others) appropriate their own surplus labor. In general terms, a class analysis implies nothing about the self-employed as a group of people. Thus, within this anti-essentialist analysis, the home day-care provider struggling to make ends meet can be *both* self-employed and the victim of a dysfunctional economic and social system, the owners of small businesses (or large ones for that matter) can be *both* self-employed and capitalist, and contract workers can be *both* self-employed and temporary employees of capitalist enterprises.

Moreover, in common usage the label "self-employed" is applied to a diversity of workers and not actually reserved for those who engage in the independent class process associated with self-employment. To deal with this ambiguity or divergence in meanings, I am not arguing for a change in usage (substituting an academic or a Marxian meaning for the common ones), but for fostering an appreciation of the variety of meanings associated with the term "self-employment." In particular, I want to reserve a place in the category "self-employed" for workers who are not self-appropriating.[10] This strategy seems more respectful of the process of self-definition and of alternative ways of reading and constructing the meaning of particular situations. While an individual may not be self-employed by *my* definition, conveying this to them will often not be appropriate, useful, or welcome.

Under what circumstances would workers who do not appropriate their own surplus call themselves self-employed? A worker might perform a variety of jobs for a variety of clients, only some of whom appropriate the surplus labor. For example, a garment maker may produce customized garments for individual clients as well as for capitalist firms and may not perceive capitalist clients as altering her or his self-employed status. Another worker might only work for capitalist firms that appropriate the surplus labor and yet identify herself or himself as self-employed because of being able to work flexible hours and able to budget time between paid work and other life work. For this worker, self-employment has nothing to do with class position, in which she or he might be completely uninterested.

Flexibility is, in fact, central to many people's definition of self-employment. In a book entitled *On Our Own: A Declaration of Independence for the Self-Employed,* Paul Dickson discusses how being self-employed enabled him to take time off from work when his father was sick (1985, 36). For him, this was decidedly different from quitting his job in order to care for his father. He was not earning any income during this period, and he was facing an uncertain future when it was time to look for work again, so what was the difference? I believe it was largely identity related. When Dickson took time off, he did not suffer the stigma attached to quitting a job, and he felt freer to make this choice as a self-employed person than he would have had he been employed. Moreover, during this break from paid work he remained self-employed. In this sense, his job would be waiting for him when he returned. Even if that meant struggling to find new clients, he would not be unemployed.

It is not only homeworkers and freelancers who might consider themselves self-employed even though someone else is appropriating their surplus. I spoke with people at a telemarketing company that hired ostensibly self-employed workers to perform its telemarketing and found that, by my definition, none of these workers actually engaged in self-appropriation. It was clear to me that the owner of the company was employing a ruse to avoid making any longterm commitment to these workers or paying his share of their social security taxes. To my surprise, however, the workers did not believe their self-employment status to be a sham.

It was their status as self-employed workers that they associated with having the freedom to take time off from work (without pay) whenever they needed it. Their self-employment was also key to their identity vis-à-vis their job as telemarketers. It enabled many of them to see telemarketing, a job that carried low social status in their eyes, as nonessential to their identity. They were not telemarketers; they were self-employed workers, who at this time were working in telemarketing and could pursue other interests or labor options at any time. Their self-employed status gave them a way of distancing their personal identity from the work they performed. Had they been employees of the telemarketing company, they would have been identified with that work in a way that did not accord with their self-image.

Attempting to organize these diverse individuals and class experiences into a union may seem a quixotic endeavor, a kind of obstacle course on the way to failure. But I am suggesting that this kind of analysis, this parsing of difference along the axis of class, is necessary for developing effective organizing strategies and can contribute to the building of an organization that is itself a point of unity among its diverse members.

Implications for Organizing the Self-Employed

It is one thing to offer an alternative way of theorizing self-employment as a unique class process as well as a grouping of diverse individuals; it is quite another to investigate the implications of this alternative theoretical position for organizing the self-employed. One cannot predict the effects of a particular theory on practice, nor does theory remain immutable as efforts are made to fashion appropriate actions. Nonetheless, different theoretical positions can open new vistas from which one can see alternative ways of addressing practical problems. The following effort to understand the practical effects of an anti-essentialist class analysis on organizing the self-employed can best be understood as a contribution to what I hope will become an ongoing effort by the labor movement to address the needs and concerns of self-employed and other nontraditional workers.

My class analysis implies that any conflation of employment and self-employment can have serious repercussions for labor unions and others hoping to effectively address the needs of the self-employed. Failing to distinguish the two, I would argue, makes it difficult if not impossible to organize self-employed people and to imagine productive ways to serve them. This observation seems straightforward but it is neither innocent nor unproblematic, and in making it I often come up against the deeply held view that theorizing/recognizing differences among workers undermines the reason for organizing them. Many people share with Linder a concern that emphasizing difference and multiplicity will serve to decrease solidarity among workers and will play into the hands of capital, which is always looking for ways to divide and conquer.

Although I understand the basis of this concern, I believe that theorizing difference rather than sameness may be more empowering for groups of people that come together for a variety of reasons to reach a common goal.[11] Theorizing sameness instead of difference has an effect, but that effect may not be unifying. Projects of creating unity that are predicated on showing people their "real" similarities beneath the facade of difference often founder on the contingencies of identity and identification.[12] I would rather entertain the notion that people with different interests, different class positions, and different theories about the way the world works could come together, albeit not without some internal struggle and debate, to pursue a common project or to pursue a variety of projects within a single organization.

But it is not enough to recognize the distinctiveness of the self-employed as a category of workers (i.e., the difference *between* wage labor and self-employed labor). I believe that the differences *among* the self-employed also need to become a key focus of attention if this group of workers is to be successfully organized. Any effort to organize the self-employed needs to recognize that a broad range of work arrangements and experiences fall under the rubric of self-employment and that none of them has any privileged claim to the label. Rather than assuming a homogeneity of interests among those workers labeled "self-employed" and targeted for organizing efforts, making the distinction between necessary and surplus labor can be used as a device for articulating difference.[13]

The complex effects that changes to the conditions of self-employment can have on self-employed workers' ability to produce surplus as well as to maintain their current standard of living can inform plans to organize these workers. As with any organizing effort, if unions foresee the contradictory effects of proposals ostensibly designed to benefit self-employed workers, they can better address the internal struggles that could arise when they try to develop such proposals. While a recognition of contradictory effects will not eradicate internal struggles, it can change the nature of those struggles by increasing members' awareness of each other's unique problems as self-employed workers.

Recent inquiries into the potential for organizing the "new work force" offer proposals that are relevant to or include strategies for organizing self-employed workers (see Heckscher 1988; Cobble 1990; Nussbaum and Sweeney 1989; Carré, duRivage, and Tilly 1993). These inquiries tend to be grounded in the theoretical literature on flexibility and post-Fordism. Thus, self-employment is generally subsumed under the category of contingent, nontraditional work arrangements (other contingent work arrangements include part-time, temporary, and home-based work) that are understood to be on the rise due to employer efforts to save money and increase flexibility. In general, the "new unionism" literature recommends that unions take a multipronged approach to representing the nontraditional work force, suggesting the following four goals: (1) promoting universal health coverage and portable pension benefits (i.e., benefits that would be associated with a person and not a particular job held by that person); (2) organizing contingent workers into bargaining units and pressing for wages and working conditions comparable to those of permanent workers; (3) encouraging a new model of craft unionism that could run hiring halls for temporary and/or self-employed workers as well as offer training and apprenticeships if appropriate; (4) pressing for changes in labor law to recognize the rights of the self-employed and other nontraditional workers under the National Labor Relations Act (NLRA).

There is little doubt that to effectively meet the needs of self-employed workers a new model of unionism is required. Developing that model is beyond the scope of this essay, but all of the recommendations enumerated above are ones that have potential. At least on the face of things, they would certainly help some of the self-employed while not overtly hurting any of them. The last recommendation, however, requires special consideration because it has been left largely unstressed in the literature and because it is crucial to furthering the effort to provide security for workers who are not traditionally employed within a capitalist enterprise.

To effectively fight for better conditions for self-employed workers, these workers would need to be legally recognized as workers. Formal recognition and protection under the NLRA would not only help unions represent the self-employed, but would establish these workers as part of the fabric of labor relations in the United States.

The experiences of the Self-Employed Women's Association (SEWA) in India, which was actually successful in changing the labor laws, may provide some valuable ideas for a similar effort in the United States. When SEWA tried to register as a trade union in India, the labor authority told them: "You cannot be a trade union because you do not have any fixed employer-employee relationship. You cannot even be called workers" (SEWA 1982, chapter 2, p. 7). In their defense, SEWA argued

> A worker is not only an employee. . . . A worker is a person who earns his/her living by his/her own effort without exploiting the labour of others. . . . A trade union is not against an employer but for the benefit of the worker. A worker is oppressed not only by an employer but by many other sections of society and a trade union can be an organisation to defend themselves against all the vested interests. It is heartening to note that the Gujarat Labour Office did accept that defence and did register SEWA as a trade union. (Ibid.)

Labor unions in the United States are not apt to have as easy a time changing the status of self-employed workers vis-à-vis the NLRA, which explicitly excludes "independent contractors" in section 2(3). The determination of independent contractor status in case law has rested on a nebulous common law test for control over working conditions. "If the alleged employer retains the right of control, the worker is an employee; if the worker has the right of control over his own working conditions, he is an independent contractor" (Getman and Pogrebin 1988, 17).

Given the express statutory exclusion of independent contractors and its common law interpretation, labor activists, like Linder, have been moved to show that all independent contractors are really dependent on their temporary employers. As I mentioned earlier, I believe that such a strategy is ultimately misguided in its implicit linking of security and legal protection to traditional employment relations, making it impossible to consider secure, legally protected work outside a capitalist enterprise. Thus, I would argue for a much more direct strategy of removing the restriction on independent contractors from the NLRA.

I understand that any recommendation that rests on a change to the NLRA, and specifically its Taft-Hartley amendments, will engender skepticism, and for good reason given recent labor history. However, should the efforts of the reinvigorated labor movement succeed in rallying a call for workers' rights to organize, and should that call be connected to the growing discourse on postindustrial labor relations, an opportunity to radically revise or completely rewrite the NLRA might arise. If such an opportunity presents itself, the United States' labor movement might look to the success of SEWA and argue for the protection of workers and not just employees.[14]

Beyond advocating for change in the NLRA and the three other recommendations enumerated above, there are a number of recommendations that do not appear in the literature on organizing and representing the contingent work force that would be appropriate for self-employed workers. These recommendations come out of an understanding of, and appreciation for, self-employment as a unique class process and a recognition of the class and nonclass diversity among the self-employed.

As I pointed out above, all workers engaged in self-appropriation are self-employed, but not all self-employed workers are engaged in self-appropriation. Because it is my contention that the class process affects the needs of workers vis-à-vis a labor organization, it will be useful to consider the needs of the self-appropriating self-employed separately from the non-self-appropriating. This does not mean that a single labor organization cannot represent both types of workers, nor that there are not areas of overlap in the needs of these two types of self-employed workers. Nonetheless, addressing class differences among members presents unique challenges.[15]

Proposals for Representing the Self-Appropriating Self-Employed

The role of a labor organization representing the self-appropriating, self-employed worker could be divided into three broad areas: (1) helping to secure the conditions of existence for self-appropriation; (2) supporting negotiations between the self-employed workers and their clients; (3) promoting collective processes of purchasing, production, and banking. Interestingly, SEWA has in fact successfully supported the self-employed in each of these areas. I will therefore draw heavily on their experiences (as they have been described in various articles, books, and pamphlets produced by and about SEWA) in formulating specific recommendations.

To meet the conditions of existence for self-appropriation, the self-employed must be able to satisfy both their necessary and surplus labor requirements, as well as replace inputs used up in the production process. Labor unions could help the self-employed both to acquire means of production and to consider alternative methods for, and effects of, changing the rate of self-appropriation.

Considering first the rate of appropriation, and specifically the necessary labor requirements, unions might help the self-employed reduce the amount of labor time required for meeting necessary labor requirements by reducing necessary labor demands. Pressing for programs like government-sponsored child care and affordable and accessible public transportation would be one way to reduce these demands. Importantly, such programs would not necessarily be in the best interests of *all* self-employed workers. Presumably, some sort of rise in taxes (or shift in tax expenditures) would be required to pay for these services, and not all self-employed (nor other workers) would benefit equally. This potential for conflicting interests is, of course, not a new problem. Understanding this problem in terms of changes in the rate of self-appropriation for the self-employed, however, may help labor unions make sense of differences of opinion among their membership. Whatever the outcome of internal struggles, a labor organization must tackle issues relating to demands on necessary labor.

SEWA recognized that as a labor organization it could not separate its members' survival needs from their needs as productive laborers. For example, SEWA realized that it must provide minimum paid leave for its members immediately before and after pregnancy and first approached insurance companies to ask for coverage for pregnant women. When the insurance companies refused, SEWA set up its own benefit scheme. Their strategy and success indicates that taking on the burden of provision of benefits can ultimately result in government policy change:

> SEWA feels that we, as women, are providing for the continuity of society. So why should motherhood be seen as a burden to be borne by women alone? With this in mind we went to the insurance companies and said "During the time of delivery a mother has to stop working and earning. Can you make a scheme which will protect her motherhood?" The insurance companies tried, but then replied, "No, women are a high insurance risk and poor women particularly so, since so many of them die. We cannot afford to insure them unless we charge a very high premium." No other agency could

help us. SEWA started its own motherhood defence—The Maternity Benefit Scheme.

The death rate among mothers under the scheme has certainly fallen. This success has made the Government of Gujarat also adopt the scheme for agricultural workers on a statewide scale. We hope that motherhood defence will reach the working mothers all over the country. (SEWA 1982, chapter 2, p. 7)

Of course, even such successful efforts to support the necessary labor requirements of the self-employed need not be the only, or even primary, goal of a labor organization. Attention might also be paid to demands on the self-employed's surplus labor production. This suggests, among other things, that labor unions might be concerned with the training requirements of the self-employed, enabling them to keep up with technological innovations. Again, SEWA provides examples of how important such training can be and how a labor organization might help provide it:

SEWA is sponsoring training programmes to develop women's skill in a number of fields. Courses in bamboo work, block printing, and sewing, traditional occupations for women, aim to upgrade women's skills in these areas. (ibid., chapter 4, p. 2)

For years, Chipa (Muslim) women have hand-printed cloth for traders on a piece rate. In recent years the market for their products has been taken over by modern designs from screen printing factories, and the women have been unemployed. A training programme supported by the All India Handicrafts Board is being run by SEWA to teach 25 women designs suited to more sophisticated markets. (ibid., p. 3)

Providing training to self-employed workers will not appeal to nor benefit equally all self-employed workers. Some workers will not have the time to take away from revenue-producing work to acquire new skills, and thus labor unions may need to consider how to subsidize training to make it feasible for more self-employed workers to obtain. Perhaps more important, not all workers will see technological innovation as a good thing. Craft workers, for example, may recognize that certain innovations will trade off quality or individual artistry for quantity production or mass-market appeal.[16] These craft workers may want the labor union to focus its energies on a public education campaign aimed at creating a market for traditional artisanry. It is not possible to theoretically judge the correct solution to such potential differences in opinion regarding union strategy. I am only suggesting that these kinds of debates might arise among members of an organization of self-employed workers.

A further problem that self-employed workers face in trying to keep up with technological change is obtaining financing for the purchase of new equipment. Unions for self-employed workers might help by working to secure loans for their membership through existing financial institutions or government programs, or even setting up a credit union for their members. A cornerstone of SEWA's success has been the development of a bank set up specifically for providing business loans to its members.

Another possible union activity involves the promotion of collective purchasing, production, and/or marketing units. Once again, SEWA has enjoyed success in this area. Recognizing that individually workers were unable to purchase raw materials directly from producers, SEWA developed several programs to help women purchase raw materials collectively. They have also helped home-based, piece-rate workers (non-self-appropriating laborers) to become self-appropriating by freeing them from the grip of merchants who supply women with raw materials to be processed and pay them at a piece rate. In a similar fashion, labor organizations in the United States could help the self-employed set up purchasing cooperatives to buy both raw materials and/or equipment directly from producers (or at least from wholesalers).

Self-employed workers might also transform their class identity and establish cooperative production units, instituting a communal class process that enables them to reap the benefits of divisions of labor and economies of scale and scope. In India, SEWA helped set up such cooperatives for home-based producers, empowering them to take control of their working environments and to strive for improved working conditions and higher earnings. Such cooperatives involved all steps of the production and distribution processes, from the acquisition of raw materials to the final sale. These cooperatives allowed the members to redefine their identity as workers:

> At first it was difficult for them to define themselves in relation to SEWA as anything but "labourer." After working for a time they would say, we are neither owners nor labourers, we are somewhere in between. But now after time and struggle, it is "our own production unit." Soon the workers hope this production unit will become a registered cooperative with the women from the community as the shareholders, the directors, the managers, and the workers . . . and they will truly have "Our Own Cooperative Units." (SEWA 1982, chapter 4, p. 6)

Organizing the self-employed could be particularly beneficial for workers providing business services to capitalist firms. In a relationship typically unbalanced in favor of the capitalist firm, a union could create the potential for a different power relation between firms and contractors. One of the greatest problems faced by self-employed workers contracting with a capitalist company is the lack of power to negotiate and enforce a fair contract. A union that combines the resources and power of its workers and is connected to the broader labor movement could shift the balance of power. Furthermore, by helping workers establish cooperatives with greater purchasing power and the benefits of mutual support, labor unions could offer their members an alternative to subcontracting through a consulting firm or other agency, which appropriates a portion (or all) of the workers' surplus labor.

Representing All Self-Employed Workers

Since not all self-employed workers are actually self-appropriating, and some would rather not be, how should unions of self-employed workers approach the problem of representing non-self-appropriating workers? I suggest, again based on the experiences of SEWA, that unions might encourage *interested* workers to become self-appropriating (or communally appropriating) by offering them the services described above. On the other hand, unions do not need to force all workers into continued self-employment, self-appropriation, or cooperative units. For those workers who would prefer employment with a capitalist enterprise, and for those who are already working for these firms, unions could pressure employers to recognize the employment status of their workers and pay them an adequate wage with benefits. These strategies, among others, have already been recommended in the current literature on organizing the self-employed.

Of course, the needs and interests of the two types of self-employed workers (self-appropriating and non-self-appropriating) will sometimes clash. Those who want to be employees may feel that the self-employed contract workers are undermining their jobs. Similarly, the self-employed contract workers may feel that those workers seeking wage employment are undermining their ability to be self-appropriating.

These differences are potentially very divisive and might call for a strategy of setting up two "locals" that work separately but also come together around issues of shared interest as well as to work through their differences. The potential for differences could surely be minimized, however, if all working arrangements were made more secure. Then, workers might actually be able to choose the work arrangement that most appealed to them without directly threatening or feeling threatened by other workers' choices.

Creating Alternatives to Capitalism

By recognizing the legitimacy of alternative forms of employment, unions could attract new membership and explore new ways to address the needs of a diverse work force, rather than fight a losing battle to maintain the status quo. The lone self-employed worker, spatially and economically isolated from other workers, is in need of organizations that can provide a link to the rest of the world. The self-employed can join forces to pressure wayward clients into paying their bills, to lobby for the linkage of social benefits to residency rather than employment status, or to form partnerships or even communal class processes of production. The list is open-ended, and I am sure that other theorists and activists will extend it in the future.

For now, however, I want simply to emphasize that a bipolar class analysis, which divides the world into capitalists and proletarians, is not necessary in order to encourage a transformative labor movement. In fact, I would argue that such a bipolarization makes transformation theoretically impossible by leaving no conceptual space for alternatives to capitalism. This is particularly problematic in the era of downsizing and restructuring, when arguably the social space for noncapitalist economic activity is growing.

By shedding permanent workers and outsourcing labor, a capitalist firm is inadvertently creating an opening for alternative modes of production including, but not limited to, individual ones. That firms may choose to shed their work force in an attempt at self-preservation—in order to become leaner and meaner or more competitive—does not change the fact that opportunities for alternative modes of production are created.

It is my intention to explore these opportunities and openings, both theoretically and politically. My project is antithetical to projects like those of Linder (1992) and Harvey (1989), who theorize "non-capitalist forms of production, such as commodity production by self-employed workers . . . as somehow taking place *within* capitalism" (Gibson-Graham 1996, 258). Though many believe that to theorize capitalism as anything but all-embracing is to refuse to see the *reality* of capitalism, that is, to attempt to wish capitalism away by refusing to see it, I would argue that to theorize capitalism as all-embracing is to refuse to see different, alternative modes of production that come together to form the complex production relations of our economy.

It is not that theorizing multiplicity more accurately reflects reality than theorizing singleness or homogeneity. Both ways of theorizing are tenable, but the theoretical choice makes a difference. Constructing a theory of production in which all forms of labor are labeled capitalist and then bemoaning the ubiquitousness of capitalism is analogous to constructing a theory of literature in which all forms of storytelling are labeled novels and then bemoaning the lack of other literary forms.

The composition of the economy is changed when capitalist firms shed their workers in favor of hiring self-employed workers. Failing to recognize this change may mean failing to drive a wedge in the dominance of capitalist exploitation. While one may argue that generating sites of individual production is not a change for the better, this is far different from arguing that the social formation is not changing at all.

It is obviously not a good thing for workers to be cast out of capitalist employment and into self-employment without appropriate legal, social, or economic protection. But attempting to secure this protection by insisting that self-employment is actually just another form of capitalist employment is highly problematic. This strategy discursively aligns security and legal protection with capitalism and traditional employment, making it difficult to consider secure, legally protected work outside a capitalist enterprise. And by failing to provide discursive space for anything but capitalism and capitalist employment, it discourages efforts to promote the creation of noncapitalist class processes.

On the other hand, focusing on the creation of noncapitalist class processes as a by-product of changes in corporate employment strategies opens up a wide array of opportunities for effecting social change. Alternatives to wage labor suddenly appear important and viable rather than futile, utopian, or old-fashioned. Refusing to give wage labor a sanctified place as the only secure form of employment, and the only basis on which workers can join together in collective action, allows room to create alternative forms of employment, which may be economically, socially, or emotionally more satisfying than traditional wage labor.

Notes

I am very grateful to Rick Wolff and Julie Graham for their assistance during the early stages of writing this paper, and to all the editors for their help in bringing the paper to its finished form.

1. This is not, of course, to suggest that diversity is absent among other types of workers (see Southern, this volume).

2. The difficulty of counting the self-employed is mainly due to a lack of consensus regarding who should be included. Most of the data used to support statistical analyses of self-employment in the United States are derived from the national census

and the *Current Population Survey*, which exclude the incorporated self-employed and workers in the informal sector from their count; on the other hand, they include "involuntarily self-employed" contract workers, often referred to as "disguised wage laborers." See Linder and Houghton's (1990) commentary on Steinmetz and Wright (1989) for an example of the debate around interpretation of the statistics on self-employment. See Aronson (1991) for an extensive empirical analysis of self-employment that tries to make sense of the existing data and concludes with a plea for additional research.

3. According to the *Occupational Outlook Quarterly*, published by the Bureau of Labor Statistics in 1990, 13 percent of the labor force was self-employed (15.6 million workers). Approximately 10 million worked in their own unincorporated businesses, 3.5 million owned incorporated businesses, and 2 million were self-employed part-time while also holding primary jobs as wage or salaried workers. Between 1983 and 1990, the total number of self-employed owners of unincorporated businesses increased by nearly 11 percent, but the proportion of self-employed in the work force fell because total employment rose 17 percent (Silvestri 1991).

More recent data published in the *Monthly Labor Review* show that 12 percent of the labor force was self-employed in 1994 (Bregger 1996). This figure includes incorporated and unincorporated but does not include those who are self-employed part-time while holding other jobs. If the latter were included, the percentage of self-employed in the labor force would probably be the same if not greater than in 1990.

4. The ILO, for example, looking at global self-employment trends, is interested in "promoting self-employment" as a partial solution to rising unemployment and underemployment (ILO 1990).

5. In Linder's words we need to "dismember the category of the self-employed and redistribute its constituent parts to the capitalist and working classes, where they objectively—and increasingly subjectively—belong" (1992, 3). A more complex class structure with room for contradictory class locations is theorized by Steinmetz and Wright (1989) who see the self-employed (petty bourgeoisie) as distinct from capitalists and wage workers. But despite the claim that the self-employed individually appropriate their own surplus, Wright does not want to rob capitalism of its exploitative power over all workers. Through a complex theory of exploitation based on game theory, he is led to note that "some petty bourgeois . . . will actually be exploited by capital (through unequal exchange on the market) because they own such minimal means of production, and some will be capitalistic exploiters because they own a great deal of capital even though they may not hire any wage earners" (Wright 1985, 103). In this way Wright once again allocates the self-employed to the two great capitalist classes.

6. See Hotch (1991) for a discussion of precariousness in atypical employment arrangements, which argues that precariousness is a socially constructed, rather than necessary, characteristic of certain types of work arrangements.

7. In much of the Marxian literature, the self-employed worker is seen as par-

ticipating in a "precapitalist mode of production" (see, for example, Wolpe 1980 and Hindess and Hirst 1975). I resist using this term because it implies that this mode of production is a precursor of capitalism and will disappear in a "fully capitalist" economy. Although this stagist implication is not always accepted by those using the term, I feel it is safer to avoid the term altogether.

8. Some theorists, like Gabriel, would disagree with me here. Gabriel uses the term "self-exploitation" to refer to the "unified production and appropriation of surplus labor in a single human being" (Gabriel 1990, 87). While I understand that this term has the advantage of emphasizing the similarities between exploitative class processes and self-employment, this emphasis may also be seen as a disadvantage. I believe the term downplays the difference between the effects of appropriating one's own surplus and the effects of having one's surplus appropriated by someone else. By this, I do *not* mean to imply that it is always (or even usually) better to appropriate one's own surplus. I do mean that whether the process of appropriation also entails the process of exploitation makes a difference. It seems "cleaner," therefore, to use the term "self-appropriation" to mean appropriating from oneself, leaving the term "exploitation" to mean the process by which one person or group appropriates surplus labor from another.

9. Gabriel identifies the ratio of surplus to necessary labor as the rate of self-exploitation (1989, 108).

10. There are, for example, homeworkers who would consider themselves self-employed but who make products (e.g., sew clothes) or perform services (e.g., enter data) for one or more companies that appropriate their surplus labor (i.e., the company pays a wage and then sells the products at a price greater than the cost of the labor and the constant capital used up in production).

11. Others associated with the labor movement, for example, Elaine Bernard, have adopted a more welcoming approach to difference, recognizing the need for the labor movement to work with organizations of self-employed workers such as the Writers Union (to which she herself belongs). She points to the example of the Teamsters union that has allowed independent truckers to join even though they do not come under its collective bargaining agreements (presentation, University of Oregon, Eugene, Oct. 1997).

12. Of course, as the line of argument goes, one is not *forcing* the self-employed to identify themselves erroneously with the working class, one is simply *enlightening* them about the ways that capitalism obscures their common interests with other workers who are also oppressed and exploited. But what if someone, or most people, do not find this vision enlightening? Do we give up on them and decide that they are not necessary for inclusion in a union, a campaign, a movement?

13. Let me make clear here that I am not saying that this is the only area of difference among the self-employed, or even the most important one; it is one of many.

14. A detailed discussion of how a new system of labor relations would operate to include all workers is beyond the scope of this paper. Some of Hecksher's (1988) ideas on "associational unionism" might be expanded to include the self-employed

(and other nontraditional employees). Unfortunately, Hecksher himself did not address these workers explicitly except to say that nontraditional workers "clearly form a massive group with no loyalties to any corporate organization." They are a "wild card in the current deck" (241).

15. On a practical note, SEWA found that in India it worked best to create homogeneous groups defined by identifiable, felt needs and then encourage communication and support between groups. In organizing women in India, they found it best to "identify felt needs of the women to be organised, which are perceived by them as critical problems. They may be economic or social issues, but must be a common difficulty for any particular group of women, so that homogeneous clusters are formed. . . . The initial issues identified for organising must be . . . tackled in a visibly successful way. . . . Then, other issues can be taken up to . . . tackle larger problems common to several groups" (SEWA 1981, 52).

16. I can imagine such criticism raised against SEWA's retraining of the block printers, described above.

7

Los Angeles:

A Postmodern Class Mapping

Enid Arvidson

Classing Los Angeles

Los Angeles is frequently cited in discussions and debates about an emerging postmodern[1] urbanism (e.g., Dear and Flusty 1998; Scott and Soja 1996). Once a mononucleated, modern, industrial metropolis, Los Angeles is now seen as transformed by global capitalist restructuring into a polycentered, postmodern service and information city. There is general agreement that production and reproduction are increasingly spatially decentralized, resulting from complex processes of regional wars for jobs, capital flight and deindustrialization, technological changes, new waves of immigration, and continued pursuit of an "American dream" lifestyle. As this literature develops, countless other cities are seen as following the L.A. model.[2]

General consensus continues on another point, that accompanying urban and economic restructuring has been class restructuring. With deindustrialization and the globalization of capital has come the decline of the traditional working class and the rise of a new class structure. No longer representable as a pyramid, this new structure is variously described as an hourglass, a dumbbell, or a pear. At the top is a flourishing "yuppie" class of highly paid producer-service, high-tech, and culture-producing workers; on the bottom is a growing underclass of workers in the low-paying consumer-service and low-tech manufacturing sectors; and in between is an increasingly squeezed and shrinking middle class (Soja and Scott 1996).

Increasing class polarization is understood to be manifest spatially in postmodern urbanism where the "haves" move out of the original urban core and central cities to new "urban villages" and "edge cities," leaving the older, increasingly blighted areas to recent immigrants and other "have-nots."

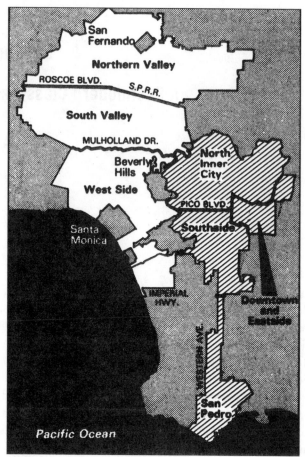

Divided city: ☐ = Anglo majority; ▨ = Non-anglo majority

Figure 1. Racial polarization. From Mike Davis, "*Chinatown,* Part Two? The 'Internationalization' of Downtown Los Angeles," *New Left Review* 164 (July/August 1987): 84. Copyright 1987; reprinted by permission of *New Left Review.*

Cartographers of postmodern Los Angeles, Mike Davis and Ed Soja, have mapped this polarization employing techniques of social area analysis that hark back to the urban ecology of the Chicago School in the 1920s (see Davis 1992). Using census data, Davis (1987) maps (figure 1) racial differences over space that indicate dramatic class spatial divisions in Los Angeles.[3] Anglo Angelenos have secured, through gated communities and home-owners' associations, the clean-air, low-density areas in the hills and along the coast, leaving the smog belt to an increasingly unemployed, non-Anglo working

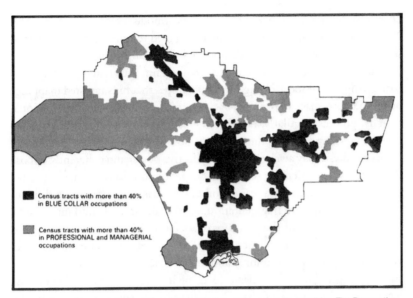

Figure 2. Occupational polarization. From Edward W. Soja, *Postmodern Geographies: The Reassertion of Space in Critical Social Theory* (New York: Verso Books, 1989). Copyright 1989; reprinted by permission of Verso Books.

class and a newer immigrant proletariat. Soja (1989) uses census data to map (see, for example, figure 2) the spatial polarization of class that has arisen with economic restructuring, where an emerging yuppie-managerial class works in producer-service and high-tech industries located in new business centers on the periphery of Los Angeles, while a diminishing or squeezed working class, disciplined by deindustrialization and a growing immigrant reserve army, remains in the older manufacturing core.

With deindustrialization and the disappearance of the traditional working class, these urban commentators point to a decline of class consciousness and class-based politics: either firms in the new producer- and consumer-service industries, such as WalMart, vow to keep unions out, or workers in these industries lack the tradition of unification and contestation that characterized the modern urban proletariat. Or both. In any case, agents are seen as increasingly oppressed and disoriented by a fragmented and commodified built environment. In place of traditional class politics has emerged a variety of new social movements based on divergent group identities that have filled the class void in increasingly polarized urban spaces (Gibson and Graham 1992; Gibson 1998).

One can detect (at least) two directions taken by cartographers of postmodern urbanism in response to these changes. One strategic response has been the call for a "cognitive mapping" of postmodern space (Jameson 1988). The political motivation of such a mapping is to resituate individuals out of the microcosmic, privatized, disoriented space of postmodern urban life back onto a more basic, collectivized, *class* terrain, thus reinvigorating class-based struggles for social change. Jameson hopes that his suggested mappings of postmodern space may put us back on track toward a true, multinational socialist politics. Similarly, Davis (1987; 1992) asserts a revolutionary hope that the working classes of the inner city, now a "sleeping dragon" marked by anomic protest, may awaken to their collective power and coherently oppose the repressive, disorienting scan/scam-scapes of postmodernism.

While some argue for a reassertion of class-based analysis and politics in the face of postmodern fragmentation, others call for its abandonment and a recognition instead of the plurality of social positions and movements in postmodern society. Gottdiener (1985, 286), for example, wants to move beyond Marxian political economy and make "a clean break with . . . some abstraction called the working class," focusing instead on transforming the variegated social relations of Late Capitalism in the spaces of everyday life. Along similar lines, Swanstrom (1993, 56) remarks that in the present context of political divergence, "Marxist notions that class solidarities will overcome" balkanized identities "seem hopelessly naive and behind the times." For purposes here, these positions represent two sides of one coin. They tend to understand postmodern spatial logics as an inversion of modernist forms; in their inverted postmodern form class structures are fragmented, communities are decentered, and agents are beguiled by Disneyfied built environments. Despite their differing calls for reassertion versus abandonment of class-based identity and struggle, cartographers of contemporary urbanism tend to agree that with postmodern restructuring comes the demise of the traditional working class and loss of its agency (Gibson and Graham 1992).

In this essay, I offer an alternative mapping of Los Angeles that shows class relations and politics not as polarized and declining but as socially prevalent and spatially ubiquitous. I use a definition of class that circumvents the conflation of identities associated with race, income, or occupational status with those derived from relationship to a class process—the production of surplus labor, its appropriation, and distribution. By identifying a range of different types of exploitation (or class processes) that coexist in any one locale, I attempt a form of social area analysis that works against the dual homogenizing and differentiating tendencies inherent in the mapping of urban ecology.[4] My purpose here is to question the commonly accepted story about social and spatial polarization with its attendant stalemate between reassertion versus abandonment of class-based identity and struggle.

The alternative mapping offered here creates a picture of spatial simultaneity and social heterogeneity that is very different from that produced via modernist techniques of urban analysis. In the "Postmodern Understandings of Urban Space" section of this chapter I attempt to demonstrate how such a disorderly and decentered sociospatial analysis might offer new possibilities for thinking about class, postmodern politics, and postmodern urban spaces.

Specifying Class

While I am not advocating reassertion of the traditional centering of class as the social foundation for analysis and change, neither am I willing to abandon class-based knowledge and politics in favor of more diverse, new social identities. But in order to constitute class as a significant feature of social experience, I must first specify what I mean by it. Despite its centrality in critical urban analysis, the meaning of "class" is slippery and often not strictly defined. The term usually refers to a group to which one belongs, based variously on one's income level, racial identity, relation to the extraction of surplus (i.e., exploitation), position in the labor market, occupation, or property ownership (specifically home ownership).[5] When it comes to mapping class, some composite of these social indicators is usually deployed to generate a pattern of class-differentiated urban space (in the style of the maps shown in figures 1 and 2). The tradition of social area analysis and urban ecology has produced clear expectations that cities are mappable into working class, or lower socioeconomic status areas, and high status areas occupied by the middle and upper classes. And studies of gentrification, like the earlier analyses of urban invasion and succession, have shown that this mapping is always in motion.

I am interested in exploring how a different meaning of class might yield a different class mapping of the city and potentially contribute to new political strategies, ones not limited by the structured dualisms of the social polarization thesis or the modernist vision of capital-labor struggle. I employ a simple (rather than composite) meaning of class, defined in terms of the production, appropriation, and distribution of surplus labor, that is, exploitation and the distribution of its fruits (Resnick and Wolff 1987). This allows me to identify city dwellers (and thereby urban space) in terms of a range of class positions associated with different class processes. The variety and "disorder" of the analysis is aimed at bringing to light current opportunities for class struggle that may have been obscured by social polarization theory and associated mappings of sociospatial "order."[6]

Class, as exploitation, is a "lacuna"[7] in most social analysis. My attempt to make it visible, to si(gh)te this meaning of class in the urban form, should be taken as a strategic anti-essentialist intervention into current debates in urban studies. The mapping presented here seeks to avoid reductionist arguments about the determining or foundational role of class in urban structure or claims about necessary relationships between class and other nonclass identities (such as those that derive from racial, cultural, or legal processes) that have burdened much of critical urban theory. This focused mapping, while eschewing essentialism, might nonetheless be seen, borrowing from feminist theory, as a "strategic essentialism" (Schor and Weed 1994).[8] It is a strategy of mapping or imposing one meaning of class onto individuals along with all their other self-known or socially imposed identities.

In imposing a mapping of class onto individuals who might not understand themselves in (these) class terms, one could say that individuals are, in the language of postmodern architecture, "double coded" (Jencks 1984). We could see a popular code, or knowledge of people's identities, roles, and motivations, overlain by an avant-garde code, deploying the neologism of "class," where class is not a foundational girder but where, rather, it may serve as a strategic focal point for knowledge and change. In borrowing the language of postmodern architecture, I do not mean to suggest that this class mapping is elitist, superimposing a privileged, "scientific" knowledge (of class) on a local, "ideological" knowledge. Rather, I recognize that many competing class knowledges coexist, each vying for a place in the political imaginary and agenda. While none can be said to be more "real" than others, my project of mapping offers an alternate class representation that might afford a different urban political imaginary.

Remapping Los Angeles

In mapping class in Los Angeles, I borrow from other cartographers of postmodern space the technique of using U.S. census data to construct social indicators that act as surrogates for class. Unlike other practitioners, however, I disentangle class (as exploitation) from race, occupation, and ownership in an attempt to leave space for the complex articulations of class with these other nonclass relations. Obviously, the U.S. census does not collect data on exploitation because class, in this sense, is not one of the realities reified by census knowledge production. Possibly because of its potentially transformative consequences, the surplus labor meaning of class has tended to be dismissed as political, biased, or propagandistic and has never gone through the inversion of becoming an independently existing object, measured by social scientists (cf. Latour and Woolgar 1986).

The transformation of census labor force categories into Marxian class categories might best be understood, borrowing from Althusser (1970a, 183–92), as a "theoretical practice" or a process of knowledge production. This production process involves generating new class "facts" by respecifying the class-ifications employed by census takers (particularly the occupational, industrial, and legal or property ownership classifications) in terms of the Marxian concepts of exploitation and surplus distribution.[9]

In the mapping presented here, I distinguish between different kinds of capitalist as well as other, noncapitalist, class positions that individuals can occupy. Not all enterprises in the city are sites of capitalist exploitation, nor are all those who work for a wage members of a capitalist working class.[10] Some firms are, of course, capitalist exploiters—including those global corporations that receive so much attention in the postmodernization/globalization literature. In these firms, direct producers and appropriators of surplus value occupy capitalist appropriative class positions; other employees, such as managers, who provide conditions for the continued existence of surplus production and are paid out of distributions of appropriated surplus, occupy capitalist distributive class positions.

Noncapitalist enterprises include the small businesses of the self-employed who appropriate their own surplus labor in an "independent" or "ancient" class process (Gabriel 1990; Resnick and Wolff 1987; Hindess and Hirst 1975). These enterprises unite the production and appropriation of surplus labor within a single individual. Still other enterprises—those that make a profit not through exploitation but through "buying cheap and selling dear" (i.e., merchanting), or that otherwise receive a distributed share of already produced surplus (e.g., in return for lending money, leasing land, etc.)—may not be involved in appropriative class relations at all. They are understood as also involved in distributive class relations, receiving a share of already produced surplus in return for providing conditions of existence for capitalist or other forms of surplus production. Employees of these enterprises are understood as involved in nonclass relations because they do not directly produce or receive distributions of surplus value. Yet other enterprises and individuals in the city may be seen as engaged in what Harvey (1989) terms "patriarchal," or what I call "feudal," relations where family members are obliged to work in the patriarch's business and are then looked after in kind by the appropriator—the business "lord." Perhaps the least documented of economic activities is that of communal or collectivist production in which the surplus labor of members of a collective enterprise is communally appropriated and distributed to agreed-upon ends. Figure 3 summarizes the different class positions associated with this range of class processes.[11]

	Class Position			
	Fundamental		Subsumed	Nonclass
Class Process	Direct Producers of Surplus	Surplus Appropriators[a]	Receivers of Distributed Shares	Second Receivers of Distributed Shares
Capitalist	Exploited sellers of labor power[b]	Capitalist appropriators	Managers, merchants, etc.[b]	Employees of merchants, etc.[b]
Independent (or ancient)	Self-exploited individuals[b]	Self-appropriators	"	"[b]
Feudal (or patriarchal)	Exploited family members[b]	Business patriarchs	"	"[b]
Communal	Members of a collective	Members of a collective	"	"

Note: Individuals can simultaneously and sequentially occupy more than one class position.
[a]Once appropriated, surplus is then distributed by appropriators to the various receivers of distributed shares.
[b]Positions empirically mapped in this paper.

Figure 3. Some Marxian class positions and occupants.

It is important to note that in this conception of class, each individual can occupy multiple class, as well as multiple nonclass, positions. For example, a worker in a capitalist enterprise may participate in an exploitative capitalist class process at work, a communal class process at home in a collectively organized household, and work on the weekends and evenings in an independent class process as a self-employed dressmaker.

This meaning of class leads to an image of the city in which class relations are seen as irreducibly heterogeneous and multiple rather than simply "convened within the plenary geography of capitalism" (Gregory 1990, 82). What this vision of class liberates in terms of the possibilities of mapping economic difference and multiple economic subjectivities is, however, way ahead of the representational capabilities of available data sets and mapping techniques. While census data can help to construct a sense of the class mosaic of the L.A. region, it may not give as complicated or accurate a mosaic as some other raw material. For example, a different census might explicitly ask about relations to surplus production and distribution, specifically recording whether one directly produces, appropriates/distributes, or receives distributed shares of surplus, and if so in what form (e.g., capitalist, independent, feudal, communal, etc.). Further, such a census might "double count" people, showing not just the primary class position with which they identify, but their multiple class positions (e.g., second and third jobs, receipt of dividends or wage premiums, household labor, and so forth). Such a census may sound like an accounting nightmare to unaccustomed ears, but all census classifications have evolved over the decades, none starting out with the clarity we (seemingly) find today (see U.S. Department of Commerce 1989).[12]

In any census schedule, those who are classified as members of the labor force provide information on their self-perceived primary source of employment while their work in households, communities, and other businesses goes unaccounted. The census classifies the labor force in three different ways: by the *industry* in which each worker is employed (i.e., by Standard Industrial Classification [SIC] code), by the *occupation* of each worker (i.e., by Standard Occupational Classification [SOC] code), and by the *class* (or type of ownership of the employing organization) of each worker (CW).[13] These classifications are summarized in figures 4, 5, and 6.

Census data does not permit a literal transformation into the class categories in figure 3. It does not provide the raw materials for seeing the multiple class positions of any one worker nor for seeing the appropriators (e.g., corporate boards of directors) as well as some receivers of distributed shares of surplus (e.g., landlords, shareholders, etc.). And while the disaggregation by class allows for the identification of those who are independent self-appropriators, there is no way of discerning the prevalence of the very sorts of class processes (viz. democratic, communal, etc.) toward which we might want to struggle.

Despite the shortcomings of U.S. census data for the purposes of this analysis, it is possible to make some approximations about the class positions occupied by those in the labor force if certain simple transformations are performed.[14] For example, looking first at the class categorization used by the U.S. census, I have made the following assumptions and translations:

1. Each for-profit wage and salary worker, CW_1, is assumed to sell his/her labor power on the labor market to a capitalist (who has thrown a sum of money into circulation to valorize it);

2. All government workers, CW_2, and all not-for-profit wage and salary workers, CW_5, can be said to occupy nonclass positions assuming, despite convincing arguments to the contrary, that these workers neither produce, appropriate, distribute, nor receive distributed shares of surplus value;[15]

3. All self-employed workers, CW_3, can be said to occupy independent class positions, assuming that each of these workers produces, appropriates, and distributes his or her own surplus labor;

4. All unpaid family workers, CW_4, can be said to occupy feudal class positions, assuming that each of these workers produces use values that are appropriated by the business lord who in turn provides food, clothing, and shelter for the worker.

SIC_1 = workers employed in industries in SIC codes 01–09 (agriculture, forestry, fisheries)
SIC_2 = workers in SIC codes 10–14 (mining)
SIC_3 = workers in SIC 15–17 (construction)
SIC_4 = workers in SIC 20–23 and 26–31 (nondurable manufacturing)
SIC_5 = workers in SIC 24, 25, and 32–39 (durable manufacturing)
SIC_6 = workers in SIC 40–47 (transportation)
SIC_7 = workers in SIC 48–49 (communications and public utilities)
SIC_8 = workers in SIC 50–51 (wholesale trade)
SIC_9 = workers in SIC 52–59 (retail trade)
SIC_{10} = workers in SIC 60–67 (finance, insurance, and real estate [FIRE])
SIC_{11} = workers in SIC 73, 75, 76 (business and repair services)
SIC_{12} = workers in SIC 70, 72, 88 (personal services)
SIC_{13} = workers in SIC 78, 79 (entertainment and recreation services)
SIC_{14} = workers in SIC 80 (health services)
SIC_{15} = workers in SIC 82 (educational services)
SIC_{16} = workers in SIC 81, 83–87, 89 (other professional services)
SIC_{17} = workers in SIC 91–99 (public administration)
SIC_{18} = unemployed workers

Figure 4. Industry of worker, SIC_i ($i = 1$–18).

SOC_1 = workers employed in occupations in SOC codes 11–14 (exec, admin, managerial)
SOC_2 = workers in SOC codes 16–34 (professional specialty)
SOC_3 = workers in SOC 36–39, 825 (technicians and related support)
SOC_4 = workers in SOC 40–44 (sales)
SOC_5 = workers in SOC 45–47 (administrative support including clerical)
SOC_6 = workers in SOC 50 (private household)
SOC_7 = workers in SOC 51 (protective service)
SOC_8 = workers in SOC 52 (other service)
SOC_9 = workers in SOC 55–58 (farming, forestry, fishing)
SOC_{10} = workers in SOC 60–69, 71 (precision production, craft, repair)
SOC_{11} = workers in SOC 73–78 (machine operators, assemblers, and inspectors)
SOC_{12} = workers in SOC 81–83 (transportation and material movers)
SOC_{13} = workers in SOC 85–87 (handlers, equipment cleaners, helpers, and laborers)
SOC_{14} = unemployed workers

Figure 5. Occupation of worker, SOC_j ($j = 1$–14).

CW_1 = for-profit wage and salary workers
CW_2 = government workers
CW_3 = self-employed workers
CW_4 = unpaid family workers
CW_5 = not-for-profit wage and salary workers
CW_6 = unemployed workers

Figure 6. "Class" of worker, CW_k ($k = 1$–6).

This initial transformation of census classes into Marxian classes is summarized in figure 7. At this point in the transformation, the category CW_1 includes a range of class positions that could be further specified using information provided by the industry and occupational classifications. Figure 8

Census Classes	Marxian Class
Self-employed (CW_3)	Independents
Unpaid family workers (CW_4)	Feudals
Government and not-for-profit wage and salary workers ($CW_2 + CW_5$)	Nonclass
Unemployed workers (CW_6)	Unemployed
For-profit wage and salary workers (CW_1)	Capitalist fundamental + capitalist subsumed + nonclass

Figure 7. Transformation of census classes into Marxian classes.

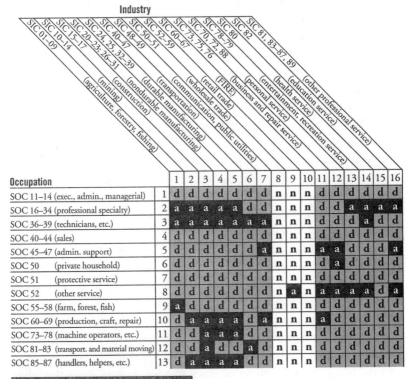

Figure 8. **C** matrix: The transformation of CW_1 into capitalist appropriative, distributive, and nonclass positions.

presents the transformational schema used to identify (from the cross tabulation of industry and occupational data) those workers assumed to occupy a capitalist appropriative class position, those occupying a capitalist distributive class position, and those who work in capitalist employment in a nonclass position. The assumptions and mechanics of this specification are detailed in the appendix.

This transformed labor-force data was calculated for all the subregions of Los Angeles and the results are presented in figure 9, which shows the prevalence of some of the identified class positions/processes in each of the census subregions of Los Angeles. Figure 9 is not a map in the conventional sense, but it shows that class in its various forms is scattered fairly evenly throughout the landscape. If we were to map the spatial distribution of class positions, a relatively homogeneous surface would result. While there are indeed racial, occupational, and income polarizations in the L.A. landscape, as Davis's and Soja's maps clearly portray, when distinguished from these other relations, class positions are, by contrast, quite uniform across all subregions of Los Angeles.

This map is based on an understanding of class position as one in the ensemble of identity positions people occupy. Like gender or ethnicity or sexuality, class is just one of the many processes in which people participate that push and pull their identities and politics in myriad, conflicting directions. Rather than using the language of polarization, the terms "ubiquitous," "heterogeneous," and "multiple" might more accurately describe the jumble of class processes and positions characterizing the late twentieth-century L.A. landscape. Los Angeles can be understood as an articulation of class and nonclass processes that interrelate and constitute one another in an unevenly developing social whole. This understanding has interesting implications for critical urban theory.

Cities, since at least the 1920s, have been represented in terms of an assortment of class and nonclass relations—socioeconomic status, ethnicity, and family status, to name the most commonly identified dimensions of differentiation. The goal of urban analysis has been to uncover a correlative and spatial order to these phenomena and to map (and explain) their changing pattern in terms of a historically evolving urban structure. Urban studies has been driven by the imperative to *differentiate* social areas within the city with the result that indicators that establish homogeneity across the urban area have been discarded as uninteresting. What, after all, does a map of sameness show?

The class mapping in figure 9 emerges from a new urban paradigm (cf. Arvidson 1995) and charts a different terrain. This paradigm is not new in the

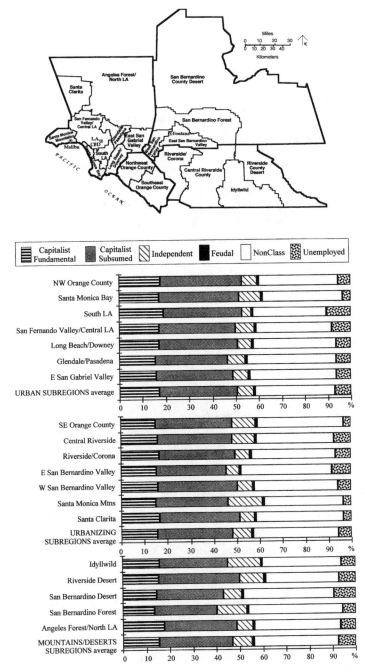

Figure 9. Labor force class positions (as a percentage of subregional labor forces). Subregional definitions are based on those of the Southern California Association of Governments (1989). Source: U.S. Bureau of the Census (1990). Map copyright 1995; reprinted by permission of EA Planning Associates.

sense that some urban theorists mean when they use the concept of a "new paradigm" to signal an emerging (postmodern) urban ontology whose truth is now captured by L.A. School theories, the way early to mid-twentieth-century urban reality was captured by Chicago School models (see, for example, Downs [1994] or Hise et al. [1996]). Rather, it is new in the sense of a novel way of understanding urban society (what Gibson and Watson [1995, 7] call a "postmodern paradigm of knowledge" or what Soja [1995, 135] terms a "simcity"). By itself a rather thin factoid, class can contribute, when overlaid with other maps of race, income, occupation, etc., to an increasingly complex knowledge of urban relations and identities. In such a layering, it becomes clear that class relations and identities (represented as ubiquitous, multiple, and heterogeneous) are articulated differently at different sites given the class and nonclass specificities of each site. These differently articulated relations and identities are always in motion, producing an unevenly developing social whole (McIntyre 1992).

The class polarization-and-decline story sees postmodern urban structure as deviating from certain established patterns and practices of modern urban society in ways that worry and anger those social critics who are invested in traditional class politics, while being accepted by others who have come to embrace a postclass politics. The mapping presented here skirts the issue of sociospatial mutation[16] by suggesting that both modern and postmodern urban society can be represented as contradictory ensembles of class and nonclass relations. Workers have always occupied a variety of class and nonclass positions that push and pull their agencies in conflicting directions. What has changed is how we might understand urban society as shaped by class processes and how we might act on that understanding.

Postmodern Understandings of Urban Space

In this section of the chapter I undertake a rereading of two subregions of the L.A. landscape in the light of the class mapping presented above. I am fortunate to have an excellent source to draw on in Mike Davis's incredibly rich and panoramic book, *City of Quartz*. This qualitative work pulls together various detailed accounts into a complex mosaic of postmodern Los Angeles. With much appreciation I attempt a class reading of Fontana (located in the East San Bernardino Valley subregion) and to a lesser extent Malibu (located in the Santa Monica Mountains subregion) based on Davis's as well as local media accounts. Figure 9 shows that these subregions are similar in the sense that slightly less than 50 percent of the labor force is employed in capitalist appropriative or distributive class positions, but Fontana's subregion has a higher percentage of unemployed and Malibu's a higher percentage of independent, self-appropriating workers.

Midcentury Fontana, described by Davis (1990, 398) as "a colorful but dissonant *bricolage*," was the site of a Kaiser Steel plant and thus home to modern industrial workers, occupying capitalist appropriative class positions. These workers sold their labor power on the market to the industrial giant Kaiser and produced surplus value that was appropriated by its board of directors. Kaiser also employed managers, bookkeepers, secretaries, sales personnel, and others who, though not directly involved in the production of steel, reproduced through their work the conditions under which steel making and the production of surplus value could continue. These workers, some of whom lived in Fontana while others (particularly upper-level management) commuted in from such neighboring genteel towns as Redlands, occupied capitalist distributive class positions.

In the 1950s Fontana was also home to a concentration of over-the-road truckers. Workers in this industry historically have tended to be either self-employed independents or wage laborers for capitalist trucking firms. Indeed the history of trucking and trucking regulation can be seen as a site of conflict between these two class processes, where the "logic" of neither destines it to eliminate or colonize the other (Fried and Wolff 1994). In addition to exploited and distributive industrial capitalist workers, independent and capitalist truckers, Fontana also was the home of a number of steel support industries as well as of merchants and professionals who serviced its generally blue-collar population. These workers occupied a variety of class as well as nonclass positions, depending on their relations to surplus production and distribution.

The class structure as articulated with the occupational and industrial structures of such a blue-collar town as midcentury Fontana is thus clearly a "bricolage" as Davis states. To further diversify this class vision, we could consider the multiple class positions any one worker may have held. For example, steelworkers at Kaiser were also members of the United Steel Workers union so that their wages contained, over and above the value of labor power, a "monopoly payment" or premium, a distribution back to them of some of the surplus value produced on the job, negotiated by the union under threat of collective withholding of labor power if such a payment was not included in the wage. They thus occupied, in addition to their capitalist appropriative class positions as producers of surplus value, capitalist distributive class positions as receivers of distributed shares of that surplus. Some steelworkers also held independent class positions moonlighting as stuntmen for the film industry or working as weekend yeoman farmers of fruit or chickens, the latter the result of an earlier real estate promotion effort by the Fontana Farms Company to bring "Jeffersonian autonomy" to the San Bernardino Valley.

Such a diversity of class relations contributed to complex individual class identities and to a class politics that was pulled in multiple directions. As self-identified exploited wage laborers, for example, workers may have had a strong sense of solidarity with each other as workers, joined the union, and tended toward radical class politics. As receivers of distributed shares of surplus, they may have also sympathized with New Deal statist support of the economy. But as independents, workers may have identified with more laissez-faire politics, questioning their union affiliations.[17] Workers' identities and struggles were thus factionalized by their various and multiple class positions.

Workers' nonclass positions, of course, also impacted their identities and actions. For example, the distribution of income in the steel workers' community politically divided the rank and file because some older workers' incomes, distributed under an incentive plan, were higher than those of younger workers distributed under a sharing plan. Such income disparities may have undermined feelings of solidarity among coworkers or also may have reinforced their self-identity as moonlighting independent. Further, despite the "aura of sunshine and prosperity, . . . there were also increasing undertones of bigotry and racial hysteria. . . . In the mill, Blacks and Chicanos were confined to the dirtiest departments—coke ovens and blast furnaces (a situation unchanged until the early 1970s)" (Davis 1990, 399).

Racist divisions of labor reinforced racist discourse among whites to justify the discrimination and protect their positions. White workers themselves were divided among ethnic identities—Poles, Slovenes, Italians, Okies, etc.—that also influenced their political allegiances in different ways. Identification with one or another racial or ethnic group may have reinforced solidarity along ethnic lines, further undermining class alliances.

The modern urban landscape of Fontana is thus clearly an ensemble of identities and political allegiances resulting from the varied and multiple class and nonclass positions of workers. Which of these sets of relations and political alignments reflects the "real" Fontana? Proletarian identifications and struggles are clearly important, but they are only one of many class and nonclass struggles in which people are involved. Only by essentializing certain aspects of reality and marginalizing others can one say that identification with, for example, capitalist wage labor and class struggles against exploitation are coherent and visionary, while other identifications with, for example, the self-employed business sector or urban environmentalists are disoriented (Gibson and Graham 1992). The role of urban theory here is not to normatively assert the primacy of proletarian class relations, but to see the multiple and contradictory realities that produce engagement with class identity and politics in some individuals and unconcern in others.

Contemporary Articulations and Implications for Class Politics

If this mapping is indeed a new way of seeing urban society, it does not necessarily then imply that there is nothing new or different about postmodern urbanism other than the gaze. Recent studies amply document the wide variety of tumultuous changes in technology, demographics, industrial and occupational structures, etc., that characterize the postmodern landscape—all fusing together in the contemporary conjuncture to produce "urban restructuring." Class structures have also been transformed, but rather than becoming polarized they could be seen as differently articulated.

In Fontana the Kaiser steel plant closed in 1983. Thousands of steelworkers lost their jobs, while a deunionized portion managed to secure capitalist class positions with the reconstituted California Steel Industries (CSI, a multinational consortium that purchased and began to run the remaining viable portions of the old Kaiser plant [Davis 1990]). While the subregion's unemployment rate is still exceptionally high, other Fontanans now hold capitalist, independent, and nonclass positions as truckers, construction workers in the Inland Empire's burgeoning construction industry, workers in incipient spectacle industries such as Fontana's new NASCAR track, and sales personnel in the growing number of consumer service establishments serving a population that has more than doubled in the past decade. Fontana's contemporary class structure, while differently articulated, is no less a bricolage than half a century ago.

Its diverse class structure is in fact, as figure 9 shows, similar to that of other subregions across Los Angeles. What distinguishes it from, say, Malibu, another "edge" city whose population more than doubled during the 1980s, is not its class structure per se but its particular articulations of class and nonclass aspects. The nonclass structures—of occupation, industry, income, race, and so on—of the Fontana area are very different from those of Malibu. While the Fontana area is racially and ethnically mixed, Malibu is strikingly homogeneous in these dimensions; Fontana is home to a relative predominance of workers in blue-collar occupations, while Malibu is home to a predominance of workers in white-collar occupations; relatively more of Fontana's residents work in construction and transportation as well as consumer service industries, while relatively more of Malibu's residents work in entertainment and professional services as well as real estate and finance industries; the median household income in Malibu is nearly twice that in Fontana. Add to these contrasts sociophysical conditions such as the fact that Malibu's only major artery, State Highway 1, radiates along the smog-free temperate coast and is closed to commercial trucks, while Fontana, situated in a smog-filled inland valley, is at the junction of two cross-country interstates.

If we were to focus on the contrasts of income, race, occupation, and environmental amenity between the two subregions and define one or more of these as indicators of class, it would be easy to produce a story of increased social polarization. And, as we have seen, just such a story is often produced. This story points to the supposed blindness to class and the eclipse of a politics of solidarity and compassion that must be addressed either by resort to a reasserted class politics or the move beyond class into more contemporary forms of struggle. With an alternative meaning of class, on the other hand, class emerges not as polarized but as both ubiquitous and variously constituted. From this perspective, struggles over surplus labor production, appropriation, and distribution are not necessarily absent but are rather invisible, in the sense of being "unread," or are hidden within other struggles that are publicly defined in nonclass terms. A number of NIMBY-inspired ("not in my backyard") movements have, for example, risen in recent years in Los Angeles, and Malibu and Fontana are no exceptions. In these movements, local self-interest and environmental concerns appear to define the nature of the struggles. These conflicts, however, can be read as also involving a number of class struggles overdetermined by the nonclass specificities of each place.

Malibu, for example, is a place where class struggle, particularly if looked for from within the traditional capital-labor opposition, seems practically absent. It was settled originally as an exurban "colony" of homes and ancillary businesses for professionals related to the movie industry, soon drawing other wealthy moguls (e.g., oil magnate J. Paul Getty), ranchers, realtors, and a variety of surfers and beach-types. Only recently incorporated as a city, it was long under the jurisdiction of the avidly prodevelopment L.A. County Board of Supervisors. In fact, its abrupt growth since the 1980s, coupled with a developer-backed county plan to build a $43 million sewer system to replace its use of septic tanks, propelled residents to ally themselves against not only the sewerage plan and progrowth efforts, but against county jurisdiction itself and for more local control. In a successful drive to incorporate, the resident coalition finally defeated the Board of Supervisors and its plan, aided by a recommendation by the California Coastal Commission against the sewerage project on environmental grounds.

From the perspective developed here, Malibu's class structure is much like Fontana's, a bricolage (see figure 9). Malibu has long been home to a disproportionately greater number of independents than other areas of Los Angeles, spanning a variety of occupational and income positions, including an assortment of writers, producers, artists, and entertainers; high-end realtors, architects, and developers; independent contractors retained by Hughes' R&D labs and other high-tech or professional service firms; and small shop owners/workers catering to the local and tourist trade. It is also home to a number of appropriative and distributive workers employed in the *capitalist* sector, working, for example, for Pepperdine University, Hughes Labs, the J. Paul Getty Museum, and the large number of Malibu restaurants. These capitalist and independent workers may also occupy other class positions (at home, on a second job, or on different tasks at their primary job), as well as a variety of nonclass positions. When articulated with its industrial, occupational, and other nonclass structures, Malibu's class structure produces identities and politics that are quite different from Fontana's.

In the late 1980s, the County Board of Supervisors, funded in part by class and nonclass revenues in the form of property tax receipts, prepared its plan and amassed backing from major developers. In support of the county plan, Pepperdine University, publicly neutral in the sewer system fight, secretly diverted shares of existing surplus value from accumulation and other allocations to purchase millions of dollars of Malibu real estate in anticipation of the new sewerage facilities and the ensuing development opportunities.

Many workers at Pepperdine, on the other hand, unaware that their appropriated surplus was going to aid development, rallied with other Malibu residents, donating time and personal income in a pitched battle against pro-development forces, fearful that with development "Vals" (people from the San Fernando Valley) and other undesirables might move in and overcrowd their coveted way of life. Key among the antigrowth coalition were many of Malibu's *independent* workers, who diverted shares of self-appropriated surplus to fund the cityhood movement. Identifying with independent ideologies of Jeffersonian autonomy, these workers resented the power of big county government and risked a squeeze on their surplus to support what they believed would be greater local control: incorporation as a city. Environmental agencies, such as the California Coastal Commission and the Santa Monica Mountains Parkland acquisition agency, also funded in part by class and nonclass revenues in the form of tax receipts, joined on this side of the battle as well.

The battle for cityhood thus involved, on one side, a coalition of state agencies and residents working in the capitalist and independent sectors who contributed time, personal income, and shares of independent surplus and, on the other side, other state agencies along with capitalist appropriators contributing shares of surplus value produced by direct laborers.

The procityhood coalition was, however, only temporary. In an ironic twist, the same independents who ardently supported incorporation are now fighting the new city hall against a proposed home-based business license and tax. The city is proposing the license and tax as a way of ensuring that otherwise unregulated home-based businesses are in compliance with zoning codes as well as a way of raising new revenues for expanding city services. Many independents are furious with the proposal, couching the issues again in environmental and anti-big-government terms. They claim, among other things, that the regulation could drive many of them out of their homes and into leased space, increasing commuting, traffic congestion, and air pollution. Yet such a regulation could also squeeze independent producers, compelling them to pump out more surplus in an effort to cover growing demands on their surplus including, in addition to the tax or increased rent, rising health insurance costs and increased technology and telecommunications costs in an increasingly electronic age. If this struggle were understood in class terms, independents, perhaps aided by city planners, might try to identify initiatives that could help them increase their rate of self-appropriation, such as reducing necessary labor relative to surplus through cheapened commuting costs (such as better public transportation). Or they might consider leasing space alongside other independents in a sort of "incubator" arrangement where surplus distributions for health insurance, telecommunications, and other conditions of production could be pooled and shared (Gibson-Graham 1996, 169–70).

In contemporary Fontana, there is also considerable conflict over NIMBY issues. An odd-couple coalition of property developers, new commuting residents, and environmentalists is opposed to any continued steel production in the area, while the small group of remaining steelworkers and other old-timers have formed an antigrowth coalition to protect their accustomed way of life. This conflict can also be read in class terms.

In 1970s Fontana, the value of workers' labor time (and the marketability of Kaiser steel) was being undermined by cheap state-of-the-art imports and a dated plant. This threat to the existence of surplus value was compounded by increased competing demands on surplus *distribution*. On one side, the union, long divided by pay inequalities, went on strike demanding shares of existing surplus for fairer payment and incentive schemes. The company agreed, temporarily quieting workers, while at the same time hedging against threats to surplus production by bleeding the existing mass of surplus to support investment in raw material sites in Australia and Canada for export to Kaiser's main competitors in Japan. The irony of this strategy was not lost on workers who, in a last-ditch effort to save the plant, demanded allocation of a portion of surplus for plant modernization. The company again agreed, then further diverted shares of surplus to hire expensive new managers and administrators to execute the plan. At the same time, other demands were made on surplus by state-mandated cleanup of land and air pollution. Indeed, in another ironic move, Kaiser reallocated over half its modernization budget to fund environmental cleanup (Davis 1990). After trying to resolve the contradictions by blaming workers, and engaging in both concessions and mass layoffs, Kaiser finally closed the plant.

Today, the remaining steelworkers employed by CSI, demoralized by two decades of pay cuts, layoffs, and union busting, are still divided among themselves and with their neighbors over what demands to make on CSI's appropriated surplus. On the one hand, the workers, their families, and other residents have experienced the consequences, including increased cancer rates, asthma cases, and so forth, of the "spreading plume of soil and groundwater contamination that is the legacy of forty years of steelmaking" (Davis 1990, 429). On the other hand, steelworkers and the local state are fearful of further capital flight if they demand that CSI distribute a larger share of surplus toward environmental cleanup. Thinking in class terms, one possibility is that steelworkers, other residents, and the local state—taking the risk of prompting further capital flight—might engage in "distributive class politics" (Gibson-Graham 1996, 165–67). In other words, in their subject positions as local stakeholders they might begin to pressure CSI to distribute shares of surplus toward environmental cleanup or toward setting up grant and loan funds to support alternative (including noncapitalist) work opportunities, particularly for current or unemployed steelworkers who may already be moonlighting or working as self-employed independents but need a boost to make their enterprises sustaining and viable.

These actual and envisioned class struggles in Fontana and Malibu have very different foci and conditions given the different nonclass relations that overdetermine class processes and politics in each place. Yet what is common to both cases is the concern for how surplus distributions are controlled and deployed. Despite the differences between the two places and the nonclass terms in which the struggles are typically defined, the analysis shows how people everywhere are involved in processes of surplus labor production, appropriation, and distribution and engaged in various types of struggle around particular aspects of the class process. This vision of similarity has the potential to reinvigorate discussions about class movements, not because these relations are deeper and more basic than others, but because they are wider and more ordinary than others. What is more, this reading of class in the L.A. landscape has the potential to break down the representation of a city polarized into two opposed "classes," fractured mirror images with the misery of one seemingly caused by the luxury of the other.

The analysis also "smashes" capitalism as a singular hegemonic formation to which all participants in class are automatically subject (Gibson-Graham 1993, 1996),[18] showing a range of class processes coexisting in any one area. Across the region as a whole, less than 50 percent of workers are engaged in capitalist class relations. By displacing capitalism as the only definer of class and by decentering social and personal identity from class, this analysis produces the potential to envision a range of alliances across class and nonclass positions in the urban scene. For instance, in Fontana it might be possible to bring new and old residents, and workers and environmentalists, together in their concerns over surplus distribution to fight for corporate and state support to facilitate environmentally sustainable community economic development that generates replacement jobs in the locality while increasing its livability. In Malibu, we could imagine both capitalist and independent workers coming together to articulate common interests around better public transportation, portability of benefits, or communal appropriation and distribution of surplus labor. Class, rather than exacerbating division and conflict, might help inform a different postmodern vision of these communities' economic futures.

Conclusion

Visibility is a complex process. Unless one understands urban reality as having an essence that can be mapped from a single vantage point (the classical epistemology rejected by Althusser and other theorists of a postmodern epistemology), then clearly multiple mappings of the city coexist, each si(gh)ting particular sets of relations, each struggling for a place in the political imaginary. The mapping presented here slices urban life along a class axis, while others slice urban reality along other axes. These multiple mappings need not necessarily be construed as mutually exclusive, but rather can be overlain to show the contradictory diversity of subject positions and regional identities.

The point of mapping class (as surplus labor appropriation and distribution) is, literally, to put it on the map. Alongside struggles against racial injustice, unfair income distribution, and occupational segmentation, this mapping hopes to "place" struggles against exploitation and struggles over surplus distribution. As this mapping shows, roughly one quarter of Los Angeles's work force is directly exploited. That is, these workers, despite their many occupational, racial, income, and locational differences, all have the fruits of their labor appropriated from them without compensation or say (in both capitalist and noncapitalist class processes). The remaining three quarters of workers all rely, directly or indirectly, on distributions of appropriated surplus as conditions for their livelihood, despite having no say in the surplus distribution process. By slicing urban life along the class axis, this mapping attempts to show that despite some stark contrasts of postmodern urbanism, exploitation and the distribution of its fruits is still common, mundane, and widespread. At a time when the focus is on urban contrasts, contributing to a discourse of polarization and decline of a politics of affinity, this mapping hopes to focus the gaze on class—not to erase urban difference, but to add a layer of commonality, specifically, class, to the multiple identities and struggles for justice people now engage in.

Appendix

To disaggregate the last entry in figure 7 and specify the capitalist appropriative, distributive, and nonclass positions of CW_1, "for-profit wage and salary workers," the census's categorization of workers by industry and occupation are useful. First, an **X** matrix is constructed, with column headings SIC 1–16 and row headings SOC 1–13.[19] Each cell, x_{ij}, of this 13 × 16 matrix, shows the jth industry's share of workers in occupation i. That is:

$$x_{ij} = SOC_i/TLF * SIC_j/TLF$$
where TLF = total labor force

Thus, x_{11} shows the percentage of workers in SOC_1 (executive, administrative, managerial occupations) that are found in SIC_1 (the agriculture, forestry, and fishing industry). In the Glendale/Pasadena subregion, for example, 13.7 percent of the total subregional labor force was employed in "executive, administrative, or managerial" occupations (SOC_1) in 1990, while 1.4 percent was employed in the "agriculture, forestry, and fishing" industry (SIC_1). Cell x_{11} for the Glendale/Pasadena **X** matrix, then, assumes that 0.2 percent (= .137 * .014) of the total subregional labor force was employed in "executive, etc." positions in the "agriculture, etc." industry in 1990. Similarly, cell x_{15} for Glendale/Pasadena assumes that 13.7 percent of the 9.1 percent employed in the "durable manufacturing" industry are in "executive, etc." positions, or 1.3 percent of the total subregional labor force. And so forth.

Because $\Sigma SOC_i = \Sigma SIC_j = \Sigma CW_k = 100\%$ of the labor force, this $\mathbf{X}$ matrix includes all census classes of workers and does not distinguish between what we've called independents, feudals, etc. The point, however, is to specifically disaggregate CW_1 by occupation and industry in order to specify the capitalist appropriative and distributive, as well as nonclass, positions of these workers. Every element in $\mathbf{X}$ is thus multiplied by the scalar (CW_1/TLF), forming a new matrix, $\mathbf{C}$. Each cell in $\mathbf{C}$, c_{ij}, shows the jth industry's share of workers in occupation i, given, or discounted by, the percentage of the labor force employed as "wage and salary workers with for-profit employers." Thus in the Glendale/Pasadena subregion, where two-thirds of the labor force is employed with for-profit employers (CW1), cell c_{15} assumes that 0.8% (= .666 * .013) of the Glendale/Pasadena labor force is employed with "for-profit employers" in "executive, etc." positions in the "durable manufacturing" industry. Constructing the $\mathbf{C}$ matrix allows some assumptions to be made about the class positions occupied by "for-profit wage and salary workers" in the different occupations employed in different industries. Figure 8 shows these assumptions.[20]

In figure 8, workers with "for-profit employers" in, for example, "executive, etc." occupations (SOC_1) employed in "manufacturing" industries (SIC_4 and SIC_5)—that is, workers in cells c_{14} and c_{15}—are assumed to hold capitalist distributive class positions.[21] Similarly, workers in "sales" occupations (SOC_4) employed in "manufacturing" industries (SIC_4 and SIC_5)— cells c_{44} and c_{45}—also are assumed to occupy capitalist distributive class positions. On the other hand, workers in "sales" occupations (SOC_4) employed in "wholesale" or "retail trade" (SIC_8 and SIC_9)—cells c_{48} and c_{49}—are assumed to hold nonclass positions.[22] Summing cells of similar class positions yields a surrogate measure of the total number of workers occupying capitalist appropriative, distributive, and nonclass positions.

Notes

The author wishes to thank each of the editors for inspiration, and Julie Graham and Kathie Gibson for invaluable guidance.

1. In urban studies the term "postmodernism" has come to mean both a new urban form and a new way of knowing the city (Gibson and Watson 1995). Postmodernism in its epistemological sense is understood as a new form of criticism often linked with anti-essentialism or poststructuralism that engages and challenges modernist forms of knowledge production and control. There is clearly no necessity, despite some theorists arguing so, that so-called postmodern cities be known via

postmodern knowledges nor modern cities via modernist knowledges. In urban studies one finds postmodern critiques of modern cities, modernist critiques of post-modern cities, and so forth, leaving the meanings of these terms anything but settled.

2. Compare this from Soja (1989, 221): "Los Angeles has, more than any other place, become the paradigmatic window through which to see the last half of the twentieth century. I do not mean to suggest that the experience of Los Angeles will be duplicated elsewhere. But just the reverse may indeed be true, that the particular experiences of urban development and change occurring elsewhere in the world are being duplicated in Los Angeles" with this from Garreau (1991, 3): "Every single American city that is growing, is growing in the fashion of Los Angeles."

3. While Davis (1987) does not explicitly define what he means by "class," it is clear that at least in this context he sees it running along race lines. I should note that neither Davis nor Soja sets out to map class in Los Angeles. They are mapping or documenting restructuring, and they offer political prognoses about class conscious-ness and agency based on their analyses. They thus operate with implicit under-standings of class, which I attempt to make explicit in this reading of their maps.

4. In studies of urban ecology any one small area of the city is mapped in terms of associated indicators so that, for instance, a high proportion of residents with low incomes, non-Anglo ethnicity, and occupying rental accommodation would result in the designation of one homogeneous area as "working class," while another, where there is a low proportion of low income residents and a predominance of Anglo eth-nicity and home ownership, would result in the designation "elite."

5. Within critical urban studies the works of, for example, Davis (1987), Katznelson (1992), Soja (1989), and Zukin et al. (1992) deploy such varied meanings of "class."

6. Class struggle, in this view, is not aimed at systemic revolution but at produc-ing more democratic and collectively fair forms of surplus extraction and distribution.

7. The word is from Althusser (1970a). For a discussion of class as a "lacuna" in urban theory see Arvidson (1995).

8. This idea of a strategic essentialism may be seen as a response to two broad concerns that have arisen in debates, both within and outside feminist theory, over anti-essentialism: "First, is it possible consistently to think in antiessentialist ways, or is some essentialist or reductionist argument inevitably reached in any constructed knowledge? Second, may essentialist modes of thought be preferred, at certain times and places, because of their specific, conjunctural effects in changing the world in particular ways?" (Wolff 1996, 151).

9. Althusser (1970a) uses the metaphor of production to understand the for-mation of knowledge and to distinguish his view from that of classical epistemology in which knowledge is a problem of abstraction of truth. In his view, the production of knowledge, like any production process, involves the transformation of a raw ma-terial (in this case, "ideological" or bourgeois knowledge—generality I) into specific products (in this case, "science" or class-focused knowledge—generality III) by set-ting in motion determinate means of production (in this case, "the corpus of concepts

whose more or less contradictory unity constitutes the 'theory' of the science at the (historical) moment under consideration, the 'theory' that defines the field in which all the problems of the science must necessarily be posed"—generality II (Althusser 1970a, 184). See Amariglio (1987) for a critical discussion of Althusser's theory of knowledge and controversial use of the science/ideology distinction.

10. In this paper I only consider class relations in the firm (or enterprise) and not in the household, the informal, or public sectors—sites that are much less visible using census data. Class analyses of these sites have been developed elsewhere (see for example, Fraad et al. [1994] and Arvidson [1996] for analyses of households).

11. This class typology is not dissimilar to Harvey's (1989, 154), who catalogs a growing array of class relations in the contemporary conjuncture, noting that struggles against exploitation will take different forms relative to different kinds of class relations. As argued below, such struggles may indeed be present but not readily visible when viewed from within the traditional capital-labor framework.

12. Qualitative data including participant observations, interviews, and other sources (such as newspaper stories) provide an alternative rich source of empirical information that can be used to garner a sense of people's multiple and contradictory class and nonclass positions. These data cannot, however, provide the coverage that a census allows. The increasing number of government sample surveys collecting statistics on such issues as household labor, and informal and voluntary community work, shows that there is a growing recognition of the contribution that a variety of labor practices (not just those in the formal sector) make to society. Were these additional practices to be included in the census schedule, there would be a much better chance for a more comprehensive class reading of individuals, households, and social areas.

13. Where $\Sigma SIC_j = \Sigma SOC_i = \Sigma CW_k = 100\%$ of the labor force.

14. Of course the labor force in this instance includes only those in the formal sector of the economy, excluding many whom we might see as participating in the economy in a broader sense, such as household labor or those who work in the informal economy.

15. Traditional Marxian theory tends to argue that the state provides conditions of existence of capitalist exploitation but that capitalist class processes themselves do not occur there. One rethinking of this position has been provided by Resnick and Wolff, who argue that the state is not only a site of political processes but also a site of class processes. However, "in the United States, relatively few individuals in the state occupy either the fundamental or subsumed class positions . . . the vast majority of state employees are involved with performing unproductive labor. . . . They do not occupy class positions qua state workers" (Resnick and Wolff 1987, 242). (Note that Resnick and Wolff use the terms "fundamental" and "subsumed" for what I have called appropriative and distributive class positions.) Despite some state workers occupying class positions, it is assumed here, for the sake of simplicity, that the state as a whole is not a site of class. It is also assumed that nonprofit corporations are not sites of exploitation despite the clear possibility of theorizing them as such.

16. Jameson (1988) uses the term "mutation" in describing the postmodernization of space.

17. Kaiser in fact deliberately located his steel plant in rural Fontana "figuring," as Davis puts it, "that hens and citrus might mitigate the class struggle" (1990, 390).

18. See also McIntyre (1996, 232): "The capitalist nature of the United States is more often presumed than proved, perhaps because the question [of whether or not the United States is capitalist] strikes the late-twentieth-century mind as absurd."

19. SOC_{14} and SIC_{18} are excluded from the X matrix because these are the unemployed and are thus assumed neither to sell their labor power on the labor market nor then occupy a capitalist fundamental, subsumed, or nonclass position. The X matrix also excludes SIC_{17} (workers employed in public administration) because all government workers, of which SIC_{17} is a subset, are assumed to hold nonclass positions. Thus the X matrix is 13×16 rather than 14×18.

20. The assumptions made in figure 8 are based on a careful reading and interpretation of the 1990 U.S. census's definitions of SOC and SIC codes in conjunction with the Marxian class literature discussed above. See Arvidson (1996, appendix B) for a detailed explanation.

21. "Managerial supervision provides certain kinds of social behavior among productive workers, without which the production and appropriation of surplus value are jeopardized. For so doing, supervisory personnel obtain subsumed class payments. The same analysis applies to all other managers: in selling their unproductive labor power, they obtain in exchange a subsumed class distribution. Thus the personnel charged with the accumulation of capital similarly comprise subsumed classes" (Resnick and Wolff 1987, 129). Note that Resnick and Wolff use the term "subsumed" to refer to what I have called "distributive" class relations.

22. On the one hand "within the industrial capitalist enterprise, . . . all sales personnel obtain distributed shares of surplus value. Their paychecks all come from the same source: the capitalist's appropriated surplus value. They are all occupants of the subsumed class position of merchant." On the other hand, "the clerks, bookkeepers, and other underlings of the independent merchant are not subsumed class members. They obtain directly no distribution of surplus value from the industrial capitalist. . . . Payments by an independent merchant to all of his or her employees are not class payments" (Resnick and Wolff 1987, 124–25). Note, again, that Resnick and Wolff use the term "subsumed" to designate what I have called "distributive" class relations.

8

Blue Collar, White Collar: Deconstructing Classification

Jacquelyn Southern

Blue collar, white collar—when we hear these words, we believe we know the actors. Who they are, where they are, what they want, how they feel toward society and one another: all these and more are familiar in the late twentieth century. Making their appearance in an extraordinary variety of narratives, these may be our most widely encountered signs of class. So pervasive are they that the vocabulary of different and conflicting collars serves both as one of the most common languages of class and as a well-established guide to social research.

In the social science of this century, the figures of the blue and white collars have played leading roles in the theaters of finance, monopoly, advanced, late, Fordist, and post-Fordist capitalism and the affluent, bureaucratic, managerial, information, and postindustrial societies. Indeed, Marxists and non-Marxists alike have emplotted the dramas of past, present, and future around conflict, contradiction, and antagonism between the two. In their stories, the collars are locked in a win/lose relationship where one gains at the other's expense; invoking their warring personages, for example, Bain says of the growth of white-collar employment that "the clerks have claimed most of the ground yielded by the manual workers" (1970, 13). Despite ambiguities in aggregate comparative trends (Form 1987; Ganzeboom, Treiman, and Ultec 1991; Giddens 1973; Hyman 1980), the blue and white collars are considered a central divide within the workforce and organizing principle of social space; arguing, for instance, that urban residential distribution, though imperfectly realized, follows "a primary bipartite split between white-collar and blue-collar social groups and neighborhoods," Scott attributes this pattern in part to "simple income differentials" between the two (1988, 219–21).

Collar conflict is so well accepted that it can be prepared and described in a casual, even perfunctory manner; thus, in an influential essay attributing the labor movement's misfortunes to sectionalism, Hobsbawm (1981) relied with equal confidence on both the decline of manual labor and the rise of the white collar as the new labor aristocracy. Most recently, collar conflict has been appropriated as the differentiating ground of the old industrial and new social movements, expanded to encompass the high-tech and service sectors, and absorbed in the story of the sea change wrought by industrial restructuring.

> [N]on-manual work grew rapidly at the expense of manual; old-fashioned engineering-type skills, for long the basis of many an area's prosperity, went into relative decline; white-collar jobs associated with burgeoning managerial functions and with the "new technology" increased in importance. The combination of decline and decentralisation destroyed the manufacturing base of many old urban areas, and the uneven distribution of service jobs—in particular of the increasingly important high-status white-collar element—became a cause for concern. (Massey 1984, 1–2)

Recounted in the dry voice of social science, illustrated with impressive statistics and graphics, and aimed most directly at the scholarly community, such theoretical and applied narratives have a specialist, even recondite tone. Yet they are strikingly similar to other narratives, produced at a variety of locations, that also tell the story of collar conflict, framing it around a historically necessary movement of rise and decline. Although the social scientific work on the blue and white collars usually is read for its internal truth values, it exists within a much larger dialogical field in which collar conflict holds sway and, by many, is understood as virtually synonymous with class conflict.

Descriptive, performative, and regulatory, the language of blue and white collars infuses a great variety of practices. For example, for many in the labor community (especially unionists, allied scholars, journalists, and writers), the blue collar has been understood as the worker pure and simple, while the white collar has been regarded as a dangerous other. Indeed, throughout this century its very presence and growth have been perceived as a threat to the working class's continued existence, its goals, and its union and political traditions. For instance, one longstanding story contrasts the class-conscious blue collar, seasoned by its history of anticapitalist struggle, with a consensual white collar stigmatized as the bearer of false consciousness. As told by Hodges,

> White-collar workers tend to be merely indifferent to politics; denim workers are irreverent, bitter, and scornful. The white-collar worker does not have

a long tradition behind him of criticism and social protest, so that his political indifference is comparatively mild. The bitter struggles of manual workers against capital, management, and the State have fostered disillusionment of an altogether different stamp. (1962, 480)

From this perspective, white-collar growth represents working-class erosion, and charting the relative strength of the collars has been considered politically and strategically important. One ready site of contest has been provided by official statistics, which bundle occupational potpourris under white-collar, blue-collar, or manual labor, service workers, and farm workers, with a line firmly drawn between private and public employment; not surprisingly, these bundles have been challenged by those who, identifying the blue collar with the working class, fear its officially sanctioned disappearance behind a veil of spurious numbers. In a familiar strategy Levison, believing that "the [class] division is basically between manual, essentially physical or menial, labor and managerial or intellectual work" (1974, 20), uncovered types of manual labor concealed by government statistics and reordered occupations under either blue or white collar; for him, the resulting numerical expansion of the blue collar gave convincing proof that the working class was not dwindling away but instead was growing.

Still, labor's collar-based stories of class difference and conflict have been too readily ascribed to the left presence and credited to a left language of class. For instance, discussing the enigma of prewar, left-led union organizing among "what most leftists saw as a problematical segment of the labor force, the 'white collars,'" Strom argues that white-collar organization "raised important conceptual problems, problems the 'workerism' ideology of the Left, focused as it was on male workers in heavy industry and manufacturing, seemed incapable of rethinking" (1990, 809). However, the vocabulary of conflictual blue and white collars is wielded across a broad spectrum of unionists, from the most radical to the most conservative, and has been enabling to many practices that converge on workers and unions—from the gathering and reporting of labor statistics through organizing, contract administration, law (such as adjudicating who is a bona fide employee under labor law or which occupations share a community of interest), and labor reporting. Even as the larger labor community has looked to the white collar to replenish the depleted ranks, it also has regarded such people as a special case of wage- and salary-earners (usually, "close to management") holding distinctively middle-class interests, values, ambitions, and characteristics; lacking in the militant, antiboss, solidaristic qualities that would suit them to join the house of labor; and in need of targeted organizing strategies that combine strategic pandering to middle-class instrumentalism and status anxiety with a helping relationship aimed at animating an otherwise timid, conformist group (see Blum 1971; Curtin 1970). In some unions, it has been believed that white-collar people would be repelled by blue-collar organizers; one highly theorized innovation has elaborated on the time-honored strategies by hiring organizers having stereotypically middle-class traits such as being college-educated, newcomers to the labor movement, and, increasingly, female (Crain 1994; Reed 1990, 1992).

That is, collar differences described as class-based also are engendered by both unionists and labor scholars (on their conflation of occupation and gender, see Forrest 1993). For example, Warskett describes a federal clerks' strike in 1980, involving the largest bargaining unit in Canada at a formative moment in the Public Service Alliance of Canada. In the largest demonstration ever by Ottawa workers, twenty thousand clerks—mostly women—led a militant, high-spirited march, yet, even as he congratulated them, a union leader asked, "Do you think the girls will be able to hold out for much longer?" As Warskett notes, "The union leader's question, with its not so hidden message that women were passive and unable to sustain militant action, raised yet again the question of 'white collar' workers—their position in the labor movement and in the class structure as a whole" (1989, 168). Nonetheless, the changing demographic and occupational composition of the workforce has been at the heart of the past twenty years' debates on the proper focus and strategies of union organizing (see Cobble 1990, 1991a; Freeman and Medoff 1984; Heckscher 1988; Shostak 1991; Sweeney and Nussbaum 1989). Studies of certification elections have found increasing losses among production workers but growing victories among white-collar and service workers (see Goldfield 1987 for a critical discussion of election findings); by comparison with white, male, blue-collar workers, survey research also has been understood to suggest a greater desire for organization among women and minorities associated with the white-collar and service workforce (DeFreitas 1993; Freeman and Medoff 1984; Leigh and Hills 1987; Schur and Kruse 1992). Rather than arguing as in the past that white-collar women are unorganizable, the newer, more feminist-inspired story represents them as labor's untapped reserve (see Nussbaum 1984). Still, despite a history of left, feminist, union, and other solidarism and organizing by white-collar women (see Allen et al. 1976; Cobble 1991b; Cross and Shergold 1987; Gilpin et al. 1988; Norwood 1990; Strom 1980, 1983; Tepperman 1976), some unions have asserted a need for special, go-slow, nonconfrontational organizing. Though the justifications turn to gender (see Crain 1994), they are indistinguishable from longstanding labor perceptions of the white collar's class-based fearfulness, conformity, submission, promanagement outlook, and newness to struggle. In organizers' eyes, as reported by Hurd and McElwain:

> [B]ecause most clericals are women who have . . . accepted the subservient role implicit in their jobs, more attention must be given to building self-confidence than in campaigns among other groups of workers. . . . [C]lericals typically have little prior personal experience with unions, and tend to view them as institutions dominated by angry groups of male employees. . . .
>
> The biggest barriers to organizing private sector clerical workers all relate to fear—fear of job loss, fear of strikes, and fear of being ostracized by fellow workers or management. Being on friendly terms with management is more important to clericals than to most other workers. . . . Fear of strikes is also more prevalent among clericals than among other workers. (1988, 362)

These and other representations of the blue and white collars are widely produced. The two have been thoroughly inscribed at many discursive sites, including politics, art, film, and literature (Bernstein 1985; Bush 1990; Freeman 1993; Gordon 1947; Melosh 1993; Wilson 1992), where they are both the objects of distinct descriptions and interpellated subjects. Despite such pervasiveness, however, this language of class is by no means a uniform field. Not everyone is saying the same thing nor does everyone speak in the same modalities or seek identical objectives. Rather, there are regions and complex dialectical relations among them.

Here, I want to interrogate a theoretical and research consensus on the bifurcated workforce, foregrounding work produced primarily in economic and industrial sociology and in industrial relations. In this effort I am not attempting directly to develop a better class analytics, study trends and forecasts, identify blue- or white-collar interests, or interpret group opinions, values, and consciousness. Instead, I hope to problematize these categories that now have such authority and currency and, of course, hope that doing so will open up a space for other class analyses, descriptions, and epistemologies. First, I explore attempts to ground the classificatory scheme in a fundamental difference between the blue and white collars. When all is said and done, the categories rest on unstable distinctions across a nexus of binaries that cannot be sustained even by those who most expertly deploy them; nonetheless, the binaries are constitutive of representations that embody and lend presence to the notion of distinct groups. Further, though the sociological scheme is buttressed by specialist terms and truth protocols, its representations of the blue and white collars are distinctly shaped and inflected by the larger discursive field. Second, I attempt a symptomatic reading of the neo-Weberians and neo-Marxists. Whereas others have focused on their theoretical differences from one another, I have identified some ways in which they have narrated class in concert. As the major competitor to neoclassical and radical postindustrial theories, which valorize the white collar, this neo-Weberian and neo-Marxist work has sustained the normativity of the blue collar. In upholding an image of the worker as the proper subject of history, this body of work has shaped a left and left-leaning politics of class and social justice. Yet they have done so at the high cost of promoting a narrow image of class within a problematic where, logically, radical change awaits the Armageddon of capitalism and its erasure of difference. Finally, I suggest that even when informed by progressive concerns to address exploitation and oppression, these categories are derogatory toward workers and others and have disabling effects both on their self-activity and on a less crabbed politics of class. They belong among those descriptions that, though voiced to uphold the centrality of class, have contributed to perceptions of workers' supersession and a declining significance of class (see Balibar 1994).

The Collar Line

Though the blue and white collars consist of occupations, the terms are not merely convenient shorthand for occupational differences. While particular jobs and titles may be debated in the academy, it is generally agreed that the blue and white collars represent objective, determinate, and integral groups within the political economy or society. Indeed, they are ontologically distinct: what must be granted is a wall between them, or what Kocka (1980) has termed a collar line. At a minimum each seems to comprise a group of people who perform similar work, but larger claims are made as well, including that their members hold similar values, share a common life style, and have distinct interests. Consequently, studies of particular occupations also serve as windows on the whole; for example, Kenney and Florida's brief look at production workers and engineers does double duty as "the blue collar/white collar divide" (1993, 231–35).

Because both blue and white collars bundle vastly dissimilar titles and occupations, the classifying impulse girds this vocabulary. Its dualism both states that occupations may be grouped and enjoins the performance of a classification, which has had aporetic effects for those who have attempted to stipulate the terms. A good part of white-collar work, then, has been invested in strategies of deferral that protect both the fundamental distinction and a canon of truthful statements and protocols that have changed remarkably little over this century.

A Nexus of Binaries

It is precisely the group nature and identity of the collars that has resisted analysis. Categorical contrasts of the blue and white collars would be meaningless without some crowning difference between them, but, while the blue collar is generally considered an unproblematic category of manual labor (or treated as background), the white collar has been the resistant object of attempts to find the key to its internal unity or essence as a group. Analytically, the problem resides in its internal complexity, including disparate economic sectors (e.g., finance, sales, advertising, corporate administration, sometimes services); disparate occupations (e.g., managers, professionals, technicians, clericals); great contrasts in education, skill, and autonomy; a large and growing spread in salaries and benefits; differential discipline; and gender, racial, and ethnic inequalities. As noted by an industrial relations expert on the white collar:

> There are some differences from country to country as to who belongs in the group as well as some changes over time. But most important, there are so many and such basic differences within the group that few generalizations apply to all sectors of the white-collar group. To find constitutive characteristics that permit speaking of a white-collar group at all has been a problem challenging sociologists for a long time. . . . There is indeed in many respects little that a top executive and a clerk in the office have in common. Yet, somehow they both belong to "white collar." (Sturmthal 1966, 386–87)

For decades, the quest has been to find some common quality underlying this diversity—whether class, status group, bureaucratic authority, mental labor, unproductive labor, or some other possibility. Among the more prominent contrasts between blue and white collars have been productive/entrepreneurial functions, mechanical/bureaucratic workplaces, distance from/proximity to authority, and working/middle class (see Hyman 1980). However, despite many attempts to define the white collar and plumb its depths, there has been noticeably little progress; one can dip into the postwar literature at any point and find substantially the same terms, questions, themes, and debates. Repeated efforts to fasten opposed and differentiating qualities to either side of the collar line have proved unsatisfactory as traits attributed to one can be shown to apply equally to both.

Thus, in a summary review of the leading candidates for a definitive difference, Bain and Price (1972) showed that those based on type or location of labor have anomalous results. For example, manual and mental labor cannot be assigned to the blue and white collar, respectively, as most occupations have aspects of both (cf. Wright 1978). Indeed, some "manual" occupations (like electricians and compositors) may require more intellectual labor than do "white-collar" occupations (such as file clerks and typists). Decisions rendered in British courts illustrate the tenuousness of the distinction; for example, one court defined a lithographic artist as a mental worker because in the course of his work he "necessarily uses his hands, but the use to which he puts them is not labour; because it involves no strenuous exercise of the muscles of his hand or his arm. The real labour involved is labour of the brain and intelligence" (quoted in Bain and Price 1972, 47). In adjudicating mental and manual labor, other courts, following what Bain and Price describe as similar "involved reasoning," have reached conflicting decisions on occupations brought before them.

Again, a distinction between objects and functions of labor—manual as goods and production, nonmanual as people and information—cannot be sustained. "Occupations that are generally considered to be typically white-collar, such as mechanical engineers, airline pilots, medical auxiliaries, and laboratory technicians, would logically have to be classified as 'material' oriented and hence blue-collar. Similarly, occupations that are generally considered to be manual, such as ticket-collectors, bus conductors, and doormen, would have to be regarded as 'person-oriented' and hence white-collar" (50). Nor do the blue and white collars fall neatly into mechanical and bureaucratic work environments; for example, it would be difficult to know where to place typists, switchboard operators, lab technicians, or draftsmen (49).

Instead, and following Lockwood (1989), Bain and Price argue that the above traits of the white collar are merely "different external symbols of a more fundamental common feature, the possession of, or proximity to, authority. . . . A process of what can be called 'assimilation by association' would seem to be at work" (1972, 50). Yet even this apparently conclusive, rigorously neo-Weberian conception turns out to be wanting when, despite having demolished the categorical distinction between mental and manual labor, Bain and Price reintroduce it as foundation: "The 'non-manual' nature of white-collar work . . . tend[s] to produce a functional proximity to authority" (50).

In this literature, it is not uncommon to find one term serving as origin for those differences theorized as essence or foundation. Most often, the manual/mental dichotomy is referenced as ultimate ground. Like Bain and Price, for example, Sturmthal argues that the distinctive property of the white collar lies in high status, but refers status back to "feudal and other prejudices against manual labor" (1966, 386). Similarly, for Poulantzas (1975) a definitive productive/unproductive distinction follows from the manual/ mental divide. The labor process literature, too, wielded this opposition in challenging postindustrial theory's prediction of a technology-driven upgrading of the occupational structure out of manual and into mental labor. Braverman (1974) argued in reply that the growth of the white collar was consistent with a general tendency toward proletarianization evidenced by technologically and organizationally induced loss of skill and autonomy— that is, the separation of manual and mental labor. Besides inspiring a host of class analyses of white-collar deskilling and routinization (see Baxandall et al. 1976; Clawson 1980; Zimbalist 1979), his work informed feminist studies further by explaining white-collar feminization as a function of deskilling (see Crompton and Jones 1984; Davies 1982; Strom 1989, 1992). Across diverse theories, there radiates from the manual/mental difference a wide variety of collar contrasts, from class, status, and authority through consciousness. This density has led some to call for ever more inclusive studies:

> A comprehensive elucidation of the historically emergent meanings of "white-collar" would require an understanding of the complex interplay of state and managerial control, material advantage, the criteria of social esteem and ideological legitimation, and the sexual division of labour. Only through a grasp of the relevance of *all* these factors . . . can the continuing practical and ideological importance of the "manual"/"non-manual" dichotomy be fully understood. (Hyman 1980, 14–15; emphasis in original)

More studies, however, will not solve the puzzle of the white collar, which is only a negative. The terms "blue" and "white collar" are constituted by their opposition; that is, the white collar consists in all that the blue collar is not and vice versa. That constitutive dualism is both stark and explicit in C. Wright Mills's classic *White Collar* (1951), a benchmark for postwar Marxist scholarship that remains assessed as an "outstanding study" (Kocka 1980, 22) that is "historically and theoretically sensitive" (Edgell 1993, 62), "exceptional . . . for the knowledge it displays of the earlier German debate on white-collar workers and the breadth of empirical material used" (Carter 1985, 33), "fresh and incisive" (Bottomore 1990, 470), even "unsurpassed in insight" (Zeitlin and Kimeldorf 1983, 19). Yet, Mills is quite clear that the white collar is an "occupational salad" constituted by a negative, its location outside goods production: "fewer individuals manipulate *things,* more handle *people* and *symbols.* . . . The one thing they do not do is live by making things" (1951, 65; emphasis in original). Citing the work of German economic sociologists, Mills terms the white collar a residual group by definition, based on both (faulty) data and the structure of the concept.

> Owing to the negative definition of the occupational function of the new middle class as "non-commodity producing," the group as a whole is quite heterogeneous. . . . To combine these heterogeneous elements into one

group and call them the "New Middle Class" would seem hazardous if it were not for the fact that by their very nature, given the census classifications with which we must work, they are residual groups and further that "other classes . . . likewise exhibit considerable lateral extensions. . . . The manual laborer's class includes the unskilled proletarians of the lowest strata . . . as well as the skilled, regularly employed and well-paid male wage earners." The white-collar group can be "comprehended as an entity only in contradistinction to the other classes." . . . [I]n a good number of cases we do not have any criteria for placing a given occupation *in* the new middle class, but we have many criteria for *not placing* it in the free enterpriser or the wage-worker. (359–60; emphasis in original, reference omitted)

Still, as Mills's method illustrates, though the essential term of difference (or presence and absence) may be disputed, the opposition between collars does not at all rest on a simple binary. The collar line is constituted by a nexus of many binaries that are interdependent. Each term is not only necessary to the collar line but relies on the support of the others and, whatever the theorized ground of differentiation, all have been invoked without theoretical prejudice over the past many decades. Among the most frequently rehearsed have been goods/services, productive/unproductive labor, manual/mental labor, unskilled/skilled, production/administration, subordination/authority, wages/status, production/consumption, strength/weakness, male/female, working class/other (usually middle or new middle class, often neoproletariat), and not least, class consciousness/self-estrangement.

irresoluble contradiction in text, argument, theory

Aporia and Deferral

Despite the centrality of classification, there remains uncomfortable ambiguity in identifying these groups or persons rigorously and demonstrably. Others have echoed Mills's confession to lacking firm criteria for consigning occupations to the new middle class. Further, not only does each differentiating criterion produce anomalies, but the bundles of group characteristics do not cohere as expected. Nonetheless, it remains acceptable to identify occupations as blue or white collar while weaving stories of conflict between these categorical "groups." Faced with aporetic choices among its terms, this literature has survived the century through a variety of devices, especially grafting and naming.

Grafting has been an important but underrecognized device. Many use but simply decline to stipulate the terms, perhaps agreeing with Jenkins and Sherman: "Our attitude is one of detestation for the semantic game of attempting to define a white-collar worker," with its "attendant exceptions and anomalies" (1979, 12). As even the attempt to stipulate terms has fallen off in recent years (though see Ganzeboom, Treiman, and Ultec 1991 on attempts to define a more meaningful construct for statistical analysis), the blue and white collars have been extended to absorb and enable new referents. For instance, the white-collar and service literatures exchange both materials and thematics; for many, as Gershuny notes, "'service workers' means more or less the same thing as the old-fashioned term 'white-collar workers' or the new and rather trendy 'information workers'" (1987, 106), which undoubtedly contributes to the conflation of occupation, industry, and product under "services" that he criticizes. Similarly, this literature continues the fuzzy tradition of distinguishing services by often dubious differences from production (Britton 1990). In short, the service literature reproduces the ontological differences affirmed by white-collar theory but under a different name. As discussed by Offe, it is a literature defined by its constitutive negativities.

> [T]he concept of service labour is in general very poorly defined; it is used as a residual category comprising all those types of work . . . or work organizations that cannot clearly be classified as either "primary" (extractive) work or "secondary" (productive) work. In cases where the characteristics of service labour are in fact stated explicitly, we find that . . . almost exclusively negative attributes predominate. Service labour produces *non*-material outcomes. . . . Service labor is *not*—or, at least, is *less*—susceptible to technical and organizational rationalization when compared with goods-producing labour. . . . Service labour is *not* "productive" (in the sense of both classical political economy and Marxism); and so on. These negative definitions developed in the field of labour economics find their counterparts in the discipline of sociology. Here, service workers are conventionally termed "middle class," which implies that they are neither classifiable as "upper" nor as "lower," or else they are categorized as "new" middle class, which simply indicates that they do *not* belong to an "old" middle class. Equally uninformative is the concept of postindustrial society introduced by Bell; this designates a social system which is "other than" or "no longer" industrial. . . . (1985, 104–5; emphasis in original)

The theme of feminization also bridges the white-collar and service literatures. Thus, scholars and unionists theorize a gendered divide between manufacturing and services (Christopherson 1989; Sweeney and Nussbaum 1989), while arguments for a new, organizing, often postindustrial model of unionism rely on the feminization of white-collar and service employment supporting, by contrast with male industrial workers, what is considered a concurrent growth of "people skills" (Conrow 1992; Milkman 1993; Needleman 1993). The story of collar difference and conflict persists, then, under many social guises, not to be interrogated too closely.

Not least among the devices of deferral has been naming, or straightforwardly labeling and grouping, occupations by reference to common sense. In one labor text the authors, confessing themselves unable precisely to locate either white-collar people or the so-called white-collar industries in the economy, concluded tautologically, "White-collar work is simply work done by white-collar workers" (Beal and Wickersham 1959, 210). Others have been more willing to get down to brass tacks. For example, in criticizing government labor statistics Spencer wrote:

> Only employees in the categories of manufacturing, mining, construction and transportation were considered blue collar workers. All others (except agricultural . . .) were listed as white collar and service employees. In this manner, millions of workers which *common sense* tells us are blue collar workers are pushed, shoved or stuffed into the white collar and service filing cabinet. . . . According to the census the white collar workers are also television repairmen, gas station attendants, auto mechanics, bus drivers (but not railroad engineers!), hotel and culinary workers, . . . hospital workers (janitors as well as therapists). Absolutely no government employment is considered as blue collar. (1977, 32–33; emphasis added)

If Spencer was willing to rely on his own common sense, some white-collar scholars have instead invoked what they consider the social or lay common sense. Thus, in his study of the extent of British white-collar unionism, Lumley announced that he had rejected the "synonyms" manual/nonmanual labor and works/staff in favor of recourse to everyday terms in "historic" usage (1973, 16).

> To attempt rigorously to define the term "white-collar labour force" would be a complex task. . . . Rather than pursuing this complex [sic], I propose to adopt a practical approach and to use terms in their common usage. . . .
>
> It will then be assumed that the labour force can be categorized into two groups, white-collar and blue-collar. Since there are numerous occupations, each one measurable on multiple criteria, this categorization must necessarily be a coarse and arbitrary process. (15)

This hardheaded pragmatism may be the most enabling device of all, allowing the authority of preconceived ideas of indeterminate origin to lay the ground for a host of studies and judgments.

Common Sense and Representations

In the more firmly Weberian work, concern for common sense is accompanied by the presumption that the prestige, status, and authority accorded the white collar are socially and subjectively determined. One might expect, then, that both lay and scholarly perceptions (i.e., common sense) would be variable. Instead, though there certainly are contested occupations, there remain strong expectations that it is not hard to know who is blue or white collar. As Hyman asked, "if many occupations are ambiguously placed in terms of authority, why is difficulty so *rarely* experienced in applying the conventional 'white-collar' label? Doubts arise as soon as the notion of 'proximity to authority' is probed. In what respect is a 'white-collar' airline pilot closer to authority than a 'blue-collar' engine driver, a laboratory technician than a garage mechanic, a shop assistant than a factory storekeeper?" (1980, 14; emphasis in original).

In the end, there is a widespread conviction that—ambiguities or no and research protocols notwithstanding—scholars and others already know who these people are; perhaps good reasons will follow. And why should it be otherwise? Whether Kitty Foyle or Stanley Kowalski, we have a century of representations of social types that visualize and locate them for us and that tell us both what they are like and how they are different from one another. Nor are these representations confined to the arts. For instance, Mills's *White Collar,* considered a sociological classic and ethnographic gem, relies extensively on fictional characters like Alice Adams to flesh out white-collar character traits and ambitions (see 1951, 198–204). His interviews and observational data lend realist detail to white-collar personality "types" drawn in broad strokes; advertising themselves on the "personality market" where "personality and personal traits become part of the means of production" (225), each type expresses an occupational function. Sited in offices and salesrooms and given modern-day attributes of costly or tawdry consumer goods, these types also are easy to picture. Mostly they are female: "compared to older hierarchies, the white-collar pyramids are youthful and feminine bureaucracies" (76). Even the men share this trait, as the white collar is a "Little Man" ("the small creature who is acted upon but who does not act" [xii]) comparable to "political eunuchs . . . without potency" (xviii). In its occupational diversity, the white collar encompasses many, specialized personality types. The "great salesroom" ranges, for example, from the "Prima Donna Vice-Presidents of corporations" (164) through the prestige- and service-oriented salespeople of small-town department stores (172–73) to the bevy of calculating salesgirls in big-city department stores who can be named even more precisely the wolf, the elbower, the charmer, the ingénue, the collegiate, the drifter, the social pretender, and the old-timer (173–78). More obliquely, as noted by Bain and Price, "Indicative of the confusion surrounding the term is the large number of synonyms which it has acquired: 'salaried employee,' 'office worker,' 'non-manual worker,' and 'blackcoated worker'" (1972, 46). These clearly are not synonymous with white collar or with each other but are an array of descriptive types given select attributes.

The extensive use of description—including visual, spatial, bodily, and gendered metaphors—is neither mistaken nor peripheral to this particular language of class. Though theory and research may fail to establish a satisfactory collar line, description gives the categories verisimilitude and is, in fact, constitutive of them. According to the second edition of *Webster's New Twentieth Century Dictionary,* the terms derive etymologically from the color of work shirts and business dress; "blue-collar" (adjective) means "designating or of industrial workers, especially the semiskilled and unskilled" while "white-collar" (adjective) means "designating or of clerical or professional workers or the like: white-collar workers are usually salaried employees engaged in work not essentially manual." The second revised edition of the *Random House Unabridged Dictionary* defines "blue-collar" (adjective, dated 1945–50) as "of or pertaining to wage-earning workers who wear work clothes or other specialized clothing on the job, as mechanics, longshoremen, and miners," while "white-collar" (adjective, dated 1920–25) means "belonging or pertaining to the ranks of office and professional workers whose jobs generally do not involve manual labor or the wearing of a uniform or work clothes." The terms, that is, already imply reference to coherent, real-world groups of people whose work and other attributes hold together in a singular unity. As summarized by a labor text:

> By one broad definition, white-collar workers are those who make their living not with their hands but with their heads. . . .
>
> White-collar occupations usually require a higher degree of general education than shop jobs. . . . White-collar workers have in the past come from "higher" social strata than the shop workers. The positions they occupy carry greater prestige than shop jobs, and generally provide greater security; they are paid a salary rather than an hourly wage. While many hourly paid manual workers today make more money in a week or in a year than certain white-collar workers, and differences in living standards have generally narrowed, more than a trace remains of the old "mentality" that holds white-collar employment preferable, and superior to shop work. (Beal and Wickersham 1959, 210)

These descriptions perfectly encapsulate the oppositions at work in this universe of dichotomous attributes, including work shirts/business dress, factory/office, hands/head, waged/salaried, and others. The dense succession of metonyms produces an imagery of concrete persons in real places; visual metaphors of color, dress, body, workplace, even paycheck and consumer basket are persuasive allusions to something we surely can all see for ourselves. Certainly, Mills put such metonyms to productive use in developing occupational statistics; working closely with Bureau of Labor Statistics (BLS) staff on their unpublished work, he reworked it to resolve discrepancies between the theorized white collar and existing government data by bringing economic, workplace, and sartorial traits into play as markers of a white-collar group.

> The distinction between white-collar and wage-worker was based in part on the [BLS's] "non-commodity-producing" character of white-collar work. [The BLS] uses, along with "fixed payment by the day, week, or month," two other criteria which I found helpful: "A well-groomed appearance"and "the wearing of street clothes at work." The broad occupational groups included within the category of "white-collar workers" . . . are quite similar to my four categories, except they omit salaried managerial employees. (1951, 359)

Spatially, too, these figures can be envisioned and mobilized beyond the factory/office sites and into a much more far-reaching geography. For Doreen Massey, for instance, class-based conflict occurs between collars located in regionally based factories or nonindustrial workplaces (1984, 67–68). Conversely, microlevel spatialization is a key device in practices affecting workers, such as determining appropriate bargaining units, including adjudicating with whom white-collar people may organize. Through Taft-Hartley restrictions and the decisions and per se rules of the National Labor Relations Board (NLRB), a patchwork of exceptional rules discourages joint bargaining units of white-collar employees and production workers or of plant and office clericals. Spatial proximity in factory or office is among the criteria crucial to demonstrating before the NLRB a legitimate "community of interest" in organizing and bargaining, potentially outweighing even a history of common bargaining or workers' preference to be represented in one unit (Abodeely, Hammer, and Sandler 1981; Grady 1978; Kaminsky 1979; Schlossberg 1967).

In other words, the linguistic matrix and often indeterminate common sense of scholarship draw up on and are intercalated with a body of representations produced by and beyond the social sciences. In these, the reified figures of collars are an effect of prosopopeia, or personification achieved by visual, spatial, and bodily attributes and conceits that envision and yoke disparate elements. Through these representational devices, the canonical blue and white collars have emerged as persons: the manual, productive, deskilled, male laboring body of the worker in the factory on the one hand and, on the other, the nonmanual, unproductive, educated, eroticized figure of borrowed authority and striving consumption in the office (or perhaps the store, hospital, or other nonfactory venue). If the white collar is a special case, it also is both endowed with group consciousness and capacity and represented by a wide range of special types given distinctive personalities. Against the fraternal masses there are the deracinated organization men, the men in gray flannel suits, the status seekers, and the lonely crowd who, without social attachments or ideology, serve another master; against the collective worker and the proletarian sister, wife, and mother—the pillars of working-class community—are the loyal office wives absorbed in preindustrial master/servant relationships and the individualist, upwardly mobile career women. Against dirt, courage, and fortitude stand antisepsis, fear, and calculation. Each collar is invested with a complex bundle of descriptions, names, and subtypes now familiar through scholarship, the arts, unionism, law, and other practices. We know them: a century of representations completes the picture even when we cannot fully make them out to be as theory would have it.

Collars and Class

In representing and debating class structure and politics, these categories are freely wielded by labor, the left, and scholars in the social sciences. Yet the critical literature is surprisingly thin, its readings repetitive. Many argue, for example, that study of the blue and white collars is politically important to particular theoretical and evidentiary debates such as embourgeoisement versus proletarianization, mobility and affluence versus inequality and impoverishment, stratification versus class, postindustrialism versus advanced capitalism or, through distribution of occupations and skill, decline versus growth of the working class (Braverman 1974; Cappelli 1993; DiPrete 1988; Edgell 1993; Watson 1980; Wright 1978, 1985). That is, the assessments repeat the problems without asking why or how they should require and support the notion of a collar line. Nor is the critical literature well ordered. In its most tendentious form it asserts a deep-seated, conservative/radical division and ideological struggle over the politics of class and class analysis among postwar neo-Weberians and neo-Marxists (Abercrombie and Urry

1983; Carter 1985), which would make their exchange and absorption of questions, materials, and thematics almost unintelligible.

Instead, I prefer to question the project in which these categories are embedded or, in Althusser's (1970b) sense, to attempt a symptomatic reading. To begin with, if neo-Weberian and neo-Marxist scholars know that the manual/mental, goods/services dichotomy does not quite hold water, why is there such persistent and resistant commitment to this ontology? For the purposes of class analysis, why should a language of collars be persuasive at all? What is accomplished by a collar line that could not be achieved by the classical concepts of class? Contrary to the dominant critical perception of their divergent roles within social theory, I argue that the neo-Weberian and neo-Marxist work share a discursive position from which they are not only the best elaborated theoretically, but are the most self-consciously concerned with a pro-worker politics of class and issues of class capacity. Each pursues the theoretical and research question: how is class formation related to class structure, and, in particular, under what conditions will the white collar be susceptible to class formation? Moreover, both schools contest the precepts of postindustrial theory and, in so doing, produce a body of similar, interrelated statements upholding workers' centrality to anticapitalist change. In order to do this, by their lights, each defends the collar line and its representations against all odds and thereby maintains the normativity of the blue collar.

Class under Advanced Capitalism

Though, of course, theory matters, an overemphasis on differences and particulars has obscured ways in which neo-Weberians and neo-Marxists participate in a shared problematic. Rather than gross disagreement, the core white-collar work of both draws on a common body of theory, works a shared narrative, and holds similar attitudes of disdain, suspicion, and sometimes animus toward the white collar. In the view of the best-known white-collar historian,

> [T]he main reason for the marked neglect of the history of white collar workers in the US is the nature of the subject itself. The characteristics of American white collar employees have inhibited rather than invited conceptualization and study by contemporaries, social scientists, and historians. . . .
> The unfavorable state of the sources also reflects the image of American white collar workers which they themselves and which others hold. (Kocka 1980, 23)

Whatever white-collar people themselves may think, being described for decades as conformist, instrumentalist, self-serving, loyal to capital, and the comfortable beneficiaries of unearned wealth neither invites nor expresses sympathetic identification. Arm's-length study is nothing if not the common province of these white-collar schools.

At the same time, there is no doubt that much of this scholarship is moved by pro-worker sympathies. The agonistic character of the neo-Weberian and neo-Marxist work emerges most clearly by comparison with postindustrial scholarship that validates or comes cautiously to terms with knowledge work and knowledge workers. To Mills (1951), for example, the postindustrial vision of a "knowledge society" of experts and technocrats was a horror. *White Collar* argued that the white collar was merely a bought-and-sold cipher in a still relevant capitalism, incapable of rousing a creative challenge to it or contributing actively to popular democracy (see especially chapter 7); implicitly, by contrast with the new middle class, his book asserted the continued primacy of the blue collar as workers who remained the real source of wealth and democratic traditions. Similarly, Goldthorpe (1982) gives short shrift to neo- and post-Marxist, postindustrial theories of the activist neo-proletariat or middle-class vanguard of new social movements. Not likely of these agents of capital, says he, who are more given to resisting their social obligations and mounting a conservative struggle against their own declassing; better look to the routinized wage-workers for any possibility of meaningful anticapitalist protest.

Finally, though it is sometimes thought that differences in class analytics mark profoundly dichotomous theoretical and political projects (usually under the rubric of economic versus social class or production- versus market-based theories in support of change versus the status quo), such differences, too, can be exaggerated. Neo-Weberians and neo-Marxists draw on a shared theoretical heritage including Marx, Weber, critical theory, Austro-Marxism, and much else; consequently, their core work explores a common bundle of processes theorized as key to shaping class structure and class formation under the conditions particular to advanced capitalism. The idea of the white collar depends on and enables a narrative of the large monopoly firm or capital driving the economy and creating a vast fund of skilled but unproductive labor to administer its needs within a highly specialized division of labor. As Hegedüs tells the story,

> [S]ince the middle of the last century managements of a bureaucratic character have gained more and more influence in the economy, especially in the larger industrial plants. Marx and Engels never perceived that the white collar

staff of the factories are the bearers of the same essential social relations as the state management apparatus, and they wrote about the increasing role of clerical workers and managers in industry only as a simple empirical fact. (1983, 58)

Fulfilling capital's delegated functions, bearing its instrumental reason, depending on its beneficence and the superexploitation of productive workers, white-collar types serve deliberately or, perhaps through false consciousness, unwittingly as capital's agents; they are weak sisters indeed to the fraternity of labor.

Though often considered late, correcting additions to the literature, the crucial processes driving class structure and formation under monopoly or advanced capitalism already are fully present in Mills (1951): concentration and centralization, automation, bureaucratization, feminization, alienation, and unionization. Better, each of these is an instance of rationalization, a central dynamic that subjects social sites and all of society to calculation and control, including the bureaucratic appropriation and centralization of specialized knowledge and authority, normalization of a minute and closely managed division of labor, the validation and spread of instrumental reason, and institutionalization of technical and administrative supports to capital accumulation. By contrast with fragmentation, instrumentalism, and alienation, unionization represents a countermovement of class formation, or achievement of working-class capacity for solidarism and collective action; thus, much of this work has theorized the white collar's prospects for collective action toward working-class goals. Whether based in bureaucratization, automation, the labor process, workplace relations of subordination and authority, or, more nearly, relations among all these sites and processes, for both neo-Weberians and neo-Marxists a master process of rationalization anchors and gives directionality to twentieth-century class structure and formation.

Producing a Working-Class Subject

Still, what has any of this got to do with a collar line, and why the stubborn consensus on a bifurcated workforce? The sectoral gaps and occupational anomalies arising from these dichotomous categories certainly are well known, yet what Wright deems "the purely ideological distinction between 'blue-collar' and 'white-collar' occupations" (1985, 153) lies at the heart of neo-Weberian and neo-Marxist theory. If these categories continue to hold sway, it must be at least in part because, no matter how shaky, they achieve something that cannot be easily relinquished.

Most obviously, the collar line accomplishes a class analysis before class analytics proper ever get off the ground. That is, the blue and white collars are constituted by an asymmetrical binary that, following Derrida, proposes "not a peaceful coexistence of facing terms but a violent hierarchy. One of the terms dominates the other (axiologically, logically, etc.), occupies the commanding position" (1981, 41). Here, if the white collar is a distasteful other, the blue collar *is* the worker—complete with specific, already known social and occupational attributes. "Blue collar" identifies, concretizes, and stabilizes the working class as male, manual, deskilled, routinized, goods-producing, industrial, productive, subordinate (outside decision making), waged, and so on. As its contrary and demoted other, under "white collar" whatever is female, mental, professional, autonomous, nongoods-producing, bureaucratic, unproductive, authoritative (inside the decision-making apparatus), or salaried already denotes the nonworker. If that satisfies what Wright calls a "general intuition among Marxists, namely that the working class consists of productive, subordinated manual wage-earners" (1985, 154), the images and attributes also transcend the Marxist and non-Marxist left and are in that sense pretheoretical.

However, that is not the end of the work. While it is widely agreed that the white collar is nonworker, for many that means "middle class" in the sense of a status hierarchy. Neo-Weberian and neo-Marxist theory inflect class differently through the addition of two terms to the conventional nexus: "propertyless" and "new." First, that the white collar is nonworker does *not* mean that its members are not workers. Paradoxically, in the Anglo-American story, the white collar emerges toward the turn of the century not from the "old," propertied middle class or petty bourgeoisie, but de novo as the "propertyless non-manual, or 'white-collar,' workers" (Giddens 1973, 177) of the nascent monopoly firm. Within its walls, the white collar participates in the Weberian pyramid of officialdom (i.e., a bureaucratic ladder of expertise and authority as well as today's occupational and class mobility structure), where it exercises capital's delegated authority and functions over and adjacent to the blue collar; congruently, the greater career and life chances associated with skill and education effect a shared status above manual workers (as manifest in high prestige and affluent life style). From this low/high vantage, the white collar simultaneously occupies *both* a working-class location and a middle-class "class situation" (Lockwood 1989; Mills 1951) or, perhaps, a "contradictory class location" (Wright 1985).

This curious nonworker who also is a worker is not just a particular case of the general, but rather is a negated worker on the wrong side of an internal class boundary. On the correct side is the propertyless worker who is manual, subordinate, goods producing, and so forth, a figure who can only be he who owns nothing but his own labor power. In inserting "propertyless" among the preexisting bundle of attributes held by the blue collar, the work of theory subtly changes the meaning of class, bringing the collar line within the purview of both Marx and Weber. In this body of theory, manual labor is deemed propertyless in the sense that it has been dispossessed of not only tools but skill, education, and craft knowledge. By contrast, the nonworker attributes of the white collar are rendered seamlessly as its endowments. Unlike the old, "propertied" middle class or petty bourgeoisie, the new middle class is propertied only in the sense of holding skill, education, and so forth; by definition, then, possession of knowledge, job-related autonomy, and decision-making authority, or personal and organizational assets (see Wright 1985), suffices to negate the white collar's propertyless condition. By bringing nonownership of the means of production and market situation into close relation, neo-Marxist and neo-Weberian theory succeeds in ranging the attributes of the blue and white collars on either side of a propertyless/propertied internal class boundary.

From that negation follows not just the difference of calculating instrumentalism and status anxiety but a conservative class outlook, achieved by contrast with the production- and status-based solidarism of the blue-collar worker. Unlike the work ethic and spirit of craftsmanship central to manual labor, the work of mental, unproductive, socially manipulative labor is spiritually "hollow"; white-collar workers must seek meaning, gratification, and status in leisure (consumption) rather than work (Mills 1951, 256). Whereas the blue collar is alienated from its product, the white collar is alienated only from itself or "self-estranged," selling itself on "the personality market" of the bureaucracies where appearance and manner function as manipulations of power (225): "emotions become ceremonial gestures by which status is claimed, alienated from the inner feelings they supposedly express" (257). Restated, blue-collar workers sell labor power; white-collar workers sell their souls to become the captives of false consciousness. Expertise and authority give the white collar a stake and psychic investment in a bureaucratic apparatus where they are only formally workers; the exchange among knowledge, power, and interest supports a bourgeois instrumental reason that subverts class capacity for solidarism and resistance (Lockwood 1989; Wright 1985).

Second, though the collar line works to stabilize a paradigmatic, normative working class, the dichotomy is not at all static. Neo-Weberian and neo-Marxist addition of the term "new" secures the worker's other within a developmental level and trajectory, periodizing the negated worker as the "new middle class" of advanced capitalism. In embryo, its presence signifies the concentration of wealth and power by monopoly capital, enactment of the delegated authority of absentee capitalists through a bureaucratic apparatus, and organizational deepening of surveillance over and routinization of workers that leads toward the industrial proletariat; in addition, its professional prerogatives and ambitions, conservative outlook, and instrumentalism introduce a fundamental societal erosion of democratic values and altruism (Lockwood 1989; Mills 1951). Yet, the new middle class itself faces persistent, systemic decay: it is both the product of rationalization and subject to its logic, whose effects appear almost simultaneously with its birth. For example, leveling is manifest almost immediately in feminization of the white-collar workforce (Mills 1951; cf. Davies 1982; Strom 1989, 1992).

As the new middle class, then, the negated worker is also a protoworker. At issue has been the question whether the white collar will be fully or partially rationalized into extinction and, whatever their particular differences, these schools have tended to agree that at least some portion of the white collar will end in declassed routinization. For instance, the labor-process literature suggested that the more technologically and organizationally rationalized the workplace, the more white-collar labor would come to resemble blue-collar workers. By extension, class consciousness and its telltale readiness to unionize would follow (see Crompton 1979; Tepperman 1976). In effect, dispossession of knowledge, skill, autonomy, and other nonworker attributes would release the true worker and genuine class capacity. As summarized by Abercrombie, Hill, and Turner:

> Proletarianization of action . . . is chiefly measured by . . . the propensity to join trade unions. The more closely white-collar workers' pay, holidays, chances of promotion, fringe benefits, relationships with employers, autonomy at work and status in the community approach that of manual workers, the more proletarianized they have become. . . . [I]n the view of many, particularly Marxist, sociologists, large sections of the middle class will become proletarianized (perhaps through de-skilling) and this will eventually lead to their increased and more militant trade-union participation and radical political action. (1988, 197)

However, the labor-process literature was criticized for producing a proletarianized labor force only by suppressing the occupational and sectoral differences in question (Hyman 1980; Watson 1980). Numerous studies have argued in response that there is no one, overriding pattern of deskilling and routinization across occupations and workplaces, but rather contrary tendencies toward reskilling and professionalization, differential effects on particular occupations, and important distinctions to be drawn between de-skilling jobs and deskilling workers (Cappelli 1993; DiPrete 1988; Form 1987; Howell and Wolff 1991; Thompson 1989). Nor does deskilling of white-collar labor necessarily lead to heightened class consciousness (Vallas 1987). More to the point, Braverman (1974) came close to messing up the story. In treating occupations as epiphenomena of the capitalist labor process, he went too far toward dissolving the raw materials of the class boundary; restating the productive/unproductive binary as productive/necessary also undermined an objection to the white collar that, for some neo-Marxists, has been the center of a class divide (Nicolaus 1967; Poulantzas 1975).

Other theoretical strategies have focused on reworking the white-collar group, redistributing and regionalizing its types within an internalist hierar-chy. In this work, the collars have provided raw material to continually re-fined class analytics, including ever more meticulous taxonomies of a discrete white collar. The low/high contrast between the collars has proved especially troublesome and difficult to attach across disparate occupations, which has confronted neo-Weberian and neo-Marxist theory with competing theories or misrecognitions of their object of knowledge (see Lockwood 1989, epi-logue). For example, the white collar's relative mobility and privilege—both socially and at the workplace—have been hard to reconcile with the practice and effects of occupational segregation, quintessentially identified with the clerical workers (Crompton and Jones 1984). The emergence of neo- and post-Marxist theories of a neoproletariat also called for fresh analysis of the professional and technical occupations, as such work threatened to pull both those occupations and skilled manual labor into a radical postindustrial nar-rative (see Mallet 1963). Since the seventies, the white collar has been re-ordered and bifurcated by gender and class. As *The Penguin Dictionary of Sociology* (Abercrombie, Hill, and Turner 1988) says of "blue-collar," "This is an American term used to describe manual workers," but "white-collar" must be qualified as follows: "A term sometimes used to describe all non-manual employees, but increasingly confined to the lower levels of this occu-pational hierarchy." Thus, neo-Weberians have pursued both low/high and inside/outside boundaries, such as by confining the term "white collar" to routinized occupations deemed working class, while ejecting the upper eche-lons into Karl Renner's service class (Goldthorpe 1982). Focusing on work-place relations of subordination/authority, neo-Marxists also have sought to locate routinized, subordinated white-collar elements resembling the blue collar, to distinguish them from an upper white collar inhabiting con-tradictory class locations, and to forecast various types' political outlook (Abercrombie and Urry 1983; Carter 1985; Oppenheimer 1985; Wright 1978,

1985). In other words, competing narratives have compelled theoretical refinements that all the more closely argue and reassert the ontology of the collar line.

Despite the driving processes, occupational studies, and predictions of occupational change and behavior, nothing ever quite happens: the more things change, the more they remain the same. Indeed, it is hard to locate the white collar in time at all. Mills, who pictured the fifties office as an entirely automated workplace, also suggested that rationalization of the office had occurred by the thirties (1951, 209) yet projected office workers' class-conscious organizing into the dim future. In this literature, as Lockwood (1989) noted of Braverman's work, trends are presented as inexorable necessities that both will occur and already have occurred. The stated aim of white-collar theory is to explain the relationship between class structure and class formation (see Lockwood 1989; Wright 1985) for which unionization serves as an index of class-conscious collective action. Repeatedly the white-collar types enact their moment of self-realization through unionization, fulfilling a prediction nicely stated during the depression: "the white collar and professional people are joining the onward march of labor. . . . [I]t is through the unions' penetration of the white collar and professional workers that the middle class will at last awaken to its place in history" (Vorse 1938, 182–83). Still, each instance is hailed as a new, even unprecedented awakening.[1] However identified and distributed and despite a long history of unionized white-collar occupations (Kassalow 1966; Kocka 1980; McColloch 1983), the white collar remains categorically and simultaneously negated and a proto-worker—perhaps resembling the blue collar in some ways but continuing to hold nonworker attributes (say, by being waged or routinized but still performing mental or unproductive labor or receiving higher pay or enjoying occupational mobility), perhaps organizing but in need of a firm directing hand to know its interests and stay the course or perhaps already unionized but in an instrumental rather than solidarist way (see Lockwood 1989; Price 1980), its attainment of full-fledged proletarianization and class capacity always just beyond the horizon (Wright 1985).

Class Epistemologies

What exactly is the epistemology of this problematic, and what is the problem that inspires it? The categories are neither self-evident nor universally deployed and, indeed, depart from many people's self-descriptions; as Jenkins and Sherman point out, "Most people do not consciously think in this idiom. . . . It is relatively rare for employees to think of, or talk of, their jobs in terms of manual or non-manual employment, let alone argue into which category their particular job fits" (1979, 14–15). Further, the terms are valued differently by neo-Weberians and neo-Marxists than in competitor theories that, by contrast, validate the white collar as the normative figure.

In the literature the baseline of the blue collar would seem to be not value-laden but merely an objective fact. For instance, Wright explained his method by reference to an indeterminate common sense: "In spite of . . . reservations, I will adopt the conventional blue-collar criterion for defining 'manual labour,' and thus the working class. Since this definition is the least self-consciously theorized of the ones we are considering and does, in fact, rely most heavily on categories given in everyday discourse, this operationalization is, I believe, faithful to usage" (1985, 154). Compared with the complicated taxonomic work devoted to the white collar, the blue collar is bracketed as a relatively simple, proletarianized mass. Yet, from other perspectives, that is an exoticized view of workers. In his polemic against blue-collar studies, for example, Spencer objected to just such stereotyping homogenization: "A steel mill has a broad mix of occupations and workers, skilled, semi-skilled and unskilled; Black, white, Latinos; ethnics and WASPs; precision workers and assembly-line workers; back-breaking labor and light machine work; outside and inside work; transporting, shipping, fabrication, forging, smelting, constructing; simple mechanical and sophisticated computerized processes" (1977, 4–5). That the deskilled, routinized, goods-producing worker should epitomize the working class is not at all obvious to everyone. Among neo-Weberians, the baseline blue collar is essentially the unionized, party-affiliated manual worker who exemplifies working-class consciousness (Lockwood 1989) (neo-Weberians may be best known, in fact, for their work on the affluent worker, which, contra the thesis of embourgeoisement, argued that the workers of advanced capitalism retain an altered but significant class identification).

In other words, there is a particular class identification at work in the selection of the blue collar as the foundational, normative worker and the white collar as a deficient worker. Clearly, the image of the worker validated by neo-Weberians and neo-Marxists has been overdetermined by a number of discourses. However dispersed and bowdlerized, their blue collar holds traces of past disputes and stances, including labor's oppositional and left-wing self-representations. Manual imagery was central to labor's self-representations long before the idea of the white collar emerged. The hand was an icon of preindustrial labor, as in the brotherly handshake that symbolizes fraternity; it has dominated labor iconography since the industrial revolution, with the clenched fist serving as an especially prominent symbol of struggle (Korff

1992). In the nineteenth-century United States, manual imagery was wedded to Protestantism to valorize the new and for many unsavory "class of permanent hirelings" that had appeared on the scene (Rodgers 1978, 32); hence, labor deployed the language of virtuous work against sinful idleness to contest "irrational, anti-republican and unchristian opinions in relation to the worth and respectability of *manual labor*" (175; emphasis in original). The work/idleness binary, too, was highly gendered, redolent of the "sons of toil" versus "idle womanhood," and the labor leader William Sylvis did not hesitate to condemn "effeminate nonproducers" (174). By the end of the century, producerism had linked the idle, effeminate nonproducers to parasitical exploitation of productive, especially manual or goods-producing, labor. If the producers were a known quantity, however, the nonproducers included a wide range of targets of resentment, from robber barons and bankers to professionals and the unemployed.

> The myth [of yeoman prosperity] began with a sense of moral loss. . . . From Thorstein Veblen's lament . . . to the anxious editorial complaint of the rush from manual work into white-collar gentility, a sense of lost virtue was inextricably entangled with discussions of work. Somewhere in the past, . . . men and women had worked hard and without complaint, had reaped what they earned, and had been happy.
>
> But for its cutting edge the myth demanded a villain. From beggar to millionaire, this figure was capable of a bewildering variety of outward guises. . . . Advocates of competitive capitalism and the socialist commonwealth, money cranks and genteel ladies bountiful joined in declaring their allegiance to a commonwealth of labor and raised their voices against the lazy and parasitic. Together they helped make idleness one of the most popular weapons in the arsenal of rhetorical invectives. (211–12)

In the thirties, these linkages coalesced in the proletarian imaginary, produced within a far-flung community of labor, the left, artists, writers, and the New Deal. Male, manual, industrial, productive, moral worth—all were canonized as distinctively proletarian. In the arts, nineteenth-century painters had envisioned unified manual and mental labor within rural idylls and the trades; when the worker appeared in paintings, prints, and murals of the thirties, it was in the image of manual labor (see Hills 1985). Those representations also were racially, ethnically, and sexually coded. While New Deal arts agencies encouraged images of white, male, manual workers painted and cast in heroic gestures, comparable images of women, minorities, and white-collar labor were actively discouraged (Melosh 1993). And if the proletarian imaginary affirmed a class line between capital and labor, it also absorbed and carried forward the producerist suspicion of motley non-producers, asserting a class boundary between manual and nonmanual labor. Authors of proletarian novels stressed "the insularity of the American working class. In their eyes it [was] blue collar, poorly educated, and pre-dominantly male," facing an "unbridgeable" divide between manual and white-collar work (Bernstein 1985, 198) that was explored through the the-matic of rising out of one's class.

Though somewhat obscured by theory and research protocols (such as reliance on occupational statistics), neo-Weberian and neo-Marxist theory reproduce important aspects of the proletarian imaginary, including de-scriptions of the valorized worker. Epistemologically, their curious psychic distance from nonmanual workers combined with sympathies toward in-dustrial workers also echoes the subject-position of that imaginary, includ-ing its exclusions, demotions, and tutelary stance toward those considered outside or in potential conflict with the working class. With the authority of social science, neo-Weberian and neo-Marxist work lends objectivity and even timeless truth-value to a body of descriptions and sentiments that emerged agonistically as one of the major achievements of the prewar left: offering a heroic image inviting identification within a compellingly epic narrative of worker-led social change.

Similarly with the class-coded image of the conservative white collar, which has its own determinations and refinements. For example, the post-war theoretical work bears traces of interwar controversies over this group in which economic sociologists, revisionists, the Comintern, and the right theorized about, projected, and struggled for its allegiance. From the 1920s through the present, as Kocka says,

> the thesis connecting industrial capitalist development, the situation of the
> lower middle class, and the development of right-wing protest tendencies has
> been advanced primarily in the context of the controversy over fascism. Parts
> of the argument have been contradicted. For the most part it is unclearly for-
> mulated, sometimes only vaguely alluded to. It appears with marked shifts of
> emphasis, in varying contexts, and is qualified with distinctions. Yet . . . this
> is still the basic thesis that prevails. . . . It tries to explain the lower middle
> classes' *potential* susceptibility to right-wing radicalization as a consequence
> of transformation processes which typically appear at advanced stages of capi-
> talist industrialization. (1980, 5; emphasis in original)

Indeed, what must be known already has been said; the literature can fairly be described as a body of repetitions and refinements. For example, in the postwar theory each theoretical gesture, each rationalizing process, each white-collar type and routinized location was fully anticipated by Mills, who himself evenhandedly quoted and cited Marx, Weber, Fabian socialists, social democrats, institutionalists, Trotskyists, critical theorists, prewar German economic sociologists, and German revisionists. In white-collar theory, the central expository strategy has been review and repetition of statements from an archive that spans this century (cf. Oppenheimer 1985), perhaps worrying a binary or incorporating recent findings to order and expand descriptions of white-collar types with greater theoretical exactitude (see Braverman 1974; Carchedi 1977; Goldthorpe 1982; Lockwood 1989; Mills 1951; Poulantzas 1975; Wright 1978, 1985). In effect, not only a historic imaginary but one hundred years of statements inspired by dimly remembered projects of social theory, the disciplines, and left-wing parties remain actively present and strategically available.

What exactly is the question posed by this problematic? Kocka ties the use of the term "white collar" to a leveling-and-decline thesis applied to the old, propertied middle class, then extended to salaried, nonmanual labor by at least 1890 in Germany and 1915 in the United States (1980, 4). The white collar's future was debated as decline and proletarianization, vestigial survival, or growth, the last prediction claimed by the revisionists who identified it as a new class transgressing the bounds of capitalism. More precisely, the roots of these categories lie in the party debates over the capitalist trajectory and consequent future of working-class action. According to Bernstein (1898), Marx had argued that at some evolutionary moment in the development of capitalism, workers and others would reach a condition of identity, represented by near universal proletarianization and immiseration. For Bernstein, if some new group or class appeared, it must prefigure a change in evolutionary direction, perhaps beyond capitalism and its simple social landscape, and he found such a group in affluent, skilled, salaried employees. Unlike the combative and culturally limited proletariat with its negative struggle (in the Hegelian sense), this new class held the creative capacity to democratize industry and the state and thereby lead a quiet evolution out of class society and its antagonisms; indeed, as a minority class, industrial workers lacked both the right and the capacity to impose or universalize a proletarian view of social change. Economic sociologists replied that the salaried were merely a social layer between capital and labor, having a distinct status and interests and an unstable class allegiance, while party theorists on the Marxist left held that they were not an independent "third force" (as argued by the right) but a vacillating group to be won over by proletarian leadership (see Carter 1985, chapter 1).

In its repetitions and elaborations, postwar theory carries forward both the prewar sociological and party theory and its dialogical stances. In the process, however, white-collar theorists have conceded the main point. Bernstein's question was, if sameness shows developmental readiness for socialism, does social difference imply a new social logic and, with it, a new vanguard agent? Though answering with a resounding affirmation of the persistent force of capitalism, white-collar theory remains well on the terrain of the revisionist problem. Thus, neo-Weberians and neo-Marxists have written a counternarrative of class structure and class formation that emphatically rejects the idea of postcapitalist and postindustrial society. Instead of an independent or quasi-independent class on a postcapitalist trajectory, they have situated the new middle class firmly within structures of capital. The white collar's trajectory does not lie outside or presage a new system but depends on and expresses the logic of rationalization, an overarching, directional master process that governs the unfolding of this late stage of capitalism and explains its class dynamics. The "new class" are mere, albeit unrealized, wage-workers who in some portion and at some moment will come to resemble the true worker, ceasing to perform as agents of capital and instead embracing their true class vocation.

However leaky this sieve, the white collar is essential to neo-Marxist and neo-Weberian narratives precisely because it is different while the worker is the same. White-collar theory ratifies the "truth" that the worker really is that fully proletarianized figure that capitalism must produce; in fact, it is its universalized condition as propertyless that is so enabling to its stature as the solidaristic subject of social change. By contrast, the white collar will be developmentally incomplete and an obstacle to change so long as it retains its differences.

In the end, neo-Marxist and neo-Weberian theory counters the claims of revisionist and postindustrial theory by reasserting both the continued explanatory power of capitalism and workers' centrality to fundamental change, but only at a very high cost. The image of the worker that is so strongly defended and in which there are such deep emotional investments is an icon ineluctably linked with a bygone discursive moment—one, moreover, that is gendered, racialized, and riddled with producerism and the worst of workerism. Further, in countering the revisionist logic of relentless organic differentiation, white-collar theory has returned us to an unfortunate "two camps" vision of capitalism in which a simple social totality is governed by a teleological master process. In its praiseworthy attempts to keep capitalism visible, white-collar theory also makes the major concession that difference does indeed constitute a developmental obstacle to a politics of class. Here it can only hold out the hope (or the dystopic vision) that, although the highest and best stage of capitalism would be the two-class model, given time, late capitalism may oblige us by sorting the wheat from the chaff. Little wonder, then, that this politics of class so often reverts to anxious scrutiny of occupational statistics, in a highly specialized accounting of a priori categorical groups.

Conclusion

I know you think I'm below the evolutionary scale.
—A former coworker to her boss

The figures of the blue and white collars—enacting their unchanging conflicts, moving through their distinctive spaces of factory and office, city and suburb—have represented for many people the quintessential social landscape of twentieth-century capitalism. There are, of course, many sites at which the collar line has been developed and a variety of statements that have been enabled by it. I have focused on that domain in sociology that has attempted to ground the classificatory scheme in identifiable occupations, types of labor, and groups of people. As it happens, though the categories are widely accepted as accurate reflections of the way things are and as rigorously supported by economic and sociological concepts, the constitutive binaries cannot be sustained. White-collar specialists rely instead on the complement of visual, bodily, and spatial metaphors and, through these, produce a panoptical tableau of class and society.

It is easy enough to see that the stories are totalizing and that, in that sense, it hardly matters that there are fissures and uncertain sites of blue- and white-collar labor. I am more concerned, however, with the effects of these categories and the problem they support than with their internal consistency, especially in the neo-Weberian and neo-Marxist theory whose influence has reached into and intersected with so many political, intellectual, and organizational practices. Most obviously, these categorical terms have been the vehicle for deprecating descriptions of a variety of workers, all herded into a group of undesirables and tarred with the same brush as unproductive, selfish, privileged, close to management, confused about their real interests, less than real workers, and so forth. Such descriptions are not only diminishing but have provided arrogant justifications for a one-way, tutelary relationship between the left and labor community and white-collar workers.

In addition, these representations are primitivizing. After decades the essential nature of the white collar remains unchanged, suspended in a systemic time that holds all the agency. As Mills said, "The white-collar people slipped quietly into modern society. Whatever history they have had is a history without events; whatever common interests they have do not lead to unity; whatever future they have will not be of their own making" (1951, ix). That is, these unloved figures have held little interest in themselves, but have been merely the vessels for representing the system of monopoly or advanced capitalism—or, rather, its visible signs within a problematic of a simple social totality moving inexorably toward completion and supersession. Seen through the labor process, workplace relations, or an interplay of knowledge, power, and interest, collectively and in its many types and descriptions, the white collar has served as a reflection, expression, and personified embodiment of developmental moments within a rationalization dynamic that governs production, administration, the state, class structure and formation, and, in short, society. Indeed, though fated from the moment of its appearance for at least partial bureaucratic and technological appropriation, the white collar's story cannot end without jeopardizing the system's fundamental dynamic; logically, fulfillment of its trajectory could only signify completion of the stage of advanced capitalism. Instead, white-collar types always remain developmentally inferior, in a state of endless becoming in which they themselves play no role.

Of course, primitivizing cuts both ways. In neo- and post-Marxist postindustrial and new social movement theory, the white collar is the normative figure and the blue collar is developmentally inferior. Here, the white-collar knowledge worker holds the spatially and culturally more extensive knowledge, altruism, and collective capacity to effect social change; the forward looking, vanguard status of the new middle class is constituted only by contrast with the rearguard role of the creaky blue collar (see Touraine 1988). From this perspective, the manual, goods-producing worker really is that debased figure—ignorant, low-skilled, masculinist—that white-collar theory celebrates. Similarly, in a major reversal and redescription, it is no longer the blue-collar worker who stands outside and subverts the apparatus. Rather, in late Frankfurt School and new social movement theory, the blue collar is a consensual participant in, defender of, perhaps a prime beneficiary of late capitalism; radical social change must emerge, then, from the blue collar's other, theorized as exterior to or marginalized by industrial production. Hence, theories of postindustrial unionism, for instance, reject the achievements of blue-collar organization as organic with a waning, bureaucratic Fordism; new, dynamic, participatory, antisexist unionism originates with the white-collar and service workforce (Cobble 1990, 1991b; Heckscher 1988; Schmidman 1979; Sweeney and Nussbaum 1989). On the wrong side of history's dynamic, blue-collar workers and their organizations are reduced to being anachronisms in their own time. In fact, this potentiality was inscribed in white-collar theory all along: if white-collar types were moving into position, the blue collar itself already was proletarianized—developmentally ready but stalled, perhaps overtaken by the enemy within the ranks (Hobsbawm 1981). Or perhaps affluence, consumerism, and productivism have undermined the blue collar's proletarian stature, raising it inconveniently above its immiserated station and corroding its moral leadership from within: "whatever house the workers might have been thought to be building has not been built. Now there are no centers of firm and uniform identification" (Mills 1951, 332). Ironically, the very imagery that constituted a powerful working class has contributed to its demotion as new and "different" figures seem to peripheralize outmoded workers and a transformative politics of class (Gibson-Graham 1996).

Finally, the underlying principle of the collar line is that any differences must arise within a contradiction. In this constitutive nexus, class is tightly knit with occupation, labor, exploitation, gender, authority, consciousness, the geographies of capitalism, and much else—all embodied in the figure of the worker and held together organically by a systemic trajectory. The problem of the collar line is one of how to value difference from an ideal—to wit, a uniform mass across work, market, and social situations as the sign of proletarianization and precondition for class struggle. Indeed, white-collar theory on class formation rests explicitly on the notion that solidarism follows from an identical condition, and, conversely, that heterogeneity creates disparate and necessarily conflicting interests and action. Such reasoning, of course, has dominated much of the neo-Marxist scholarship. As neatly summarized by Gordon, Edwards, and Reich,

> The disunity of the U.S. working class persists in large part as a result of objective divisions among workers in their production experiences; these objective divisions constitute both a consequence of continuing capitalist development in the United States and a barrier to a unified anticapitalist working-class movement. (1982, 8)

Subtly, the collar line supports the dangerous idea that only like people can organize and work together; almost imperceptibly, solidarity across differences great and small becomes virtually oxymoronic.

There is much that can be said of the collar line—that it gives us only a rigidly bounded, essentialist construct for class, for instance, one that fosters scientism and teleologism. And despite the great number of types, names, and descriptions, this construct leaves remarkably few moves for workers or others to make, no new or transformative subject positions for them to create and fill. Though it has never ruled political practice in any simple way, this language of class has supported unhappy descriptions and unfortunate practices, trivializing and rejecting the struggles and aspirations of a wide variety of workers who fall short of the normative worker known from labor iconography and the proletarian imaginary. Equally, the ideal of the self-identical class has thrown almost insuperable hurdles in the path of a transformative politics, burdening it with numerous, near metaphysical conditions people must satisfy in order to be recognized and validated by a politics of class, raising obstacles and even self-satisfied objections to the negotiation of difference, and subordinating the mandates of political practice to the logic of a big, impersonal motor of change beyond the power of human intervention. Despite the many beautiful resonances of the proletarian imaginary, it was an agonistic device and historic product that demoted and failed to speak to or for large numbers of workers. Today, maybe this is neither the class imaginary nor the politics of class that we want.

Notes

This essay is based in part on my master's thesis at the University of Massachusetts, Amherst, of which I was fortunate in my advisor, Patricia Greenfield, and two committee members, Richard Wolff and Julie Graham, all of whom contributed generously with their time and helpful criticisms. A somewhat new line of argument was greatly facilitated by discussion at the AESA Workshop on Class Analysis and written comments from David Ruccio. Julie Graham, who has supported this work through all its ups and downs, also has enriched it immeasurably with her own theoretical skills and judgment. In addition, I am grateful to Mark Gould at Haverford College, who always listens, encourages, and comments. Finally, my husband, Christopher Couch, read and commented on each draft. At each stage he reworded white-collar theory in plain English, which proved an often hilariously funny antidote to an otherwise glum subject.

1. For instance, in 1997 nearly ten thousand reservation takers, gate agents, and ticket sellers employed in 110 cities by US Airways voted to form a union, joining the Communications Workers of America. Though this was the largest private-sector union election in a decade, it was instantly framed as a novel and special case of unionism. As Kate Bronfenbrenner, a progressive labor educator and specialist, said, "The victory . . . is very significant. It's not just because it involved so many workers, but it's the kind of workers that people questioned whether the labor movement could organize. These are white-collar workers" (Greenhouse 1997, A1). Though the union drive had been precipitated by a restructuring that deepened the disparities in pay, benefits, and voice between nonunion and union employees (including organized

"white-collar" pilots and flight attendants), the specter of white-collar submission and newness to struggle refused to go away. In the opinion of Richard Bensinger of the AFL-CIO, "These are highly educated, white-collar workers, part of the information age, knowledge-based new economy. What's interesting is they were so supportive of the union. One woman there told me, they want to be players, not pawns" (A16). The unintended irony of this judgment should hardly escape anyone familiar with the Communications Workers: one of the oldest white-collar unions, tracing its roots to union organizing by women telephone operators at the turn of the century, affiliated with the CIO at midcentury, and having a longstanding base among "information workers," including telephone workers, office workers, technicians, and professionals (Kassalow 1966; Norwood 1990).

Bibliography

Abercrombie, N., and J. Urry. 1983. *Capital, Labour, and the Middle Classes*. Boston: George Allen and Unwin.

Abercrombie, N., S. Hill, and B. S. Turner. 1988. *The Penguin Dictionary of Sociology*. 2d ed. London: Penguin.

Abodeely, J. E., R. C. Hammer, and A. L. Sandler. 1981. *The NLRB and the Appropriate Bargaining Unit*. Rev. ed. Labor Relations and Public Policy Series, no. 3. Philadelphia: Industrial Research Unit, Wharton School, University of Pennsylvania.

Adorno, T., ed. 1950. *The Authoritarian Personality*. New York: Harper.

Alexander, P. 1996. "Bathhouses and Brothels: Symbolic Sites in Discourse and Practice." In *Policing Public Sex*, ed. Dangerous Bedfellows, 221–41. Boston: South End Press.

———. 1997. "Feminism, Sex Workers, and Human Rights." In *Whores and Other Feminists*, ed. J. Nagle, 83–97. New York: Routledge.

Allen, P., et al. 1976. *Jean Maddox: The Fight for Rank and File Democracy*. Berkeley, Calif.: Union WAGE Educational Committee.

Allison, D. 1992. *Bastard out of Carolina*. New York: Penguin.

Althusser, L. 1970a. *For Marx*. New York: Vintage Books.

———. 1970b. "From *Capital* to Marx's Philosophy." In *Reading Capital*, L. Althusser and E. Balibar, 11–69. Trans. B. Brewster. London: New Left Books.

———. 1977. *For Marx*. London: NLB.

———. 1993. *The Future Lasts Forever*. Trans. R. Veasey. New York: New Press.

Amariglio, J. 1984. *Economic History and the Theory of Primitive Socioeconomic Development*. Ph.D. diss., Department of Economics, University of Massachusetts, Amherst.

———. 1987. "Marxism against Economic Science: Althusser's Legacy." In

Research in Political Economy, vol. 10, ed. P. Zarembka. 159–94. Greenwich, Conn.: JAI Press.

———. 1997. "Subjectivity, Class and Marx's 'Forms of the Commune.'" Unpublished paper, Department of Economics, Merrimack College, North Andover, Mass.

Amott, T. L., and J. A. Matthaei. 1991. *Race, Gender and Work: A Multicultural Economic History of Women in the United States.* Boston: South End Press.

Aronson, R. L. 1991. *Self-Employment: A Labor Market Perspective.* Ithaca: ILR Press.

Arvidson, E. 1995. "Cognitive Mapping and Class Politics: Towards a Nondeterminist Image of the City." *Rethinking Marxism* 8, no. 2: 8–23.

———. 1996. *An Economic Critique of Urban Planning and the Postmodern City: Los Angeles.* Ph.D. diss., Department of Economics, University of Massachusetts, Amherst.

Baber, K., and K. Allen. 1992. *Women and Families: Feminist Reconstructions.* New York: Guilford.

Bain, G. S. 1970. *The Growth of White-Collar Unionism.* Oxford: Clarendon Press.

Bain, G. S., and R. Price. [1972] 1983. "Who Is a White-Collar Employee?" Reprinted in *The New Working Class? White-Collar Workers and Their Organizations,* eds. R. Hyman and R. Price, 46–51. London: Macmillan.

Balibar, E. 1994. *Masses, Classes, Ideas: Studies on Politics and Philosophy before and after Marx.* Trans. J. Swenson. New York: Routledge.

Barkley Brown, E. 1990. "African American Women's Quilting: A Framework for Conceptualizing and Teaching African-American Women's History." In *Black Women in America: Social Science Perspectives,* eds. M. R. Malson et al., 9–18. Chicago: University of Chicago Press.

Barron, C. 1995. "The Economics of Incest." *Incest Survivors Information Exchange* 12, no. 4 (March): 6.

Barry, K. 1979. *Female Sexual Slavery.* New Jersey: Prentice-Hall.

———. 1984. "International Politics of Female Sexual Slavery" and "The Network Defines Its Issues: Theory, Evidence, and Analysis of Female Sexual Slavery." In *International Feminism: Networking against Female Sexual Slavery,* eds. K. Barry, C. Bunch, and S. Castley, 21–48. New York: International Women's Tribune Center.

———. 1995. *The Prostitution of Sexuality.* New York: New York University Press.

Baxandall, R., et al. 1976. Special issue of *Monthly Review* 28, no. 3. "Technology, the Labor Process, and the Working Class."

Baxter, J. 1990. "Domestic Labour: Issues and Studies." *Labour and Industry* 3, no. 1: 112–45.

———. 1993. *Work at Home: The Domestic Division of Labour.* St Lucia, QLD: University of Queensland Press.

Beal, E. F., and E. D. Wickersham. 1959. *The Practice of Collective Bargaining.* Homewood, Ill.: Richard D. Irwin.

Bell, L., ed. 1987. *Good Girls/Bad Girls: Sex Trade Workers and Feminists Face to Face.* Toronto: Women's Press.

Bell, S. 1994. *Reading, Writing, and Rewriting the Prostitute Body.* Bloomington: Indiana University Press.

———. 1995. *Whore Carnival.* New York: Autonomedia.

Beneria, L. 1996. "Thou Shalt Not Live by Statistics Alone, But It Might Help." *Feminist Economics* 2, no. 3: 64–83.

Benner, P., and J. Wrubel. 1989. "Caring Comes First." In *The Primacy of Caring: Stress and Coping in Health And Illness,* eds. P. Benner and J. Wrubel, 1–5. New York: Addison-Wesley.

Bernstein, E. [1898] 1961. *Evolutionary Socialism: A Criticism and Affirmation.* Trans. E. C. Harvey. Reprint, New York: Schocken Books.

Bernstein, I. 1985. *A Caring Society: The New Deal, the Worker, and the Great Depression.* Boston: Houghton Mifflin.

Bittman, M., and F. Lovejoy. 1993. "Domestic Power: Negotiating an Unequal Division of Labour within a Framework of Equality." *Australian and New Zealand Journal of Sociology* 229, no. 3: 302–21.

Blum, A. A. 1971. "The Office Employee." In *White-Collar Workers,* A. A. Blum et al., 3–45. New York: Random House.

Blume, E. S. 1990. *Secret Survivors.* New York: John Wiley & Sons.

Bohlen, C. 1997. "Exotic Imports Have Captured Italy's Sex Market." *New York Times,* 9 July, A4.

Bottomore, T. 1990. "Charles Wright Mills (1916–62)." In *Encyclopedia of the American Left,* eds. M. J. Buhle, P. Buhle, and D. Georgakas, 470–71. Urbana: University of Illinois Press.

Braverman, H. 1974. *Labor and Monopoly Capital: The Degradation of Work in the Twentieth Century.* New York: Monthly Review Press.

Bregger, J. 1996. "Measuring Self-Employment in the United States." *Monthly Labor Review* 119, no. 1 and 2 (January/February): 3–9.

Brewer, R. M. 1993. "Theorizing Race, Class, and Gender." In *Theorizing Black Feminisms,* eds. S. James and A. Busia, 13–30. New York: Routledge.

Britton, S. 1990. "The Role of Services in Production." *Progress in Human Geography* 14(4): 529–46.

Brown, G., and J. Jenski. 1997. "Two Modes of Child Nurturing." *Journal of Psychohistory* 24, no. 4 (spring): 339–52.

Brown, W. 1995. *States of Injury: Power and Freedom in Late Modernity.* Princeton: Princeton University Press.

Burr, C. 1996. "Supporting the Helpers." *Nursing Clinics of North America* 31, no. 1 (March): 69–76.

Bush, G. 1990. "'I'd Prefer Not To': A Research Note on Resistance to Office Work in Some Post World War II American Films." *Labor History* 31, no. 3: 361–72.

Butler, J. 1990. *Gender Trouble: Feminism and the Subversion of Identity.* New York: Routledge.

———. 1992. "Contingent Foundations: Feminism and the Question of 'Postmodernism.'" In *Feminists Theorize the Political*, eds. J. Butler and J. W. Scott, 1–21. New York and London: Routledge.

———. 1993. *Bodies That Matter: On the Discursive Limits of "Sex."* New York: Routledge.

———. 1995. "Contingent Foundations." In *Feminist Contentions: A Philosophical Exchange*, S. Benhabib et al., 35–58. New York: Routledge.

Callari, A., and D. F. Ruccio. 1996. "Introduction." In *Postmodern Materialism and the Future of Marxist Theory*, eds. A. Callari and D. F. Ruccio, 1–48. Hanover, N.H.: University Press of New England.

Callon, M., and B. Latour. 1981. "Unscrewing the Big Leviathan: How Actors Macro-structure Reality and How Sociologists Help Them to Do So." In *Advances in Social Theory and Methodology: Toward an Integration of Micro- and Macro-Sociologies*, eds. K. Knorr-Cetina and A. V. Cicourel, 277–303. London: Routledge and Kegan Paul.

Cameron, J. 1996/1997. "Throwing a Dishcloth into the Works: Troubling Theories of Domestic Labor." *Rethinking Marxism* 9 (summer): 24–44.

———. 1997. "Turning the Household Inside Out: Homosexuality, Heterosexuality, and Housework." In *Institute of Australian Geographers: Conference Proceedings, 1997*. Hobart, Tasmania.

Cappelli, P. 1993. "Are Skill Requirements Rising? Evidence from Production and Clerical Jobs." *Industrial and Labor Relations Review* 46, no. 3: 515–30.

Carby, H. V. 1987. *Reconstructing Womanhood: The Emergence of the Afro-American Woman Novelist*. New York: Oxford University Press.

Carchedi, G. 1977. *On the Economic Identification of Social Classes*. Boston: Routledge and Kegan Paul.

Carotenuto, A. 1982. *A Secret Symmetry*. Trans. A. Pomerans, J. Shepley, and K. Winston. New York: Pantheon Books.

Carré, F. J., V. L. duRivage, and C. Tilly. 1995. "Piecing Together the Fragmented Workplace: Unions and Public Policy on Flexible Employment." In *Unions and Public Policy: The New Economy, Law, and Democratic Politics*, ed. L. G. Flood, 13–37. Westport, Conn.: Greenwood Press.

Carter, B. 1985. *Capitalism, Class Conflict, and the New Middle Class*. Boston: Routledge and Kegan Paul.

Chant, S., and C. McIlwaine. 1995. *Women of a Lesser Cost: Female Labour, Foreign Exchange, and Philippine Development*. London: Pluto Press.

Chapkis, W. 1995. *Prostitution Politics and Policies: An Examination of the Commercial Sex Trade*. Ph.D. diss., University of California, Santa Cruz.

———. 1997. *Live Sex Acts: Women Performing Erotic Labor*. New York: Routledge.

Children's Defense Fund. 1992. *The State of America's Children Yearbook, 1992*. Washington, D.C.: CDF Press.

————. 1997. *The State of America's Children, 1997*. Washington, D.C.: CDF Press.

Childress, A. 1956. *Like One of the Family: Conversations from a Domestic's Life.* Brooklyn: Independence Publishers.

Chira, S. 1994. "Murdered Children: In Most Cases a Parent Did It." *New York Times*, November 5, 9.

Chodorow, N. 1978. *The Reproduction of Mothering.* Berkeley and Los Angeles: University of California Press.

————. 1989. *Feminism and Psychoanalytic Theory.* New Haven: Yale Press.

————. 1994. *Femininities, Masculinities, Sexualities.* Lexington: University Press of Kentucky.

Christopherson, S. 1989. "Flexibility in the U.S. Service Economy and the Emerging Spatial Division of Labour." *Transactions of the Institute of British Geographers, N.S.* 14, no. 2: 131–43.

Clark-Lewis, E. 1994. *Living In, Living Out: African Domestics in Washington, D.C., 1910–1940.* Washington: Smithsonian Institution Press.

Clawson, D. 1980. *Bureaucracy and the Labor Process.* New York: Monthly Review Press.

Cobble, D. S. 1990. "Union Strategies for Organizing and Representing the New Service Workforce." Paper presented at the 43rd annual conference of the Industrial Relations Research Association, Washington, D.C.

————. 1991a. "Organizing the Postindustrial Work Force: Lessons from the History of Waitress Unionism." *Industrial and Labor Relations Review* 44, no. 3: 419–36.

————. 1991b. *Dishing It Out: Waitresses and Their Unions in the Twentieth Century.* Urbana: University of Illinois Press.

Cohen, E. 1993. "Are We (Not) What We Are Becoming? Gay 'Identity,' 'Gay Studies,' and the Disciplining of Knowledge." In *Knowledges: Historical and Critical Studies in Disciplinarity*, eds. E. Messer-Davidow, D. R. Shumway, and D. J. Sylvan, 397-421. Charlottesville: University Press of Virginia.

Collins, P. H. 1990. *Black Feminist Thought: Knowledge, Consciousness, and the Politics of Empowerment.* New York: Routledge.

Conrow, T. 1992. "Contract Servicing from an Organizing Model." *Labor Research Review* 17: 45–59.

Coontz, S. 1992. *The Way We Never Were.* New York: Basic Books.

Corbin, A. 1987. "Commercial Sexuality in Nineteenth-Century France: A System of Images and Regulations." In *The Making of the Modern Body: Sexuality and Society in the Nineteenth Century*, eds. C. Gallagher and T. Laqueur, 209-19. Berkeley and Los Angeles: University of California Press.

————. 1990. *Women for Hire: Prostitution and Sexuality in France after 1850.* Cambridge, Mass.: Harvard University Press.

Cornell, D. 1991. *Beyond Accommodation.* New York: Routledge.

———. 1995. *The Imaginary Domain: Abortion, Pornography, and Sexual Harrassment.* New York and London: Routledge.

Coser, L. 1974. "Servants: The Obsolescence of an Occupational Role." *Social Forces* 52: 31–40.

Crain, M. 1994. "Gender and Union Organizing." *Industrial and Labor Relations Review* 47, no. 2: 227–48.

Crompton, R. 1979. "Trade Unionism and the Insurance Clerk." *Sociology* 13, no. 3: 403–26.

Crompton, R., and G. Jones. 1984. *White-Collar Proletariat: Deskilling and Gender in Clerical Work.* Philadelphia: Temple University Press.

Cross, G., and P. Shergold. 1987. "'We Think We Are of the Oppressed': Gender, White Collar Work, and Grievances of Late Nineteenth-Century Women." *Labor History* 28, no. 1: 23–53.

Curtin, E. R. 1970. *White-Collar Unionization.* Personnel Policy Study No. 220. New York: National Industrial Conference Bulletin.

Curtis, P., et al. 1995. *Child Abuse and Neglect: A Look At The States.* Washington, D.C.: Child Welfare League of America.

Daly, G. 1991. "The Discursive Construction of Economic Space: Logics of Organization and Disorganization." *Economy and Society* 20, no. 1: 79–102.

Davies, M. W. 1982. *Woman's Place Is at the Typewriter: Office Work and Office Workers, 1870–1930.* Philadelphia: Temple University Press.

Davis, A. 1981. *Women, Race, and Class.* New York: Vintage Books.

Davis, M. 1987. "Chinatown, Part Two? The 'Internationalization' of Downtown Los Angeles." *New Left Review* 164: 65–86.

———. 1990. *City of Quartz: Excavating the Future in Los Angeles.* London: Verso.

———. 1992. *Beyond Blade Runner: Urban Control, the Ecology of Fear.* Pamphlet no. 23. Westfield, N. J.: Open Magazine Pamphlet Series.

Dear, M., and S. Flusty. 1998. "Postmodern Urbanism." *Annals of the Association of American Geographers* 88: 50–72.

Deckard, G., B. Rountree, and L. Hicks. 1988. "Nursing Productivity: A Qualitative View of Performance." *Nursing Economics* 6, no. 4 (July/August): 184–88.

DeFreitas, G. 1993. "Unionization among Racial and Ethnic Minorities." *Industrial and Labor Relations Review* 46, no. 2: 284–301.

Delacoste, F., and P. Alexander. 1987. *Sex Work: Writings by Women in the Sex Industry.* Pittsburgh: Cleis Press.

Delphy, C., and D. Leonard. 1992. *Familiar Exploitation: A New Analysis of Marriage in Contemporary Western Societies.* Cambridge: Polity.

deMause, L., ed. 1975. *The History of Childhood.* New York: Harper & Row.

Derrida, J. 1981. *Positions.* Trans. A. Bass. Chicago: University of Chicago Press.

Dickson, P. 1985. *On Our Own: A Declaration of Independence for the Self-Employed.* New York: Facts On File Publications.

Dill, B. T. 1988. "Our Mothers' Grief: Racial Ethnic Women and the Maintenance of Families." *Journal of Family History* 13, no. 4: 418.

———. 1994. *Across the Boundaries of Race and Class: An Exploration of Work and Family among Black Female Domestic Servants.* New York: Garland Publishing.

Dimock, W. C., and M. T. Gilmore, eds. 1994. *Rethinking Class: Literary Studies and Social Formations.* New York: Columbia University Press.

DiPrete, T. A. 1988. "The Upgrading and Downgrading of Occupations: Status Redefinition vs. Deskilling as Alternative Theories of Change." *Social Forces* 66, no. 3: 725–46.

Dorenkamp, A. G., et al., eds. 1995. *Images of Women in American Popular Culture.* 2nd ed. Fort Worth, Tex.: Harcourt Brace College Publishers.

Downs, A. 1994. *New Visions for Metropolitan America.* Washington, D.C.: Brookings Institution.

Du Bois, W. E. B. 1899. *The Philadelphia Negro.* Millwood, N.Y.: Kraus-Thomson Organization Limited.

Edgell, S. 1993. *Class.* New York: Routledge.

Engels, F. 1972. *The Origin of the Family, Private Property, and the State.* New York: International Publishers.

———. 1978. "The Origin of the Family, Private Property, and the State." In *The Marx-Engels Reader,* ed. R. Tucker, 734–59. New York: W. W. Norton.

Fagin, C., and D. Diers. 1983. "Occasional Notes: Nursing as Metaphor." *New England Journal of Medicine* 3, no. 9: 116–17.

Flint, A. 1996. "Skin Trade Spreading across U.S." *Sunday Boston Globe,* December 1, A1.

Folbre, N. 1987. "A Patriarchal Mode of Production." In *Alternatives to Economic Orthodoxy,* eds. R. Albelda, C. Gunn, and W. Waller, 323–38. New York: M. E. Sharpe.

Folbre, N., and M. Abel. 1989. "Women's Work and Women's Households: Gender Bias in the U.S. Census." *Social Research* 56, no. 3: 545–69.

Form, W. 1987. "On the Degradation of Skills." *Annual Review of Sociology* 13: 29–47.

Forrest, A. 1993. "Women and Industrial Relations Theory: No Room in the Discourse." *Relations Industrielles/ Industrial Relations* 48, no. 3: 409–40.

Forst, M., and M. Blomquist. 1991. *Missing Children.* New York: Lexington.

Foucault, M. 1981. "Friendship as Lifestyle: An Interview with Michel Foucault." *Gay Information* 7 (spring): 4–6.

———. 1988. "The Ethic of Care for the Self as a Practice of Freedom." In *The Final Foucault,* eds. J. Bernauer and D. Rasmussen, 1–20. Boston: MIT Press.

———. 1990. *The History of Sexuality,* vol. 1. New York: Vintage Books.

Fraad, H. 1995. "Children as an Exploited Class." In *Marxism in the Postmodern Age,* eds. A. Callari, S. Cullenberg, and C. Biewener, 375–384. New York: Guildford Press.

———. 1996/1997. "At Home with Incest." *Rethinking Marxism* 9, no. 4: 16–39.

Fraad, H., S. Resnick, and R. Wolff. 1989. "For Every Knight in Shining Armor, There's a Castle Waiting to Be Cleaned." *Rethinking Marxism* 2, no. 4: 10–69.

———. 1994. *Bringing It All Back Home: Class, Gender, and Power in the Modern Household.* London: Pluto Press.

Frankenberg, R. 1993. *The Social Construction of Whiteness: White Women, Race Matters.* Minneapolis: University of Minnesota Press.

Freeman, J. B. 1993. "Hardhats: Construction Workers, Manliness, and the 1970 Pro-War Demonstrations." *Journal of Social History* 26, no. 4: 725–44.

Freeman, R. B., and J. L. Medoff. 1984. *What Do Unions Do?* New York: Basic Books.

Frenza, L. 1993. "An Early Intervention Approach to Ending Child Abuse and Neglect." *Journal of Psychohistory* 21, no. 1 (summer): 29–36.

Fried, G., and R. Wolff. 1994. "Modern Ancients: Self-Employed Truckers." *Rethinking Marxism* 7, no. 4: 103–15.

Gabriel, S. 1989. "Ancients: A Marxian Theory of Self-Exploitation." Ph.D. diss., Department of Economics, University of Massachusetts, Amherst.

———. 1990. "Ancients: A Marxian Theory of Self-Exploitation." *Rethinking Marxism* 3, no. 1: 85–106.

Ganzeboom, H. B. G., D. J. Treiman, and W. C. Ultec. 1991. "Comparative Intergenerational Stratification Research: Three Generations and Beyond." *Annual Review of Sociology* 17: 277–302.

Garreau, J. 1991. *Edge City: Life on the New Frontier.* New York: Doubleday.

Gershuny, J. 1987. "The Future of Service Employment." In *The Emerging Service Economy,* ed. O. Giarini, 105–24. Oxford: Pergamon.

Gertler, M. S. 1988. "The Limits to Flexibility: Comments on the Post-Fordist Vision of Production and Its Geography." *Transactions of the Institute of British Geographers, N.S.* 13: 419–32.

Getman, Julius G., and Bertrand Pogrebin. 1988. *Labor Relations: The Basic Processes, Law, and Practice.* New York: Foundation Press.

Gibson, K. 1992. "Hewers of Cake and Drawers of Tea." *Rethinking Marxism* 5, no. 4: 29–56.

———. 1998. "Social Polarization and the Politics of Difference: Discourses in Collusion or Collision?" In *Cities of Difference,* eds. R. Fincher and J. Jacobs, 301–16. New York: Guilford.

Gibson, K., and J. Graham. 1992. "Rethinking Class in Industrial Geography: Creating a Space for an Alternative Politics of Class." *Economic Geography* 68, no. 2: 109–27.

Gibson, K., and S. Watson. 1995. "Postmodern Spaces, Cities, and Politics: An Introduction." In *Postmodern Cities and Spaces,* eds. S. Watson and K. Gibson, 1–10. Oxford: Blackwell.

Gibson-Graham, J. K. 1993. "Waiting for the Revolution, or How to Smash Capitalism While Working at Home in Your Spare Time." *Rethinking Marxism* 6, no. 3: 10–24.

———. 1994. "'Stuffed If I Know!': Reflections on Post-Modern Feminist Social Research." *Gender, Place, and Culture* 1, no. 2: 205–24.

———. 1996. *The End of Capitalism (As We Knew It): A Feminist Critique of Political Economy.* Oxford: Blackwell.

Giddens, A. 1973. *The Class Structure of the Advanced Societies.* New York: Harper & Row.

Gilman, C. P. 1966. *Women and Economics.* New York: Harper & Row.

———. 1972. *The Home: Its Work and Influence.* Champagne: University of Illinois Press.

Gilpin, T., et al. 1988. *On Strike for Respect: The Clerical and Technical Workers' Strike at Yale University (1984–85).* Chicago: Charles H. Kerr Publishing.

Giobbe, E. 1990. "Confronting the Liberal Lies about Prostitution." In *The Sexual Liberals and the Attack on Feminism,* eds. D. Leidholdt and J. Raymond, 67–81. New York: Pergamon Press.

Goldfield, M. 1987. *The Decline of Organized Labor in the United States.* Chicago: University of Chicago Press.

Goldman, E. 1970. *The Traffic in Women and Other Essays on Feminism.* New York: Chicago Times Press.

Goldthorpe, J. 1982. "On the Service Class, Its Formation and Future." In *Social Class and the Division of Labour: Essays in Honour of Ilya Neustadt,* eds. A. Giddens and G. Mackenzie, 162–85. New York: Cambridge University Press.

Goodnow, J. 1989. "Work in Households: An Overview and Three Studies." In *Households Work: Productive Activities, Women, and Income in the Household Economy,* ed. D. Ironmonger, 38–58. Sydney: Allen and Unwin.

Goodnow, J., and J. Bowles. 1994. *Men, Women, and Household Work.* Melbourne: Oxford University Press.

Gordon, D. M., R. Edwards, and M. Reich. 1982. *Segmented Work, Divided Workers: The Historical Transformation of Labor in the United States.* New York: Cambridge University Press.

Gordon, M. M. 1947. "*Kitty Foyle* and the Concept of Class as Culture." *American Journal of Sociology* 53, no. 3: 210–17.

Gottdiener, M. 1985. *The Social Production of Urban Space.* Austin: University of Texas Press.

Grady, J. T. 1978. "Collective Bargaining Units in the Transportation Industry." *Labor Law Journal* 29, no. 2: 118–25.

Greene, L., and C. Woodson. 1930. *The Negro Wage Earner.* New York: Van Ress Press.

Greenhouse, S. 1997. "Union Strategy Results in Coup at US Airways." *New York Times,* September 30, A1, A16.

Gregory, D. 1990. "Chinatown, Part Three? Soja and the Missing Spaces of Social Theory." *Strategies: A Journal of Theory, Culture, and Politics* 3: 40–103.

Greven, P. 1992. *Spare the Child.* New York: Vintage Books.

Grosz, E. 1990. "Conclusion: A Note on Essentialism and Difference." In *Feminist Knowledge as Critique and Construct,* ed. S. Gunew, 332–44. London: Routledge.

Guy-Sheftall, B. 1995. *Words of Fire: An Anthology of African-American Feminist Thought.* New York: New Press.

Hall, J. R., ed. 1997. *Reworking Class.* Ithaca, N.Y.: Cornell University Press.

Harmer, B., and V. Henderson. 1960. *Textbook of the Principles and Practice of Nursing.* New York: Macmillan.

Harris, B. 1993. "Don't Be Unconscious, Join Our Ranks." *Rethinking Marxism* 6, no. 1: 44–76.

Harris, T. 1982. *From Mammies to Militants: The Portrayal of Domestics in African American Literature.* Philadelphia: Temple University Press.

Harvey, D. 1989. *The Condition of Postmodernity.* Oxford: Basil Blackwell.

Haynes, E. R. 1923. "Negroes in Domestic Service in the United States." *Journal of Negro History* 8 (October): 384–442.

Heckscher, C. 1988. *The New Unionism: Employee Involvement in the Changing Corporation.* New York: Basic Books.

Hegedüs, A. 1983. "Bureaucracy." In *A Dictionary of Marxist Thought,* ed. T. Bottomore, 57–59. Cambridge: Harvard University Press.

Herman, J. 1981. *Father-Daughter Incest.* Cambridge: Harvard University Press.

Higginbotham, E. B. 1995. "African American Women's History and the Meta-language of Race." In *We Specialize in the Wholly Impossible: A Reader in Black Women's History,* eds. D. C. Hine, W. King, and L. Reed, 3–24. Brooklyn: Carlson Publishing.

Hills, P. 1985. "The Fine Arts in America: Images of Labor from 1800 to 1950." In *Essays from the Lowell Conference on Industrial History, 1982 and 1983,* ed. R. Weible, 120–64. North Andover, Mass.: Museum of American Textile History.

Hindess, B. 1997. *Discourses of Power: From Hobbes to Foucault.* Oxford: Blackwell.

Hindess, B., and P. Hirst. 1975. *Precapitalist Modes of Production.* London: Routledge and Kegan Paul.

Hise, G., M. Dear, and H. E. Schockman. 1996. "Rethinking Los Angeles." In *Rethinking Los Angeles,* eds. M. Dear, H. E. Schockman, and G. Hise, 1–14. Thousand Oaks: Sage.

Hobsbawm, E. 1981. "The Forward March of Labour Halted." In *The Forward March of Labour Halted?,* eds. M. Jacques and F. Mulhern. London: Verso.

Hochschild, A. R. 1983. *The Managed Heart.* Berkeley and Los Angeles: University of California Press.

———. 1997. *Time Binds.* New York: Metropolitan.

Hodges, D. C. [1962] 1977. "Cynicism in the Labor Movement." Reprinted in

American Society, Inc.: Studies of the Social Structure and Political Economy of the United States, 2d ed., ed. M. Zeitlin, 480–86. Chicago: Rand McNally College Publishing Company.

Hofman, L., and B. van Zoggel. 1995. "Barriers and Throughways 1992–1994." Trans. E. Lap. Utrecht, Netherlands: Foundation against Trafficking in Women (STV).

Hogan, L. 1984. *The Principles of Black Political Economy.* Boston: Routledge.

hooks, b. 1981. *Ain't I a Woman: Black Women and Feminism.* Boston: South End Press.

———. 1992. *Black Looks: Race and Representation.* Boston: South End Press.

Hotch, J. 1991. "Deconstructing Precariousness in Fixed-Term Employment." Unpublished paper, University of Massachusetts, Amherst.

———. 1994. "Theories and Practices of Self-Employment: Prospects for the Labor Movement." M.S. thesis, Department of Labor Studies, University of Massachusetts, Amherst.

Howell, D. R., and E. N. Wolff. 1991. "Trends in the Growth and Distribution of Skills in the U.S. Workplace, 1960–1985." *Industrial and Labor Relations Review* 44, no. 3: 486–502.

Hoy, S. 1995. *Chasing Dirt: The American Pursuit of Cleanliness.* New York: Oxford University Press.

Hunter, T. 1995. "Domination and Resistance: The Politics of Wage Labor in New South Atlanta." In *We Specialize in the Wholly Impossible: A Reader in Black Women's History,* eds. D. C. Hine, W. King, and L. Reed, 343–57. Brooklyn: Carlson Publishing.

———. 1997. *To 'Joy My Freedom: Southern Black Women's Lives and Labors after the Civil War.* Cambridge: Harvard University Press.

Hurd, R. W., and A. McElwain, A. 1988. "Organizing Clerical Workers: Determinants of Success." *Industrial and Labor Relations Review* 41, no. 3: 360–73.

Hyman, R. [1980] 1983. "White-Collar Workers and Theories of Class." Reprinted in *The New Working Class? White-Collar Workers and Their Organizations,* eds. R. Hyman and R. Price, 3–45. London: Macmillan.

Hyman, R., and R. Price, eds. 1983. *The New Working Class? White-Collar Workers and Their Organizations.* London: Macmillan.

ILO. 1990. *The Promotion of Self-Employment: Report VII.* Geneva: International Labour Conference.

Jagger, A. 1980. "Prostitution." In *Philosophy of Sex: Contemporary Readings,* ed. A. Soble, 348–68. Totowa, N.J.: Rowman and Littlefield.

Jameson, F. 1988. "Cognitive Mapping." In *Marxism and the Interpretation of Culture,* eds. C. Nelson and L. Grossberg, 347–57. Champagne-Urbana: University of Illinois Press.

———. 1995. "Marx's Purloined Letter." *New Left Review* 209 (January/February): 75–109.

Jencks, C. 1984. *The Language of Post-Modern Architecture.* 4th ed. New York: Rizzoli.

Jenkins, C., and B. Sherman. 1979. *White-Collar Unionism: The Rebellious Salariat.* Boston: Routledge and Kegan Paul.

Jenness, V. 1993. *Making It Work.* New York: Walter de Gruyter.

Jones, J. 1985. *Labor of Love, Labor of Sorrow: Black Women, Work, and the Family: From Slavery to the Present.* New York: Vintage Books.

Joseph, G. 1981. "The Incompatible Ménage à Trois: Marxism, Feminism, and Racism." In *Women and Revolution: A Discussion of the Unhappy Marriage of Marxism and Feminism,* ed. L. Sargent, 91–106. Boston: South End Press.

Joyce, P., ed. 1995. *Class.* Oxford: Oxford University Press.

Kaminsky, R. A. 1979. "Overview of the Law, and the Basic Manufacturing Unit." In *Appropriate Units for Collective Bargaining,* eds. P. G. Nash and G. P. Blake, 1–37. New York: Practising Law Institute.

Kassalow, E. M. 1966. "White-Collar Unionism in the United States." In *White-Collar Trade Unions: Contemporary Developments in Industrialized Societies,* ed. A. Sturmthal, 305–64. Urbana: University of Illinois Press.

Katzman, D. M. 1978. *Seven Days a Week: Women and Domestic Service in Industrializing America.* New York: Oxford University Press.

Katznelson, I. 1992. *Marxism and the City.* Oxford: Oxford University Press.

Kayatekin, S. A. 1990. "A Class Analysis of Sharecropping." Ph.D. diss., Department of Economics, University of Massachusetts, Amherst.

———. Forthcoming. "Sharecropping in Post-Bellum Mississippi Delta: The Extraction of Feudal Rent." In *Re-Presenting Class: Essays in Postmodern Political Economy,* eds. J. K. Gibson-Graham, S. Resnick, and R. Wolff. Durham, N.C.: Duke University Press.

Kelley, R. D. G. 1994. *Race Rebels: Culture Politics and the Black Working Class.* New York: Free Press.

Kempe, C. H., et al. 1962. "The Battered Child Syndrome." *Journal of the American Medical Association* 181: 17–24.

Kenney, M., and R. Florida. 1993. *Beyond Mass Production: The Japanese System and Its Transfer to the United States.* New York: Oxford University Press.

Kocka, J. 1980. *White Collar Workers in America, 1890–1940: A Social-Political History in International Perspective.* Trans. M. Kealey. Beverly Hills, Calif.: Sage Publications.

Kollontai, A. 1971. *Communism and the Family.* London: Pluto.

———. 1977a. *Alexandra Kollontai Selected Writings.* Trans. A. Holt. New York: W. W. Norton.

———. 1977b. *Love of the Worker Bees.* London: Virago.

———. 1977c. *Selected Writings.* London: Allison & Busby.

Korff, G. 1992. "From Brotherly Handshake to Militant Clenched Fist: On Political Metaphors for the Worker's Hand." *International Labor and Working-Class History* 42: 70–81.

Kuhn, R. 1982. *Corruption in Paradise.* Hanover, N.H.: University Press of New England.

Kumar, A., ed. 1997. *Class Issues.* New York: New York University Press.

Lacan, J. 1968. *The Language of Self.* Trans. Anthony Wilden. New York: Delta Dell.

Laclau, E. 1984. "The Controversy over Materialism." In *Rethinking Marx,* eds. S. Hanninen and L. Paldan, 39–43. New York: International General/ IMMRC.

————. 1996. *Emancipation(s).* London: Verso.

Laclau, E., and C. Mouffe. 1985. *Hegemony and Socialist Strategy.* London: Verso.

Latour, B. 1986. "The Powers of Association." In *Power, Action and Belief: A New Sociology of Knowledge?,* ed. J. Law, 264–80. London: Routledge and Kegan Paul.

Latour, B., and S. Woolgar. 1986. *Laboratory Life: The Construction of Scientific Facts.* Princeton, N.J.: Princeton University Press.

Lee, F. 1993. "Tracking Leads When the Young Disappear." *New York Times,* 9 February, B1–2.

Lee, W. 1991. "Prostitution and Tourism in South-East Asia." In *Working Women: International Perspectives on Labour and Gender Ideology,* eds. N. Redclift and T. Sinclair, 79–103. New York: Routledge.

Leibin, V. 1993. "Freudianism, or the 'Trotskiite Contraband.'" In *Late Soviet Culture,* eds. T. Lahusen and G. Kuperman, 177–86. Durham, N.C.: Duke University Press.

Leigh, D. E., and S. M. Hills. 1987. "Male-Female Differences in the Potential for Union Growth outside Traditionally Unionized Industries." *Journal of Labor Research* 8, no. 2: 131–42.

Lenin, V. 1975. "Capitalism and Female Labor," and "The Fifth Congress against Prostitution." In *The Lenin Anthology,* ed. R. Tucker, 682–84. New York: W. W. Norton.

Levison, A. 1974. *The Working-Class Majority.* New York: Coward, McCann, and Geoghegan.

Levitas, R. 1990. *The Concept of Utopia.* Syracuse, N.Y.: Syracuse University Press.

Lewin, T. 1995. "Parent's Poll Shows Child Abuse to Be More Common." *New York Times,* December 7, 16.

Linder, M. 1992. *Farewell to the Self-Employed: Deconstructing a Socioeconomic and Legal Solipsism.* New York: Greenwood Press.

Linder, M., and J. Houghton. 1990. "Self-Employment and the Petty Bourgeoisie: Comment on Steinmetz and Wright." *American Journal of Sociology* 96, no. 3: 727–35.

Lockwood, D. 1989. *The Blackcoated Worker: A Study in Class Consciousness.* 2d ed. Oxford: Clarendon Press.

Lumley, R. 1973. *White-Collar Unionism in Britain: A Survey of the Present Position.* London: Methuen and Company.

Mallet, S. 1963. *La nouvelle classe ouvrière.* Paris: Editions du Seuil.

Marable, M. 1992. "Race Identity and Political Culture." In *Black Popular Culture,* ed. G. Dent, 292–302. Seattle: Bay Press.

Marcus, S. 1992. "Fighting Bodies, Fighting Words: A Theory and Politics of Rape Prevention." In *Feminists Theorize the Political,* eds. J. Butler and S. Scott, 385–403. New York: Routledge.

Marx, K. 1951. *Theories of Surplus Value.* Trans. G. Bonner and E. Burns. London: Lawrence and Wishart.

———. 1976. *Capital,* vol. 1. New York: Vintage Books.

———. 1977. *Capital,* vol. 1. Trans. B. Fowkes. New York: Random House.

———. 1978. "The Critique of the Gotha Program." In *The Marx-Engels Reader,* ed. R. C. Tucker, 525–41. New York: W. W. Norton.

———. 1981. *Capital,* vol. 3. Trans. D. Fernbach. New York: Random House.

———. 1987. *Capital,* vol. 1. Trans. S. Moore and E. Aveling. New York: International Publishers.

———. 1988. *Economic and Philosophic Manuscripts of 1844.* Buffalo, N.Y.: Prometheus Books.

Marx, K., and F. Engels. 1988. *Economic and Philosophic Manuscripts of 1844.* Trans. M. Milligan. New York: International Publishers.

Massey, D. 1984. *Spatial Divisions of Labor: Social Structures and the Geography of Production.* New York: Methuen.

Massumi, B. 1996. "The Autonomy of Affect." In *Deleuze: A Critical Reader,* ed. P. Patton, 215–39. Oxford: Blackwell.

Matlock, J. 1994. *Scenes of Seduction: Prostitution, Hysteria, and Reading Difference in Nineteenth-Century France.* New York: Columbia University Press.

McClintock, A. 1995. *Imperial Leather: Race, Gender, and Sexuality in the Colonial Contest.* New York: Routledge.

McColloch, M. 1983. *White Collar Workers in Transition: The Boom Years, 1940–1970.* Westport, Conn.: Greenwood Press.

McFarland, R., and J. Fanton. 1997. "Moving towards Utopia: Prevention of Child Abuse." *Journal of Psychohistory* 24, no. 4 (spring): 320–31.

McIntyre, R. 1992. "Theories of Uneven Development and Social Change." *Rethinking Marxism* 5, no. 3: 75–105.

———. 1996. "Mode of Production, Social Formation, and Uneven Development, or Is There Capitalism in America?" In *Postmodern Materialism and the Future of Marxist Theory: Essays in the Althusserian Tradition,* eds. A. Callari and D. Ruccio, 231–53. Hanover, N.H.: Wesleyan University Press.

McNaron, T., and Y. Morgan. 1982. *Voices in the Night.* San Francisco: Cleis.

Melosh, B. 1993. "Manly Work: Public Art and Masculinity in Depression America." In *Gender and American History since 1890,* ed. B. Melosh, 155–81. New York: Routledge.

Milkman, R. 1993. "The New Gender Politics in Organized Labor." In *Proceedings of the Forty-Fifth Annual Meeting, Industrial Relations Research*

Association, ed. J. F. Burton, 348–57. Madison, Wis.: Industrial Relations Research Association.

Miller, A. 1982. *The Drama of the Gifted Child.* Trans. R. Ward. New York: Basic Books.

———. 1984. *For Your Own Good.* Trans. H. Hannum and H. Hannum. New York: New American Library.

———. 1990. *Banished Knowledges.* Trans. L. Vennewitz. London: Virago.

Mills, C. W. 1951. *White Collar: The American Middle Classes.* New York: Oxford University Press.

Mitchell, J., and J. Rose, eds. 1982. *Feminine Sexuality: Jacques Lacan and the École Freudienne.* Trans. J. Rose. New York: W. W. Norton.

Morrison, T. 1970. *The Bluest Eye.* New York: Penguin Books.

Mouffe, C. 1995. "Post-Marxism: Democracy and Identity." *Environment and Planning D: Society and Space* 13, no. 3: 259–66.

Nagle, J., ed. 1997. *Whores and Other Feminists.* New York: Routledge.

Nakano, E., G. Chang, and L. Forcey, eds. 1994. *Mothering.* New York: Routledge.

Needleman, R. 1993. "Building an Organizing Culture of Unionism." In *Proceedings of the Forty-Fifth Annual Meeting, Industrial Relations Research Association,* ed. J. F. Burton, 358–66. Madison, Wis.: Industrial Relations Research Association.

Nicolaus, M. [1967] 1978. "Proletariat and Middle Class in Marx: Hegelian Choreography and the Capitalist Dialectic." Reprinted in *Marx: Sociology/ Social Change/Capitalism,* ed. D. McQuarie, 230–52. New York: Quartet Books.

Nielsen, K., and R. Ware, eds. 1997. *Exploitation.* Atlantic Highlands, N.J.: Humanities Press.

Nordhoff, C. 1966. *The Communistic Societies of the United States.* New York: Dover Publications.

Norwood, S. H. 1990. *Labor's Flaming Youth: Telephone Operators and Worker Militancy, 1878–1923.* Urbana: University of Illinois Press.

Nussbaum, K. 1984. "Women Clerical Workers and Trade Unionism." *Socialist Review* 49: 151–59.

Nussbaum, K. and J. Sweeney. 1989. *Solutions for the New Work Force.* Cabin John, Md.: Seven Locks Press.

Offe, C. 1985. *Disorganized Capitalism: Contemporary Transformations of Work and Politics.* Ed. J. Keane. Cambridge, Mass.: MIT Press.

Office of the Status of Women. 1991. *Selected Findings from Juggling Time: How Australian Familes Use Time.* Canberra: Office of the Status of Women, Department of the Prime Minister and Cabinet.

Okin, S. 1989. *Justice, Gender, and the Family.* New York: Basic Books.

Oppenheimer, M. 1985. *White Collar Politics.* New York: Monthly Review Press.

Overall, C. 1992. "What's Wrong with Prostitution? Evaluating Sex Work." *Signs* 17, no. 4 (summer): 705–24.

Palmer, P. 1989. *Domesticity and Dirt: Housewives and Domestic Servants in the United States, 1920–1945.* Philadelphia: Temple University Press.

Pateman, C. 1988. *The Sexual Contract.* Stanford: Stanford University Press.

————. 1990. "Defending Prostitution: Charges against Ericsson." In *Feminism and Political Theory,* ed. C. Sunstein, 201–6. Chicago: University of Chicago Press.

Peiss, K. 1989. "'Charity Girls' and City Pleasures: Historical Notes on Working-Class Sexuality, 1880–1920." In *Passion and Power: Sexuality in History,* eds. K. Peiss and C. Simmons with R. Padgug, 57–69. Philadelphia: Temple University Press.

Petry, A. 1946. *The Street.* Boston: Houghton Mifflin.

Pheterson, G., ed. 1989. *A Vindication of the Rights of Whores.* Seattle: Seal Press.

Pheterson, G. 1996. *The Prostitution Prism.* Amsterdam: Amsterdam University Press.

Pina, D., and V. Bengtson. 1993. "The Division of Household Labor and Wives' Happiness: Ideology, Employment, and Perceptions of Support." *Journal of Marriage and the Family* 55 (November): 901–12.

Poulantzas, N. 1975. *Classes in Contemporary Capitalism.* Trans. D. Fernbach. London: New Left Books.

Price, R. [1980] 1983. "White-Collar Unions: Growth, Character, and Attitudes in the 1970s." Reprinted in *The New Working Class? White-Collar Workers and Their Organizations,* eds. R. Hyman and R. Price, 147–83. London: Macmillan.

Quadagno, J. 1994. *The Color of Welfare: How Racism Undermined the War on Poverty.* New York: Oxford University Press.

Reed, T. F. 1990. "Profiles of Union Organizers from Manufacturing and Service Unions." *Journal of Labor Research* 11, no. 1: 73–80.

————. 1992. "Incidence and Patterns of Representation Campaign Tactics: A Comparison of Manufacturing and Service Unions." *Relations Industrielles/Industrial Relations* 47, no. 2: 203–17.

Renard, J. [1893] 1967. *Poil de Carotte.* Trans. Ralph Manheim. Reprint, New York: Walker and Co.

Resnick, S. and R. Wolff. 1986. "Power, Property, and Class." *Socialist Review* 86, 97–124.

————. 1987. *Knowledge and Class: A Marxian Critique of Political Economy.* Chicago: University of Chicago Press.

————. 1988. "Communism: Between Class and Classless." *Rethinking Marxism* 1, no. 1:14–49.

Roberts, N. 1993. *Whores in History: Prostitution in Western Society.* London: HarperCollins.

Rodgers, D. T. 1978. *The Work Ethic in Industrial America, 1850–1920.* Chicago: University of Chicago Press.

Rodgers, G., and J. Rodgers, eds. 1989. *Precarious Jobs in Labour Market Regulation: The Growth of Atypical Employment in Western Europe*. Geneva: International Institute for Labour Studies.

Rohter, L. 1996. "Area Codes, Caribbean Style." *New York Times*, May 26, section 4, 2.

Rollins, J. 1985. *Between Women: Domestics and Their Employers*. Philadelphia: Temple University Press.

Romero, M. 1992. *Maid in the U.S.A.* New York: Routledge.

Rubin, G. 1975. "The Traffic in Women: Notes on the 'Political Economy' of Sex." In *Toward an Anthropology of Women*, ed. R. Reiter, 157–210. New York: Monthly Review.

———. 1984. "Thinking Sex: Notes for a Radical Theory of the Politics of Sexuality." In *Pleasure and Danger: Exploring Female Sexuality*, ed. C. Vance, 267–319. Boston: Routledge and Kegan Paul.

———. 1994. "Sexual Traffic: Interview with Judith Butler." *Differences* 6 (summer/fall): 62–99.

Ruddick, S. 1995. *Maternal Thinking*. Boston: Beacon Press.

Rush, F. 1980. *The Best Kept Secret*. New York: McGraw Hill.

Schlossberg, S. I. 1967. *Organizing and the Law*. Washington, D.C.: Bureau of National Affairs.

Schmidman, J. 1979. *Unions in Postindustrial Society*. University Park: Pennsylvania State University Press.

Schor, N., and E. Weed. 1994. *The Essential Difference*. Bloomington: University of Indiana Press.

Schur, L. A. and D. L. Kruse. 1992. "Gender Differences in Attitudes toward Unions." *Industrial and Labor Relations Review* 46, no. 1: 89–102.

Scott, A. J. 1988. *Metropolis: From the Division of Labor to Urban Form*. Berkeley: University of California Press.

Scott, A., and E. Soja, eds. 1996. *The City: Los Angeles and Urban Theory at the End of the Twentieth Century*. Berkeley and Los Angeles: University of California Press.

Scott, K. Y. 1991. *The Habit of Surviving: Black Women's Strategies for Life*. New Brunswick: Rutgers University Press.

Sedgwick, E. K. 1993. *Tendencies*. Durham, N.C.: Duke University Press.

Sedgwick, E. K., and A. Frank. 1995. *Shame and Its Sisters: A Silvan Tomkins Reader*. Durham, N.C.: Duke University Press.

Self-Employed Women's Association. 1981. *Report of National Workshop on Organising Self-Employed Women in India, Ahmedabad, March 17–18, 1981*. Ahmedabad: Self-Employed Women's Association.

———. 1982. *We, the Self-Employed*. Ahmedabad: Self-Employed Women's Association.

Shostak, A. B. 1991. *Robust Unionism: Innovations in the Labor Movement*. Ithaca, N.Y.: ILR Press.

Shrage, L. 1994. *Moral Dilemmas of Feminism: Prostitution, Adultery, and Abortion*. New York: Routledge.

Silvestri, G. T. 1991. "Who Are the Self-Employed? Employment Profiles and Recent Trends." *Occupational Outlook Quarterly* (spring): 26–36.

Singer, L. 1993. *Erotic Welfare: Sexual Theory and Politics in the Age of Epidemic*. New York: Routledge.

Sleeth, P., and J. Barnsley. 1989. *Recollecting Our Lives*. Vancouver: Press Gang Publishers.

Smith, B. 1983. *Home Girls: A Black Feminist Anthology*. Latham, N. Y.: Kitchen Table, Women of Color Press.

Soja, E. 1989. *Postmodern Geographies: The Reassertion of Space in Critical Social Theory*. New York: Verso.

———. 1995. "Postmodern Urbanization: The Six Restructurings of Los Angeles." In *Postmodern Cities and Spaces,* eds. S. Watson and K. Gibson, 125–37. Oxford: Blackwell.

Soja, E. and Scott, A. 1996. "Introduction to Los Angeles: City and Region." In *The City: Los Angeles and Urban Theory at the End of the Twentieth Century,* eds. A. Scott and E. Soja, 1–21. Berkeley and Los Angeles: University of California Press.

Southern California Association of Governments. 1989. *Regional Growth Management Plan*. Los Angeles: SCAG.

Spencer, C. 1977. *Blue Collar: An Internal Examination of the Workplace*. Chicago: Lakeside Charter Books.

Spitz, R. A. 1945. "Hospitalism, an Inquiry into the Genesis of Psychiatric Conditions in Early Childhood." *Psychoanalytic Studies of the Child* 1: 53–74.

———. 1946a. "Hospitalism: A Follow-Up Report." *Psychoanalytical Studies of the Child* 2: 113–17.

———. 1946b. "Anaclitic Depression." *Psychoanalytical Studies of the Child* 2: 313–42.

Spivak, G. 1994. Introduction to *Bringing It All Back Home: Class, Gender, and Power in the Modern Household,* H. Fraad, S. Resnick, and R. Wolff, ix–xvi. London: Pluto Press.

Stedman Jones, G. 1983. *Languages of Class: Studies in English Working Class History, 1832–1982*. Cambridge: Cambridge University Press.

Steinmetz, G., and E. O. Wright. 1989. "The Fall and Rise of the Petty Bourgeoisie: Changing Patterns of Self-Employment in the Postwar United States." *American Journal of Sociology* 94 (March): 973–1018.

Stigler, G. 1946. *Domestic Servants in the United States, 1900–1940*. Occasional Paper 24. New York: National Bureau of Economic Research.

Strasser, S. M. 1987. "Mistress and Maid, Employer and Employee: Domestic Service Reform in the United States, 1897–1920." *Marxist Perspectives* 1, no. 4: 52–67.

Streety, R. 1990. "Getting Back to the Heart of Nursing." *Nursing* 20, no. 5 (May): 34–35.

Strom, S. H. 1980. "Florence Luscomb: For Suffrage, Labor, and Peace." In *Moving the Mountain: Women Working for Social Change*, ed. E. Cantarow, 2–51. Old Westbury, N.Y.: Feminist Press.

———. 1983. "Challenging 'Woman's Place': Feminism, the Left, and Industrial Unionism in the 1930s." *Feminist Studies* 9, no. 2: 359–86.

———. 1989. "'Light Manufacturing': The Feminization of American Office Work, 1900–1930." *Industrial and Labor Relations Review* 43, no. 1: 53–71.

———. 1990. "United Office and Professional Workers of America." In *Encyclopedia of the American Left*, eds. M. J. Buhle, P. Buhle, and D. Georgakas, 809–10. Urbana: University of Illinois Press.

———. 1992. *Beyond the Typewriter: Gender, Class, and the Origins of Modern American Office Work, 1900–1930*. Urbana: University of Illinois Press.

Sturmthal, A. 1966. "White-Collar Unions: A Comparative Essay." In *White-Collar Trade Unions: Contemporary Developments in Industrialized Societies*, ed. A. Sturmthal, 365–98. Urbana: University of Illinois Press.

Sullivan, B. 1995. "Rethinking Prostitution." In *Transitions: New Australian Feminisms*, eds. B. Caine and R. Pringle, 184–97. Sydney: Allen & Unwin.

Swanstrom, T. 1993. "Beyond Economism: Urban Political Economy and the Postmodern Challenge." *Journal of Urban Affairs* 15, no. 1: 55–78.

Sweeney, J. H., and K. Nussbaum. 1989. *Solutions for the New Work Force: Policies for a New Social Contract*. Cabin John, Md.: Seven Locks Press.

Tepperman, J. 1976. *Not Servants, Not Machines: Office Workers Speak Out*. Boston: Beacon Press.

Thompson, P. 1989. *The Nature of Work: An Introduction to Debates on the Labour Process*. 2d ed. London: Macmillan.

Touraine, A. 1988. *Return of the Actor: Social Theory in Postindustrial Society*. Trans. M. Godzich. Minneapolis: University of Minnesota Press.

Truong, T. 1990. *Money and Morality: Prostitution and Tourism in South-East Asia*. London: Zed Books.

U.S. Bureau of the Census. 1990. *Census of Population and Housing*. STF 3A.

U.S. Department of Commerce. 1989. *200 Years of U.S. Census Taking: Population and Housing Questions, 1790–1990*. Washington, D.C.: U.S. Government Printing Office.

Unger, R. M. 1987a. *False Necessity: Anti-Necessitarian Social Theory in the Service of Radical Democracy*. Cambridge: Cambridge University Press.

———. 1987b. *Plasticity into Power: Comparative-Historical Studies on the Institutional Conditions of Economic and Military Success*. Cambridge: Cambridge University Press.

Vallas, S. P. 1987. "White-Collar Proletarians? The Structure of Clerical Work and Levels of Consciousness." *Sociological Quarterly* 28, no. 4: 523–40.

Van Raaphorst, D. L. 1988. *Union Maids Not Wanted: Organizing Domestic Workers 1870–1940.* New York: Praeger Publishers.

Vorse, M. H. 1938. *Labor's New Millions.* New York: Modern Age Books.

Walby, S. 1990. *Theorising Patriarchy.* Oxford: Basil Blackwell.

Walkowitz, J. 1980. "The Politics of Prostitution." *Signs* 6, no. 1: 123–35.

Walsh, J. 1996. "The World's First Prostitutes' Union." *Marie Claire* (January): 48–51.

Warskett, R. 1989. "Women and Clerical Work: Revisiting Class and Gender." *Studies in Political Economy* 30: 167–82.

Watson, S., and K. Gibson, eds. 1996. *Postmodern Cities and Spaces.* Oxford: Blackwell.

Watson, T. J. 1980. *Sociology, Work, and Industry.* Boston: Routledge and Kegan Paul.

Welter, B. 1976. *Dimity Convictions: The American Woman in the Nineteenth Century.* Athens: Ohio University Press.

Wheelock, J. 1990. "Capital Restructuring and the Domestic Economy: Family, Self-Respect and the Irrelevance of 'Rational Economic Man.'" *Capital and Class* 41: 103–41.

White, L. 1990. *The Comforts of Home: Prostitution in Colonial Nairobi.* Chicago: University of Chicago Press.

Williams, R. 1983. *Keywords.* London: Fontana Paperbacks.

Wilson, C. P. 1992. *White Collar Fictions: Class and Social Representation in American Literature, 1885–1925.* Athens: University of Georgia Press.

Wilson, M. G. 1979. *The American Woman in Transition: The Urban Influence, 1870–1920.* Westport: Greenwood Press.

Wolff, R. 1996. "Althusser and Hegel: Making Marxist Explanations Anti-essentialist and Dialectical." In *Postmodern Materialism and the Future of Marxist Theory: Essays in the Althusserian Tradition,* eds. A. Callari and D. Ruccio, 150–63. Hanover, N.H.: Wesleyan University Press.

Wolff, R., and S. Resnick. 1986. "What Are Class Analyses?" *Research in Political Economy* 9: 1–32.

Wolpe, H., ed. 1980. *The Articulation of Modes of Production.* London: Routledge and Kegan Paul.

The Workers Council Bulletin. 1937. "The Need of Organization among Household Employees." YWCA National Board Archives, New York. Records File Collection, Sophia Smith Collection.

Wray, M., and A. Newitz. 1997. *White Trash: Race and Class in America.* New York: Routledge.

Wright, E. O. 1978. *Class, Crisis, and the State.* London: New Left Books.

———. 1985. *Classes.* London: Verso.

Yeandle, S. 1984. *Women's Working Lives: Patterns and Strategies.* London and New York: Tavistock.

Zatz, N. 1997. "Sex Work/Sex Act: Law, Labor, and Desire in Constructions of Prostitution." *Signs* (winter): 277–308.

Zeitlin, M., and H. Kimeldorf. 1983. "How Mighty a Force? The Internal Differentiation and Relative Organization of the Working Class." In *How Mighty a Force? Studies of Workers' Consciousness and Organization in the United States,* ed. M. Zeitlin, 1–64. Los Angeles: University of California, Institute of Industrial Relations.

Zimbalist, A., ed. 1979. *Case Studies on the Labor Process.* New York: Monthly Review Press.

Zukin, S., et al. 1992. "The Bubbling Cauldron: Global and Local Interactions in New York City Restaurants." In *After Modernism: Global Restructuring and the Changing Boundaries of City Life,* ed. M. P. Smith, 105–32. New Brunswick: Transaction Publishers.

Contributors

Enid Arvidson, a Los Angeles native, teaches urban studies at the University of Texas at Arlington. She holds a masters degree in regional planning and a Ph.D. in economics from the University of Massachusetts. Her published work focuses on rethinking postmodern urbanism as well as on urban impacts of federal government devolution.

Jenny Cameron is a research fellow in the School of Public Policy at Monash University, Australia. She is collaborating with Katherine Gibson on a major grant from the Australian Research Council to study class, regional development, and economic citizenship; their project involves working closely with groups of retrenched workers, unemployed young people, and single parents to develop new economic and community-based initiatives.

Harriet Fraad is a psychoanalytic psychotherapist with a private practice in New Haven, Connecticut. She was a founding mother of the Women's Liberation Movement in New Haven. Her work focuses on extending Marxism into the arena of intimate life. She coauthored (with Stephen A. Resnick and Richard D. Wolff) *Bringing It All Back Home: Class, Gender, and Power in the Modern Household.*

J. K. Gibson-Graham is the pen name of Katherine Gibson and Julie Graham, feminist economic geographers who work, respectively, at the Australian National University in Canberra and the University of Massachusetts, Amherst. They coauthored *The End of Capitalism (As We Knew It): A Feminist Critique of Political Economy,* and their current work uses conceptions of class (especially of noncapitalist class relations) to rethink the economy and economic possibility.

Janet Hotch is a special program coordinator and activist based in Chicago. Until recently, she was the executive director of Chicago Jobs with Justice. She has also been the director of publications for the Midwest Center for Labor Research, where she was the editor of *Labor Research Review.* She has a masters degree in labor studies.

Susan Jahoda, professor of art at the University of Massachusetts, Amherst, is an interdisciplinary artist whose work includes performance, installation, images/text, and photography. She has received grants and awards from the National Endowment of the Arts and the New York Foundation for the Arts, and her work has been exhibited and published widely in Europe and North America.

Amitava Kumar is associate professor of English at the University of Florida. A widely published poet, he is the author of *No Tears for the N.R.I.* and *Passport Photos.* He is the editor of *Poetics/Politics: Radical Aesthetics for the Classroom* and *Class Issues: Pedagogy, Cultural Studies, and the Public Sphere.* His writings and photography have appeared in *In These Times, The Nation, Guardian, Cultural Studies, Rethinking Marxism, Critical Inquiry, Minnesota Review, Journal of Advanced Composition, Modern Fiction Studies,* and *Socialist Review.*

Stephen A. Resnick has been a professor of economics at the University of Massachusetts, Amherst, since 1973. With Richard D. Wolff he coauthored the books *Knowledge and Class* and *Economics: Marxian vs. Neoclassical;* with Wolff and Harriet Fraad he coauthored *Bringing It All Back Home: Class, Gender, and Power in the Modern Household.* He has published numerous articles on class, and currently he is completing a class analysis of communism, capitalism, and the Soviet Union, coauthored with Richard Wolff.

Cecilia Marie Rio is completing her doctorate in economics at the University of Massachusetts, Amherst. Her work focuses on the intersection of race, class, and domestic labor. She is a staff economist of the Center for Popular Economics and an advocate for women and children at the university.

Jacquelyn Southern is completing a Ph.D. in geography at Clark University. She has experience in the labor and the environmental movements, and has a masters degree in labor studies. She is former managing editor of *Rethinking Marxism*.

Marjolein van der Veen is a Ph.D. candidate in economics at the University of Massachusetts, Amherst. Her work explores the economics of prostitution through the lens of class.

Richard D. Wolff is professor of economics at the University of Massachusetts, Amherst, and serves on the editorial board of *Rethinking Marxism*. He has published widely in the fields of political economy, philosophy, and economics, often in collaboration with Stephen A. Resnick. His latest work with Resnick is a class analysis of the rise and fall of the USSR.

Index

African American domestic workers,
17, 24, 42nn.1,3; class analysis of,
31–32; and class transition, 17, 24,
38, 40; as free workers, 23; and importance of family life, 24; and the
mammy, 27–28; and new identity,
39; as paid domestic workers,
23–39; as producers and sellers
of labor, 24–25; and slavery, 23

African American women: and class
struggle, 35–36; employment after
slavery, 26; and a new class identity,
24, 32, 39; and oppression, 25, 28;
and self-empowerment, 41; union
movements, 45n.22

Althusser, L.: aleatory materialism, 7;
autobiography of, 70, 82; and
childhood, 69–70; and the family,
69–70; his theory of knowledge,
187n.9; idealism, 7; overdetermination, 6–7, 21n.10

Amott, T. L., 42n.1, 43n.4

Ancient class process. *See* Independent
class process

Anti-economism, ix

Anti-essentialism, 6, 7, 17; and class,
10, 25, 31; and the household, 65;

and prostitution, 123; and self-
employment, 148

Appropriation of surplus labor. *See*
Surplus labor

Appropriative class position, 188n.15

Arvidson, E., 163–89, 187n.7,
188n.10

Bain, G. S., 191, 197–98, 204

Barry, K., 125, 138n.3, 139n.11

Beal, E. F., 202, 204

Beijing Women's Conference, 139n.13

Bell, S., 130, 138n.8, 140n.21

Bernstein, I., 218–19

Black feminist theory, 31

Black racial identity, 31

Blue collar: and class, 206–10; as a class
division, 193; definitions, 192, 204,
213; historical meaning of, 191–92;
neo-Weberian and neo-Marxist theory, 213, 215, 217, 219; and new
social movement theory, 221; problems in categorizing, 197–200, 206;
and union organization, 193–95,
221. *See also* Collar conflict; Collar
line; Collars, the

Bluest Eye, The (Morrison), 40

251